KIRK KAZANJIAN & AMY JOYNER

Making Dough

The 12 Secret Ingredients of Krispy Kreme's Sweet Success

Foreword by Dick Clark

WILEY

John Wiley & Sons, Inc.

Copyright © 2004 by Literary Productions. All rights reserved.

Published by John Wiley & Sons, Inc., Hoboken, New Jersey.
Published simultaneously in Canada.

No part of this publication may be reproduced, stored in a retrieval system, or transmitted in any form or by any means, electronic, mechanical, photocopying, recording, scanning, or otherwise, except as permitted under Section 107 or 108 of the 1976 United States Copyright Act, without either the prior written permission of the Publisher, or authorization through payment of the appropriate per-copy fee to the Copyright Clearance Center, Inc., 222 Rosewood Drive, Danvers, MA 01923, 978-750-8400, fax 978-750-4470, or on the web at www.copyright.com. Requests to the Publisher for permission should be addressed to the Permissions Department, John Wiley & Sons, Inc., 111 River Street, Hoboken, NJ 07030, 201-748-6011, fax 201-748-6008, e-mail: permcoordinator@wiley.com.

Limit of Liability/Disclaimer of Warranty: While the publisher and author have used their best efforts in preparing this book, they make no representations or warranties with respect to the accuracy or completeness of the contents of this book and specifically disclaim any implied warranties of merchantability or fitness for a particular purpose. No warranty may be created or extended by sales representatives or written sales materials. The advice and strategies contained herein may not be suitable for your situation. You should consult with a professional where appropriate. Neither the publisher nor author shall be liable for any loss of profit or any other commercial damages, including but not limited to special, incidental, consequential, or other damages.

For general information on our other products and services, or technical support, please contact our Customer Care Department within the United States at 800-762-2974, outside the United States at 317-572-3993 or fax 317-572-4002.

Wiley also publishes its books in a variety of electronic formats. Some content that appears in print may not be available in electronic books.

For more information about Wiley products, visit our web site at *www.wiley.com*.

ISBN 0-471-43209-1

Printed in the United States of America

10 9 8 7 6 5 4 3 2 1

To all the Krispy Kreme fans around the world who helped to make this incredible story possible.

—KK

To my parents, whose loving support is the sweetest treat of all.

—AJ

Contents

Foreword

I first came to know and love Krispy Kreme when I was in my twenties. Each summer, I went on tour with Dick Clark's Caravan of Stars. I hopped on a bus and circled the country with some of the biggest acts of the 1960s, including The Shirelles, The Supremes, Freddy Cannon, The Rip Cords, Duane Eddy, Gene Pitney, and Paul Anka, just to name a few. We'd perform nonstop to sold-out crowds for months at a time.

Although every city was great, we especially looked forward to playing in the South and, in particular, North Carolina. Why, you ask? Well, that was the home of Krispy Kreme.

The music world's top names and I would look out the window of our bus hoping—even praying—that we'd find a Krispy Kreme along the road. That was a sure sign we'd find hot doughnuts cooking inside. Once the bus pulled up, we'd run through the front door and buy boxes and boxes of the tasty treats. It was definitely an event to remember.

The smell and taste of those doughnuts was amazing. They simply melted in your mouth. It was an experience unlike any other. For me, getting the chance to bite into those Krispy Kreme doughnuts was by far one of the most memorable parts of the Caravan of Stars tour. To be honest, that delicious flavor stands out in my mind more clearly than many of the concerts we played.

Early in my career, I got involved in the fast-food industry. I have owned an Arby's franchise and ran a small chain of hamburger stands in the 1950s. Currently, I operate Dick Clark's American Bandstand Grills. But a couple of years ago, I set my sights on a new venture. After 40 years of traveling and eating those incredible doughnuts, I decided I wanted my own Krispy Kreme franchise. I'm not sure why I didn't think of it sooner.

I got in touch with the company and expressed my strong interest in joining their team. Unfortunately, I quickly learned that the area I wanted to develop had already been taken. In fact, Krispy Kreme is no longer even accepting franchise applications in the United States because every state is spoken for. Hearing this news was a major disappointment.

Granted, I didn't need to take on another business opportunity. I'm very busy as it is, hosting a number of shows, producing many popular TV programs, and running my own existing companies and restaurants. Still, I was determined to have my own Krispy Kreme store because of my passion for the product. I kept calling the company's chairman and CEO, Scott Livengood, telling him how much I longed to become a franchisee. After bugging him for months on end, he finally realized that I was really serious. He probably also figured that I'd never stop bothering him until he somehow found a way for us to work together. I'm pretty persistent. You have to be to make it in the entertainment business.

When the company began considering international markets in 2002, Scott asked if I'd be interested in acquiring the rights to develop Krispy Kreme stores in the United Kingdom. I immediately said yes and formed a partnership with two other partners. We're now working together to build 25 stores throughout Britain over the next several years.

The restaurant and fast food business in general is very profitable. If run well, you can receive a good return on your investment. I'm convinced Krispy Kreme's best years are yet to come.

I believe that one reason Krispy Kreme is so popular is because it's a throwback to the good old days of innocence when you spoiled yourself with a treat every now and then. Visiting a Krispy Kreme store—and biting into a fresh, hot original glazed doughnut—is a mystical and nostalgic experience that's pretty hard to duplicate. As a result, I view Krispy Kreme as a truly untapped resource.

How has the company been able to build such an incredible business since founder Vernon Rudolph served his first doughnut more than 60 years ago? That's the key question Kirk Kazanjian and Amy Joyner explore in this fine book. I think it's safe to say that just about every company would love to know the secret ingredients of Krispy Kreme's sweet success. After all, it doesn't advertise, it is a revered member of the community, and it keeps growing like crazy. What an extraordinary business! Without doubt, you should pay attention to what Krispy Kreme is doing, especially if you want to prosper in today's competitive world.

When people ask me why Krispy Kreme's popularity seems to keep getting stronger, even after all of these years, I tell them that's like asking what makes someone a real star in the music business. If you knew the exact reason, you could bottle it. Or, in the case of Krispy Kreme, you could box it.

Reading *Making Dough* will no doubt bring you closer to finding the answer to this interesting question. It will help you to discover some of the reasons this company continues to shine, and I'm sure you'll find the stories along the way to be most entertaining indeed.

It's hard to believe that a company I fell in love with four decades ago is now more celebrated than ever. I expect great things from Krispy Kreme in the years to come and hope you'll stop by one of our stores the next time you're in the United Kingdom. Who knows? You may even find me behind the counter!

—Dick Clark
Producer, Entertainer, and Krispy Kreme Franchisee

Introduction

It's an overcast, but still hot and humid, July day in Old Salem, North Carolina. Hundreds are gathered around a tent where a 10-tiered birthday cake that took more than six hours and 20 volunteers to build is sheltered from both the bees and the hungry onlookers swarming around it.

Cameras snap as children and adults pose by the 2,413-pound confectionery spectacle that, to say the least, is no ordinary cake. It is made out of 14,832 glazed doughnuts, 1,000 pounds of icing, and 330 pounds of gumdrops, ice cream jimmies, mints, gummy fish, and other kinds of candy.

Volunteers keep shooing celebrants away as they try to swipe an early bite of the cake. A sultry-voiced blues diva sings in the middle of a town square near downtown Winston-Salem, while kids with painted faces run around carrying helium-filled balloons tied to their wrists with curly ribbon. All of a sudden, Congressman Mel Watt begins leading everyone in a chorus of "Happy Birthday."

An outside observer might assume that all of this hoopla is being staged for a very famous person, perhaps even the most special citizen in all of North Carolina.

That's not far from the truth.

This event, and all of the festivities taking place around the historic village square, is being held to mark an important milestone by a hometown favorite company. Today, Krispy Kreme is celebrating its sixty-fifth year of making melt-in-your-mouth doughnuts.

A COMPANY LIKE NO OTHER

Old Salem is a restored Moravian village in North Carolina's fourth-largest city. In 1937, just across the street in a rustic clapboard building on South Main Street, Vernon Rudolph fried up the first original glazed Krispy Kreme doughnut. What began as a modest wholesale business has, in a little more than six decades, grown into one of the nation's most successful specialty restaurant chains.

"I don't care where I go, I don't find no doughnuts to compare with Krispy Kreme," says party attendee Mattie DeBerry. She worked as a maid at Krispy Kreme's corporate office for 30 years before retiring in 1977. Though tiny and 90 years old, DeBerry can still eat three glazed doughnuts in a sitting.

"I think these are the best doughnuts in the world," she says with much enthusiasm.

Millions of others agree.

The hometown crowd gathered for this birthday celebration pales in comparison to the legions of fans who show up at new Krispy Kreme store openings. People with jobs, families, and presumably more important places to be often wait in line hours for a new store to open its doors.

Major celebrities are constantly fawning over the confections. Rosie O'Donnell and actor George Segal sang a love song to the glazed dessert on her former talk show. Filmmaker Nora Ephron mooned over her beloved "sugar babies" in the *New Yorker.* And southern humorist Roy Blount Jr. sermonized on the goodness of Krispy Kremes in a 1996 *New York Times Magazine* essay, shortly after the chain's first store opened in the Big Apple.

Legend also has it that the King himself, Elvis Presley, kept a dozen fresh jelly-filled Krispy Kreme doughnuts on hand at Graceland at all times. Even former president Bill Clinton is a fan. He had boxes delivered to the White House until his fitness trainers found out about it.[1]

Krispy Kreme doesn't pay any celebrities to endorse its doughnuts, but it does partner with some of them. Performer Jimmy Buffett, who sings about Krispy Kreme doughnuts as well as cheeseburgers and margaritas, owns a franchise in Palm Beach, Florida. In 2002, he merged his territory with another Krispy Kreme franchisee and now shares in a joint development agreement with the company. Hall of Fame baseball player Hank Aaron, also a successful restaurateur and business owner, owns a Krispy Kreme shop in an impoverished, mainly minority neighborhood in Atlanta. And former *American Bandstand* host Dick Clark plans to open a number of stores throughout the United Kingdom.

DOING THE RIGHT THING

In addition to being a purveyor for the famous, Krispy Kreme has built a reputation as a good corporate citizen, helping charitable groups raise tens of millions each year through doughnut fund-raising sales and donations. Such goodwill originated with founder Vernon Rudolph. Former employees describe Rudolph as a good, helpful soul who genuinely cared about improving the lives of his employees and his customers.

Mattie DeBerry, who began cleaning Krispy Kreme's offices in 1947, was often the recipient of Rudolph's kindness. "He was an angel sent from heaven," says DeBerry, who still lives in Winston-Salem. "We were one devoted family. If you had a problem, everybody at Krispy Kreme would reach out and help you out," including Rudolph.

Once, on a cold winter morning, Rudolph discovered DeBerry huddled over the office radiator.

"What's wrong, Mattie?" he asked with a voice of real concern.

"I just walked from the bus stop," DeBerry answered. "I'm trying to keep my knees and legs warm."

When he learned one of his employees was suffering just to get to work, Rudolph told the widowed DeBerry, who had always depended on her husband to take her to work, that if she got a driver's license he would give her the keys to a company car. "I never did learn to drive," DeBerry admits, but she has never forgotten Rudolph's offer or his many other acts of kindness.

Another time, Rudolph handed DeBerry a $50 check and a voucher for an airline ticket. He was sending her to Buffalo, New York, to be with her pregnant daughter. "Everybody in the office was just like that," she said. "Whatever they could do for you, they would do it."

GROWTH FROM MODEST BEGINNINGS

What began as a hole-in-the-wall has now blossomed into the world's premier doughnut company, a global cult icon, and the world's most intriguing brand. Krispy Kreme currently has nearly 300 retail doughnut shops across the United States and Canada, and will soon open more in Australia, New Zealand, Europe, Mexico, and other foreign markets. These stores produce more than 2 billion doughnuts each year, about three times the number needed to encircle the Earth. By comparison, archrival Dunkin' Donuts, with more than 5,000 outlets in 40 countries, makes only slightly more doughnuts—2.3 billion per year.

This is a far cry from the company's modest beginnings.

Founder Vernon Carver Rudolph was born on June 30, 1915, in rural Marshall County, Kentucky. Rudolph was the oldest son of mother Rethie Nimmo Rudolph and father Plumie Harrison Rudolph. He was a good student and athlete, who always had a strong work ethic. He did chores for neighbors and helped out in his father's general store. But Vernon Rudolph found his true calling after high school when he went to work with his uncle, Ishmael Armstrong.

Armstrong owned a doughnut shop in Paducah, Kentucky, a city on the Illinois border a few counties northwest of Rudolph's hometown. In the middle of the Great Depression, Armstrong made the deal of a lifetime with Joe LeBeau, a French chef from New Orleans. He bought LeBeau's doughnut shop, along with the name "Krispy Kreme" and a secret recipe handwritten on a scrap of paper. That same scribbled recipe, now locked in a safe at Krispy Kreme's headquarters in Winston-Salem, is still followed today.

In 1933, Armstrong hired his nephew, Vernon, to hawk the golden fried cakes, drenched in a glaze of sugar, door-to-door. During the Depression, people didn't buy enough of Armstrong's tempting, nearly addictive doughnuts to keep the business strong and profitable. So

Armstrong took his idea south to Nashville, Tennessee, and opened a doughnut shop there. He stayed in Nashville only briefly. In 1935, Armstrong sold the business to Vernon Rudolph's father and moved back to Paducah. The Rudolphs—Vernon, his father, and his brother Lewis—found success opening doughnut shops in Charleston, West Virginia, and later Atlanta, Georgia.

The family doughnut business was doing well, but it wasn't enough for ambitious young Vernon Rudolph. He had always dreamed of owning a doughnut shop of his own, but never seemed to have enough cash to get into business.

In 1937, Rudolph was finally able to borrow and save enough money to pursue his dream. He loaded up his 1936 Pontiac with two friends, some doughnut-making equipment, and $200 and headed toward his destiny.

Company legend has it that Rudolph and his buddies didn't know exactly where they were going, only that they were bound for business success.

As they loitered one summer evening on a street corner in Peoria, Illinois, the three friends teemed with frustration, disappointed because they were nearly broke and still hadn't found the right place to build their Krispy Kreme. Rudolph fished a pack of Camel cigarettes out of his pocket and absentmindedly read the label. The cigarettes were made in a place called Winston-Salem, North Carolina, the home of R.J. Reynolds Tobacco Company.

"Why not Winston-Salem?" asked Rudolph, according to legend. "A town with a company producing a nationally advertised product has to be a good bet."[2]

Thus, history was made on an Illinois street corner, thanks to providence and a package of cigarettes.

By the time the four men made it to Winston-Salem, they had only $25 remaining, just enough to rent a building on Winston-Salem's Main Street, across from Salem Academy and College. They borrowed potatoes, sugar, milk, and the other necessary ingredients from a local grocery store and cooked up their first batch of Krispy Kreme doughnuts from scratch. The doughnuts were packed into Rudolph's Pontiac and sold to local grocery stores. In no time, the poor entrepreneurs had made enough money to repay the grocer who loaned them ingredients for the inaugural batch.[3]

Before long, local residents began showing up outside the modest bakery, lured by the scent of Rudolph's secret and rather unusual doughnut mix.

Rudolph was no fool. He decided that if people wanted doughnuts hot and fresh from the cooker, he would oblige them. He cut a hole in the side of his retail shop and started selling doughnuts through a walk-up window: two for five cents, one dozen for a quarter.

Within 10 years, Rudolph had built Krispy Kreme from a single restaurant into a business with doughnut shops in seven southern cities. Like the original, these shops sold doughnuts directly to retail customers and in bulk to a number of wholesale buyers, including several grocery stores. Krispy Kreme incorporated in 1947. Soon after, the mix department, laboratory, and the equipment department—important divisions that are still in operation today—were created.

KEEPING TO ITS ROOTS

Vernon Rudolph died on August 17, 1973, when Krispy Kreme was still just a southeastern chain with a little more than 60 units. About three years after his death, Beatrice Foods of Chicago bought the company.

"That was a dark day for Krispy Kreme,"[4] said Joseph "Mac" McAleer, a major shareholder and member of the company's board of directors. The new owner fiddled with the sacred recipe to create a bigger, but certainly not better, doughnut. Beatrice, highly focused on increasing Krispy Kreme's profits, added sausage biscuits, soup, and sandwiches to the menu.

"Our soul is in the doughnut business, and Beatrice just didn't get that," current Krispy Kreme chairman and chief executive officer Scott Livengood said.[5]

In February 1982, McAleer's father, Joseph Sr., led other longtime franchisees in a $22 million leveraged buyout of Krispy Kreme and brought the company back to its roots. Under Beatrice, Krispy Kreme "got somewhat sidetracked," according to Joseph McAleer Sr., who is now deceased. "We reverted to our 1967 mix formula, putting all the basic ingredients . . . back in."[6] The leveraged buyout saddled Krispy Kreme with hefty debt, which delayed nationwide growth for almost a decade.

Today, Krispy Kreme is run by Livengood, a tall, thin man in his early fifties. Livengood was raised in Salisbury, North Carolina, and grew up eating Krispy Kreme doughnuts. For his sixteenth birthday, he had a plateful of chocolate-covered, cream-filled Krispy Kreme doughnuts instead of a cake. "I have memories, but I can't remember the first time [I had a Krispy Kreme]," he says. "That would be like remembering the first time you went to your grandmother's house. It really was a part of your life. It's really a part of your family and part of your culture growing up."[7]

Livengood, who joined Krispy Kreme in 1977, never worked for Vernon Rudolph. But he follows a business plan of product commitment and innovation developed by the founder.

After six decades, a simple round cake of dough with a hole in the middle is still the most important thing at Krispy Kreme. The company, as it maps out an aggressive growth strategy as a public firm, has absolutely no intention of expanding its menu much beyond coffee and doughnuts.

"Commitment" is the company's driving force, says chief operating officer John Tate. "Rather than expand into things other than doughnuts, you will see us continue to look for ways to bring the hot doughnut experience closer to our customers."[8]

"The one thing that has not changed is that hot, original doughnut," Livengood adds. "That really is the foundation of Krispy Kreme."[9]

A TASTY BRAND WITH AN AMAZING BUSINESS

More than six decades after the first doughnut was handed to a customer through a tiny window, Krispy Kreme has grown into one of the world's premier brands and most admired companies. It has even earned a place in the Smithsonian Institution's National Museum of American History.

How has Krispy Kreme managed to build such a successful brand and business, especially since it spends almost no money on advertising? What does the future hold for this unique corporation? And what can other businesses do to emulate Krispy Kreme's amazing accomplishments?

You'll read about these issues and more in *Making Dough.* This is the first major book-length profile of this phenomenal organization. In the following chapters, you'll find exclusive insider interviews and colorful stories showing how the company has evolved through the years. Each chapter also thoroughly examines one key trait the company uses to pummel the competition.

Among Krispy Kreme's secrets: It mixes good taste with show business by creating a theatrical atmosphere where customers can watch the whole doughnut-making process up close. It's picky about its people, subjecting both potential franchisees and employees to a rigorous screening process. The company operates its stores around the clock and has turned most of them into mini-factories. By making every minute count, Krispy Kreme stores churn out thousands of doughnuts each day that are sold to retail customers and distributed to a number of wholesale accounts. It is constantly looking for ways to expand its brand—most recently with coffee—while at the same time protecting the Krispy Kreme name. The company thinks big, but is careful not to grow too fast. It's a guerrilla marketer, using low- or no-cost techniques to generate millions of dollars in free publicity. It maintains the highest standards and harnesses the power of technology in all aspects of its operations. What's more, Krispy Kreme gives back to the community, trains and treats its employees well, continually builds on its past successes, and, in turn, keeps loyal fans coming back again and again.

CHAPTER 1

Mix Good Taste with Show Business

From the moment you step inside a Krispy Kreme store, be it in Las Vegas, New York, or Tuscaloosa, Alabama, you know you're not in an ordinary doughnut shop. In fact, customers are often fond of calling a visit to Krispy Kreme a "Disney-like" experience that can be had for the price of a glazed doughnut. This is no run-of-the-mill trip to the bakery or your typical fast-food restaurant. Visiting Krispy Kreme is an *event*—one that is just as exciting for adults as it is for kids.

Just ask Phil Averitt, a 36-year-old pharmacist from Greensboro, North Carolina, not far from Krispy Kreme's Winston-Salem corporate headquarters. Averitt was raised in North Carolina, where Krispy Kreme is entrenched. The company's doughnuts are sold in nearly every convenience shop and grocery store in the state. The treats are even found in some mass-merchandise stores, such as Target. Krispy Kreme's hot glazed doughnuts were a special part of Averitt's childhood and the source of many fond, fun memories. That's why, on this warm summer afternoon, Averitt has decided to take his four-year-old son, Peyton, to their local Krispy Kreme.

Averitt and Peyton hop into the car and drive down the highway hoping to come face-to-face with the famous bright red glow that brings excitement to their stomachs and a glisten of joy to their eyes.

The glow they're looking for is the round, red neon, "Hot Doughnuts Now" sign that's turned on outside of Krispy Kreme stores whenever fresh original glazed doughnuts are being made. It's a guarantee that when you walk inside, you can savor a hot treat so fresh it sticks to your fingers and melts in your mouth.

But you get much more than that. Once you step through the doors, you enter what Krispy Kreme calls its "doughnut-making theater," the company's way of combining good taste with show business by inviting customers into the kitchen to share in the fun. For starters, kids—and adults, if they wish—get paper Krispy Kreme chef's hats to wear in the store and to take home as a souvenir. Then, instead of having its doughnut makers work in a closed kitchen, Krispy Kreme has built glass walls around the preparation area so customers can see exactly what's going on behind the scenes. That means customers are able to watch as the doughnuts are made and then sent down an assembly line for the final touches of glaze.

OFFER A MULTISENSORY EXPERIENCE

Krispy Kreme strives to create a multi-sensory experience for its customers by teasing and satisfying their every sense. A trip to a Krispy Kreme store guarantees to leave you not only fed but also entertained, and both elements are equally important to the company.

"They've been clever about creating something that differentiates them besides just the taste," observes Charles Moyer, former dean of the Wake Forest University Babcock Graduate School of Management in Krispy Kreme's hometown of Winston-Salem, North Carolina.

The company has created an experience out of something as ordinary as buying a doughnut. The see-through wall, an integral design feature in every store, is merely one of the ways in which Krispy Kreme, only a fraction of the size of archrival Dunkin' Donuts, has distinguished itself from the competition and built a brand of mythical proportions.

For young Peyton Averitt, the whole show is too awesome for words. Through the large, clean glass, he watches as dozens of golden doughnuts chug their way down a conveyor belt, like a train without a caboose. There are so many of the tasty confections, he can't possibly count them all. And, as is typical of almost any Krispy Kreme store, once a kitchen worker spots Peyton's freckled face staring at the factory from the other side of the glass, the child is asked if he'd like a behind-the-scenes tour.

While Peyton's dad, Phil, instantly answers, "Yes," Peyton hesitates. The conveyor belt frightens him. His child's mind envisions a cartoon-like scene in which he gets stuck on the conveyor and dunked into the hot glaze. After hearing reassurances that he won't be turned into a doughnut, Peyton follows his father and the sales clerk into the kitchen. It's a little bit like being invited backstage at a Broadway production to see the show behind the show. While the Averitts have watched the doughnut-making process through the glass wall many times before, it's exciting to cross over to the other side and actually become part of the experience.

It all begins in a big, clean back room with an uncluttered tiled floor. Pallets of ingredients are stacked neatly along the wall. This Krispy Kreme store, like every other one in the chain, receives deliveries of fresh ingredients each week from one of the company's three distribution centers in North Carolina, Illinois, and California. The mix comes in 50-pound paper sacks labeled with all of the secret ingredients needed to make a Krispy Kreme doughnut. But even if you read the list and wrote down the ingredients, you wouldn't be able to replicate the recipe. The secret is in the proportions used and in the carefully timed preparation, claims John Underwood, a Krispy Kreme manager who compares his store to Willy Wonka's chocolate factory.

"The big secret is the way it's done. Everything's a matter of timing," Underwood insists.

Other equally large bags hold granulated sugar and what's known as 6-X powdered sugar that, in the right proportions, make up the glaze that coats Krispy Kreme's most famous doughnuts—the original glazed. Big plastic barrels, the kind that elementary school cafeteria workers recycle and use as mop buckets, line another wall. A stainless steel walk-in refrigerator, so big and cold inside that you shiver as the door opens, keeps gallons of fresh milk chilled.

When it's time to make a new batch of doughnuts, these ingredients are wheeled from the storage room into the kitchen. It takes about 70 minutes for these ingredients to become dough and, ultimately, glazed doughnuts.

Few bakeries other than Krispy Kreme will let you watch the production process this closely. There are trade secrets to protect, after all. But such things don't concern Krispy Kreme.

Peyton and his father watch the process intently. A worker dumps a bag of yeast mix into an industrial-sized mixer. A poof of flour sprays into the air. Milk is added to the dry ingredients. A button is punched, and the computerized mixer comes to life.

The glaze is made nearby. First, granulated sugar is cooked until it becomes a boiling hot liquid. Another worker opens a faucet on the tank and warm, half-made glaze whooshes out into a container. It is then transferred to another big mixer, and the powdered sugar is folded in. The glaze rests for 10 minutes before it is poured into a hopper on the stainless steel patented Krispy Kreme doughnut fryer and glazing machine.

Averitt and his son, who, of course, is wearing a paper Krispy Kreme hat, watch as a hook lifts the raw dough into yet another machine, called an *extruder*. The air-powered tool punches out perfectly formed doughnut rings, which weigh about 1.17 ounces raw, onto trays that go in the proof box. The proofer is a tall, rectangular structure with glass windows on each side. The box contains just the right amount of heat and humidity to activate the yeast, making the dough rise, or proof. Raw doughnuts travel up and down inside the box for 30 minutes, until they're just puffy and airy enough to be Krispy Kremes.

Once the dough has completely risen, the rings fall into a bath of vegetable shortening. The doughnuts, six astride and still uncooked on top, travel through a river of oil, up a slight hill. Then, they plummet off a little cliff and land golden side up so the other side can cook, too. The oil is hot, about 360 degrees Fahrenheit. And the doughnuts cook quickly, browning in just over three minutes. The golden doughnuts glide under a waterfall of warm glaze, then make a brief trip through a stainless steel tunnel that allows them to cool just enough so they won't burn the tongue. Krispy Kreme employees use plastic sticks to hook hot doughnuts through their holes and serve them directly to customers or place them into cardboard boxes.

SATISFY YOUR AUDIENCE

Visitors to Krispy Kreme haven't always been treated to such an awe-inspiring show. When Krispy Kreme founder Vernon Rudolph started the company in 1937, he planned to only be a wholesaler, selling his pastries directly to local grocery stores. He was pushed into the retail business almost by accident. The residents of Winston-Salem, where the company is still based, were lured to his kitchen by the constant sweet aroma of Rudolph's secret mix of flour, yeast, shortening, potatoes, and sugar. Eager fans lined up outside his door each morning hoping for a taste of what smelled like something from heaven.

Rosalee Moore, who was born the same year as the company, lived two blocks away from the original Krispy Kreme store as a child. She remembers the smell of cooking doughnuts as if she were sniffing it today. Sometimes the sweet scent hung so thickly in the air that Moore felt intoxicated by it. The sensory assault made Moore's stomach feel heavy, as though she had gorged on all those doughnuts herself. But even when the odor was overwhelming, it didn't keep Moore, her family, or other doughnut pilgrims away. They trekked to Rudolph's kitchen and clamored for a taste.

"I just liked them then, and still do," says Moore, who anticipates her frequent Krispy Kreme visits now as much as she did in the company's early days.

Rudolph satisfied his public by selling doughnuts hot and fresh through a walk-up window that he cut in the front of his shop.

For more than a half century after that, Krispy Kreme continued to operate with basically the same kind of setup. While bulk sales to grocery stores, convenience stores, and fund-raising groups were the company's main revenue drivers, retail customers weren't turned away. But they weren't courted and pampered the way they are today.

KEEP 'EM ENTERTAINED

For decades, the only seats found inside a Krispy Kreme store were those stray counter stools that were usually filled with coffee-drinking, gossip-sharing regulars. Yes, there was a small glass window inside many stores that provided customers with a partial glimpse of the doughnut production process. But most of the work still went on out of public view. The kitchen was just that—a kitchen. It wasn't the huge stage that is found in Krispy Kreme stores today. That innovation wasn't implemented until the late 1980s.

J. A. "Mac" McAleer Jr. was among the first to realize that people didn't come to Krispy Kreme just for the doughnuts. McAleer, who was 38 when selected in May 1988 to serve as president and chief operating officer of the company, had good reason to love Krispy Kreme doughnuts. The company was literally in his blood.

His father, for whom he is named, began working for founder Vernon Rudolph as an intern making $1 an hour in 1951. Joseph McAleer, who was dubbed "the doughnut king" in newspaper obituaries after his December 1998 death from lung cancer, was working at another job when he spotted an classified ad promising "excellent profit opportunities in the doughnut business."[1] The senior McAleer decided that this could be a potentially more lucrative career than his current job at an Alabama news agency. He also felt it would be a better way for him to provide for his growing family, which eventually included five daughters and two sons. McAleer responded to the ad and, after a short stint as an intern, soon had the chance to open his own Krispy Kreme store in Alabama under the direction of Rudolph. Ultimately, his holdings grew into a large franchise group, where he oversaw several stores.

In 1982, the Alabama native led a group of men credited with saving Krispy Kreme from what they considered destruction by a big business that they felt was more concerned about profits than it was about consistency or customers. McAleer and other visionary franchisees borrowed money and pooled their savings to buy the company back from conglomerate Beatrice Foods, which had changed the famous doughnut recipe and added soups and sandwiches to the menu after buying the company in 1976, three years after Rudolph's death. McAleer also brought his two sons, Mac and Jack, into the business.

Mac McAleer started out washing doughnut delivery trucks behind his father's store in Mobile, Alabama. As a result, stories about Krispy Kreme have filled his memory bank from the time he was a small child.

CREATE MEMORIES

Through years of watching his father at work and later as an associate franchisee himself, Mac McAleer learned that other people, with much more tenuous connections to the company, had special Krispy Kreme memories, too. He discovered that the taste of a hot doughnut triggered fond recollections for many loyal customers. For others, Krispy Kreme had become an important part of family rituals.

North Carolinians Nancy Gates, Meg Scott Phipps, and Mel Watt are just three of the thousands of customers who feel a unique kinship with Krispy Kreme.

When her children were young, Nancy Gates began a Christmas morning ritual that has lasted for nearly 40 years. For children especially, Christmas is as much about the anticipation as it is about unwrapping gifts. Once all those presents are stripped of their shiny wrapping, much of the day's excitement is gone.

Not at Nancy Gates's house. There was always one box left after all of the others had been opened—a Krispy Kreme box filled with fresh doughnuts. The family ate them for Christmas breakfast, along with cereal, fresh orange juice, and cold milk.

"Those doughnuts got us going [all of those Christmases]," Gates wrote in a letter to Krispy Kreme. Gates is now a widow, and only two of her adult children live close enough to spend Christmas morning with their mom. But Gates, her daughter, her son, and her daughter-in-law still always have Krispy Kreme doughnuts for their Christmas breakfast. "Our holiday just wouldn't be the same without them," Gates says.

Meg Scott Phipps has lots of stories to tell about growing up in the North Carolina governor's mansion. Phipps, who was elected as secretary of agriculture in North Carolina in 2000, is the daughter of the state's former governor, Bob Scott, and the granddaughter of yet another governor, Kerr Scott. But one of her favorite memories is not about politics, but rather about Krispy Kreme doughnuts.

Phipps, along with four of her siblings, lived in the state governor's mansion during her father's term, from 1969 to 1973. There was a lot for young Meg to be excited about during that time. She was the governor's daughter, living in a huge, brick Victorian home in Raleigh. Even then, Raleigh was a place with a lot more going on than in her hometown of Haw River, a small village northwest of the capital in mostly rural Alamance County. But what Phipps, who spent most of her childhood on a dairy farm, loved most about living in the North Carolina executive mansion was being across the street from a Krispy

Kreme doughnut shop. Late at night, while their father was crafting state policy in his office (and sometimes even when their parents were asleep), the Scott children would scale the security wall that wraps around the governor's mansion, sneak across the street, and order hot doughnuts at Krispy Kreme. They carried the boxes back over the wall and took them to their rooms. Phipps, who is now in her forties with two children of her own, says neither her parents nor the governor's security agents ever found out about their late-night escapes. But, she surmises, they surely must have smelled the still-hot snacks.

"That is one of my favorite memories. I'm a true fan of Krispy Kreme. It is the best doughnut in the world. You can tell by looking at me," she jokes, patting her stomach.

Congressman Mel Watt remembers taking dates to Krispy Kreme in Charlotte during the late 1960s and early 1970s. Watt, whose Twelfth Congressional District includes Charlotte, North Carolina's largest city, says Krispy Kreme was "the place to go" after a night on the town. Decades ago, when few restaurants stayed open past 9, much less all night, Krispy Kreme would be cooking into the wee hours. You could drive down Independence Boulevard, then a main drag through Charlotte, and see the glow from the hot light and the fluorescents burning inside, he recalls. "There used to be people lined up at two or three o'clock in the morning. Even in a city the size of Charlotte, that was the only place where you could get them hot off the line."

EXCEED EXPECTATIONS

Mac McAleer heard many stories like these during his time at Krispy Kreme. They all had a unifying theme: Customers associated Krispy Kreme not just with good doughnuts, but also with wholesome, positive, fun family times. Maybe, McAleer mused, Krispy Kreme could play a more active role in making these experiences more robust. Perhaps it could even bring them to life.

McAleer set out to make this happen. It's an idea that now infuses the company and guides Krispy Kreme in every aspect of its business.

"Everything we do, we create it more and more around the experience," notes Jay Jung, the company's creative director of concept development. Each day, Jung works alongside Mac McAleer's younger brother, Jack, who is vice chairman and executive vice president of concept development.

"People connect to Krispy Kreme for our doughnuts, but not necessarily only because of our doughnuts. What we found is that they connect to the experience of Krispy Kreme. We have the best doughnuts. We know that, and people have told us that. And no matter what the environment looks like, people will come for our doughnuts," explains Jung, who tasted his first Krispy Kreme in 1984 after moving to the South and now talks about his employer with breathless, boyish exuberance.

"But we also realized that they come for the experience around the doughnut. So if people are celebrating winning a hockey game, they come to Krispy Kreme. If they just want to talk, they come to Krispy Kreme. If they're not feeling great, and they want a little pick-me-up, they come to Krispy Kreme."

MAKE CAREFULLY CALCULATED CHANGES

Mac McAleer, who is now a major Krispy Kreme franchisee in Texas and a former member of the company's board of directors, decided in the late 1980s that Krispy Kreme should change its look as well as its focus. These were not changes made lightly or quickly, but ones that were studied carefully and thoroughly picked apart. The changes were eventually implemented to make Krispy Kreme more marketable to customers and potential franchisees. It was all designed with a new goal in mind: to make the company as powerful and successful a retailer as it was a wholesaler.

"We're leaning toward retail now. It's something that we hope to franchise,"[2] McAleer said when Krispy Kreme was building its first stores with doughnut theaters inside.

"We have some pretty ambitious growth plans if this works like we expect that it will,"[3] said Scott Livengood, then senior vice president of administration and corporate development, and now the company's chief executive officer.

"The whole multi-sensory part of the experience is not something that came about overnight," observes Charles Moyer, the Wake Forest

University dean, who knows many Krispy Kreme executives personally. "I think what they were trying to define at that point in time was what one of these places would really look like. What's the optimal layout? And how do you present it to people so it catches their attention?"

In fact, executives were examining every part of the company. They studied years of consumer research—some collected formally, but much of it from spontaneous conversations with customers. They were seeking to find the essence of the brand. They set out to define what made Krispy Kreme different from other doughnut makers and to brainstorm ways they could expand on that.

"In the late 1980s and early 1990s, as we started listening to consumers and understanding what made Krispy Kreme special to them, we heard them tout the hot doughnuts," says Stan Parker, the company's senior vice president of marketing. "The first thing we did during that time period was to redesign the store and bring the doughnut-making theater out to make it part of the store experience. We also enlarged the seating area. We started to add drive-throughs. And very importantly, we had this 'Hot Doughnuts Now' neon sign that said, 'We're going to turn this on as a guarantee that we're making our original glazed doughnuts at that time. We're going to take a large block of time in the morning and the evening, and dedicate it to the retail customer and the hot doughnut experience.' So, that started elevating the brand in the early '90s."[4]

Beginning with a new store on High Point Road in Greensboro, a city about 40 minutes from the company's headquarters, McAleer began transforming Krispy Kreme into a true retail company in 1989. No longer would Krispy Kreme be a wholesaler that just happened to do some retail sales. The company would instead be a retailer with a secondary sales channel to food markets.

"The business model for the history of the company until the mid-1990s was a wholesale business model," according to Livengood, who worked for Mac McAleer and his father. Back then, the wholesale side of the business generated about 70 percent of Krispy Kreme revenues, and stores were built as factories.

"And sometimes these plants—we called [stores] plants then—had multiple lines in them. So we could make a lot of doughnuts,"[5] Livengood said. The doughnuts that weren't boxed up and put on grocery store delivery trucks were sold directly to consumers through "a little glass box that was built on the front of the plant."[6]

Yet what was an afterthought for the company was an important feature to its customers. Many Krispy Kreme fans began their reminiscences the same way: "I remember watching the doughnuts being made through that little window." McAleer grabbed onto that repeated detail and made the doughnut cooker the centerpiece of the newly designed Krispy Kreme stores that were meant to satisfy a customer's every sensory need—sight, smell, taste, touch, and sound.

As Livengood explains, "The one thing that we are very intentional about is making sure that the doughnut-making process is visible and that the Krispy Kreme experience is a multi-sensory experience. There are certain elements of our brand that are captivating. Once in the store, we have our doughnut-making theater. We have that glass wall where you can see the entire doughnut-making process going on."[7]

Though Krispy Kreme's recipe is a vaulted secret, every part of the cooking process is on display and well detailed in every store. Words printed on the glass describe what's happening as the doughnuts— between 4,000 and 10,000 dozen a day, depending on the size of the store—move through the cooker.

"You wouldn't think it's just a doughnut," says Robbie Davis, another Krispy Kreme manager. His employees' chatter and lively, laughter-tinged banter with customers is all part of the performance. "We're here to create magic moments. We're actually in the entertainment business. For us, the show we put on is almost as important as the doughnut."

Though Krispy Kreme employees are usually very business-minded when describing the purpose of the doughnut-making theater, even Livengood sometimes becomes as philosophical and hyperbolic about it as his customers.

"The movement of the products on the conveyor through our proof box has this relaxing, almost mesmerizing effect," he points out. "The only other thing like it is standing on the ocean front and watching the tide come in. It has that same consistent, relaxing motion that is really positive to people who may or may not understand what is happening to them."[8]

The glass-encased cooker is a keystone of the Krispy Kreme brand. But what the company describes as the "Krispy Kreme experience" actually begins long before a customer even steps inside.

TURN ON THE HOT LIGHT

Twice a day, with the regularity of the rising and setting sun, a round red light is flipped on at every Krispy Kreme store around the world. Between 5:30 A.M. and 11 A.M. and again between 5:30 P.M. and 11 P.M.— according to market research, the hours of peak demand for dough-nuts—Krispy Kreme cooks batch after batch of its glazed treats. Cus-tomers know this because the sign tells them so: "Hot Doughnuts Now." The hot light is like a marquee at the movie theater; it tells cus-tomers what they can expect if they push through the plate-glass door at their local Krispy Kreme.

"When you see that hot sign on, you start getting certain sensations in your mouth," notes Tom Ogburn, professor at Wake Forest Univer-sity. As director of the school's Family Business Center, he helps to coach owners and employees of family-run businesses. "The company looks at it as an experience. It is not selling a product. It is selling an experience. Everything it does from a marketing standpoint is designed to reinforce that experience."

People like Mac McAleer and Scott Livengood realized that one of the things customers liked best about Krispy Kreme, and something that differentiated their company from competitors, was the chance to get a hot doughnut. But before the hot light, only serendipity guaran-teed that a customer would get one. In the company's past, store managers cooked doughnuts at various times, with no day-to-day reg-ularity.

"The best thing they ever did for their marketing is to create the hot sign," claims Crystal DeBerry, a student lured away from her studies at North Carolina Agricultural and Technical State University by the red light. Krispy Kreme CEO Livengood agrees. "It was one of those great things that a company has to be around long enough to have," he says. "It's the essence of great marketing."[9]

The neon light idea, like many other Krispy Kreme innovations, was inspired by an entrepreneurial franchisee, who discovered it himself almost by accident.

During the 1970s, Chattanooga, Tennessee, franchisee Bob Glidden set out to find a way to let customers know when fresh doughnuts were available in his store. "On his own, he went to a J.C. Penney store and bought a window shade," Livengood notes. "He had a sign company print, 'Hot Doughnuts Now' on it, and when the doughnuts were hot he'd pull down the window shade."[10] The corporate office soon latched onto the good idea and had lighted neon signs produced for all of its stores. That light, which has been redesigned and stylized in recent years, is now a hallmark of the Krispy Kreme brand. "The hot light is well recognized as a sign that we're serving the original glazed doughnuts hot," Parker says. "The essence of the brand is the hot doughnut experience."

Apparently, consumers wish more companies would copy Krispy Kreme's strategy. At a recent international conference for companies in the dairy, deli, and bakery businesses, eight consumer panelists said they'd like to see bakeries turn on an in-store light to signify when items are fresh-baked, just like Krispy Kreme, according to Dan Malovany, a reporter for *Snack Food & Wholesale Bakery* who was at the event. "Hot and fresh really hits a spot with American consumers," he says.

TEMPT AND SATISFY THE SENSES

A true multi-sensory Krispy Kreme experience begins with the sight of the hot light and the wide-open kitchen. Customers can hear the sound of friendly, happy employees and watch the doughnuts sizzling in hot vegetable oil. Then there's that smell—distinctive yet so difficult to describe. Just a whiff of fresh, active yeast, but not enough that it smells like bread dough baking. The aroma is more like colored sugar being spun into cotton candy or sugar caramelizing on the stove. There's a tiny reminder of grandma's house in that scent, especially on those days when her kitchen was hot and busy with holiday baking. The deep-frying batter gives off a fragrance you might encounter at a county fair midway near the booths that serve sugar-sprinkled funnel cakes and elephant ears. But none of these descriptions really capture what a Krispy Kreme store smells like twice a day when the glazed doughnuts are cooking. The doughnuts have an aroma more like a complex perfume, a blend of many different scents, each associated with a distinct memory.

Krispy Kreme doughnuts also have a unique effect on the skin. You sense it first when the clerk hands over a green polka-dot box filled with hot doughnuts. The box is so broad you have to carry it with both hands, most likely cradling the bottom with your open palms. The cardboard prevents the sticky residue that's clinging to the freshly fried, glazed doughnuts from seeping through the box. But it's too thin to provide any insulation. The heat slowly infuses the hands, then starts warming you all over, like a sweatshirt fresh from the clothes dryer.

It's all you can do to make it to the table or car before ripping into the package and sneaking a bite. But Krispy Kremes aren't like French fries eaten from a fast-food bag. There's no such thing as a clandestine nibble. Every consumed doughnut leaves a souvenir in the box—an oily, sugar-flaked silhouette. Then there's the evidence that is left on your fingers: glaze as sticky as paste that you can't help but lick off.

Despite all of the other sensory pleasures, the climax of the Krispy Kreme experience doesn't come until you get that hot doughnut in your mouth. The taste is another elusive sensation. Is a Krispy Kreme like sugar-encrusted air? A bit of heaven on the tongue? Fifty-nine cents of pure pleasure? A sinful featherweight confection? Unbridled ecstasy? Writers, customers, company employees, and financial analysts have all stretched the boundaries of metaphor searching for words vivid enough to explain what eating a Krispy Kreme doughnut is like.

Some people devour the hot treat and moan as the last bite slips down the throat. Others linger, making a meal out of a single doughnut, sighing contentedly with each nibble. Some let the powerfully tasty doughnut possess them; their heads loll and their eyes roll at the taste. Others have even cried in joy at the taste, tearing up like a happy bride and groom on their wedding day. But nearly all customers come back for more, drawn again and again to the carefully crafted and supremely satisfying Krispy Kreme experience.

And that's really the point. By entertaining customers, the company not only gives people a reason to come into the store, but also creates lasting memories. In turn, customers return again and again to relive these memorable experiences and to fill their stomachs with Krispy Kreme's terrific treats, behavior that continues to boost the company's revenues and reputation.

CHAPTER 2

Be Picky about Your Partners

Gerard Centioli, the president and chief executive officer of Chicago-based ICON, is about as experienced a restaurateur as you can find. He learned the business at the knee of his father, Gil Centioli, a burger baron in the Pacific Northwest and an original Kentucky Fried Chicken franchisee who worked closely with that company's legendary founder, Colonel Harland Sanders.

Centioli and two partners had long dreamed of building a business that would develop and run a group of iconic restaurant chains. They began putting their plan into action with the March 1999 founding of ICON. The company is affiliated with the already successful Lettuce Entertain You Enterprises, which operates 31 popular restaurant concepts around the country.

ICON's goal: to form partnerships with bona fide restaurant icons and develop multiple units of these special eateries. "ICON partners with existing restaurants and grows them,"[1] Centioli explains.

ICON's first partnership was with Joe's Stone Crab, a legendary Miami restaurant that is open only from mid-October to mid-May each year, the height of Florida's stone crab season. The original restaurant, which opened in 1913, doesn't take reservations. But during the peak season, close to 1,200 patrons wait up to two hours each night to dine in the 450-seat restaurant. Their devotion translates into average revenues of $20 million during the seven months Joe's is open each year.[2]

ICON opened its own version of the restaurant concept, which it calls Joe's Seafood, Prime Steak & Stone Crab, in Chicago in October 2000.

But the big prize ICON coveted was gaining rights to develop a string of Krispy Kreme franchises. ICON's partners first approached Krispy Kreme about becoming an area developer in September 1998, at a time when the doughnut company wasn't actively recruiting franchisees. As a result, ICON's letters and phone calls were rebuffed for some time. When Krispy Kreme was finally willing to listen to the company's pitch a few years later, the partners had to convince senior vice president of franchise development Philip Waugh and chief executive officer Scott Livengood that they were worthy of joining the elite fraternity of Krispy Kreme franchisees.

"We knew they had the best doughnuts," says Centioli, who claims he has never been able to eat just one hot original glazed ring. Four at a sitting is more his style. "What we didn't know was how thorough that management team was. And we didn't know that until they were done examining us."

Though ICON's partners had achieved success with other restaurants and in other businesses, Krispy Kreme didn't give them an automatic pass. They were subjected to the same scrutiny every potential franchisee undergoes, including such celebrities as singer Jimmy Buffett, entertainer Dick Clark, and baseball star Hank Aaron. "They checked us out. They didn't take anything for granted. And we've had success," Centioli says, adding that Krispy Kreme executives visited various Lettuce Entertain You Restaurants as both invited guests and undercover diners during the investigative process.

"My impression is they didn't take any of that [our past successes] for granted. They came out to Chicago. They—and this includes Scott—went through our restaurants with us, front to back. They met our people. They wanted to know exactly who we were and how we operated.

"We have a pretty high profile in this industry. We're accustomed to people taking that reputation for granted and accepting it on its face. They didn't do that," Centioli observes. "They went through the restaurants, which others have done. But what they did that no one else ever did is they asked us for references. So, we gave them a list of roughly ten personal and professional references for each of the three principals of ICON. I had to really scratch my head. I think the last time I had to provide anybody references was when I was buying a house.

"To their credit, they didn't know us," adds Centioli, who remains impressed with Krispy Kreme's thorough screening process. "And they were going to get to know us before they were going to do business with us. That level of detail and commitment is evident in everything that we do with them."

In early 2000, ICON was finally granted the right to develop Krispy Kreme stores in the markets of Seattle, Washington; Portland, Oregon; Anchorage, Alaska; Honolulu, Hawaii; and Vancouver, British Columbia, in Canada. In Chicago, ICON opened one store in the River North area and another in the suburban North Shore area in a joint partnership with another Chicago-area developer. As part of the deal, Krispy Kreme took an equity interest in ICON's development territory so it can share in the profits generated by the group's doughnut shops. Such an equity arrangement is now standard operating practice for the company.

TAKE A GAMBLE

Lincoln Spoor had a somewhat different, but similarly daunting, journey to becoming a Krispy Kreme franchisee. Spoor is a former New York City investment banker who had his first Krispy Kreme hot original glazed in 1992. Spoor had been making his own doughnuts with Pillsbury dough since the age of seven. He even considered himself to be a doughnut connoisseur of sorts. But the doughnut he had at the Krispy Kreme store in Alexandria, Virginia, during a business trip to the nation's capital was the best he'd ever devoured. "I fell in love," he recalls. "I had the best doughnut I'd ever had in my life."[3]

Spoor grew up in Minneapolis, graduated from the Tuck School of Business at Dartmouth in Hanover, New Hampshire, and ultimately became managing director of high-yield investments for Bank of America. He spent a lot of time traveling to places like Las Vegas and realized he really liked the West. Around 1995, he began questioning what he wanted to do with the rest of his life, and had a hard time getting the thought of Krispy Kreme out of his mind.

"I can't let go of this dream I have," he thought. "My mind keeps coming back to it, over and over again. I want to take those doughnuts out of the South."[4]

Spoor contacted Krispy Kreme headquarters to ask about starting a franchise. Although he was invited to discuss the idea with company officials in North Carolina, the company wasn't looking to add franchisees at the time. Two years later, Spoor called the company again and talked with head of franchising Philip Waugh. Spoor told Waugh he was thinking about leaving the bank and heard that Krispy Kreme was entertaining the idea of selling some new franchises. If so, Spoor was ready to buy. The response from Waugh was an unequivocal no.

"He didn't fit our profile," Waugh reflects. "And that's what I told him. The regions he wanted were too far west; he had no management team in place . . . and no franchising experience. We have a qualification process, and he didn't pass."[5]

Crushed, Spoor still held on to his dream. He kept calling Waugh and continued negotiating for months. Finally, in March 1997, Spoor convinced Krispy Kreme to give him a deal that would allow him to build stores in Nevada and Utah. This would become the company's first foray into the West.

Spoor decided to build his initial store at the corner of Rainbow Boulevard and Spring Mountain Road in the gambling capital of the world, Las Vegas. The building process didn't go as smoothly as he had planned. The store's original opening date was set for October 1997. Because of construction delays and higher than anticipated costs, the actual opening date was delayed five months, until March 3, 1998.

To get the store opened, Spoor wound up having to borrow against his home, max out his credit cards, and liquidate his stock portfolio. It was definitely going to cost more to realize his Krispy Kreme dream than he first imagined.

"I had soaked everything into the store, and the numbers were more than I'd ever guessed they'd be. I underestimated by a long shot," Spoor admits.[6]

He realized he'd be broke if the store was unsuccessful. As a result, anticipation was high on opening day. Would anyone care that Las Vegas had a Krispy Kreme?

By 5:30 on the morning of the opening, the answer to that question was clear. A long line of customers waited outside, and cars were already parked in the drive-through. As one reporter on the scene that morning wrote, "The doors of Lincoln's Krispy Kreme store opened and quickly became a blur of doughnuts and bodies. I saw an old man weep as he bit into a hot glazed. I saw two women embrace in delight. I heard a trucker with sugar frosting on his upper lip yell out, 'Good God almighty!' I saw a woman eating a doughnut and screaming in her car, pounding her feet on the floor. I saw the fat and the thin, the old and the young, the timid and the bold."[7]

Yes, Las Vegas was thrilled that Lincoln Spoor convinced Krispy Kreme to let him open a store in Sin City. By midnight, the store had sold 72,000 doughnuts, an opening record at the time. By the end of the week, that number jumped to 360,000.

Today, Krispy Kreme stores are found throughout Las Vegas, including in many popular casinos, such as Treasure Island, Excalibur, Palace Station, and Circus Circus.

HAVE AN ENTREPRENEURIAL SPIRIT

Brad Bruckman's road to gaining the rights to develop more Krispy Kreme's in the West was equally storied. Bruckman has been an entrepreneur his whole life. In addition to running several small companies in high school, he built a multi-million-dollar network of eight pizza shops in Pittsburgh, Pennsylvania, while still in his twenties. As a student at South Carolina's Clemson University, he became a delivery driver for Domino's Pizza and quickly rose to management trainee. By age 21, Bruckman owned his first Domino's outlet, and he opened seven more within a few years.

After selling his business and earning a master's degree in business administration at the University of Pittsburgh, Bruckman joined the corporate world, creating a venture for PepsiCo in Russia worth $12 million per year. His job? Selling Taco Bell burritos to thousands of Muscovites. Even though he didn't speak a word of Russian, he built the Taco Bell operation in Moscow from scratch, serving a simple menu of Pepsi soft drinks, Frito-Lay chips, Taco Bell burritos, and American-style hot dogs. Over a two-year period, Bruckman opened 15 locations and oversaw 300 employees.[8]

"Nobody thought we could do it," Bruckman reflects. "Most folks thought in that environment we couldn't do that much that fast. Lines would literally form before we opened in the morning. It was very well accepted."[9]

Bruckman met his wife, Maria, in Moscow. She's the daughter of a

Russian diplomat who worked as an administrator with Ernst & Young. PepsiCo eventually moved Bruckman and his wife to Dallas, Texas, where he was responsible for negotiating the multi-million-dollar cheese contract for PepsiCo restaurants.

"When we came back to the U.S., I started to say to Maria that I thought I needed to go out to a small company and do something different," Bruckman says. "I had that entrepreneurial itch."[10]

In February 1997, one of Bruckman's former colleagues suggested that he take a look at running a Krispy Kreme franchise. The thought of getting up before dawn to fry doughnuts was far from appealing. But the colleague persisted and convinced Bruckman and his wife to visit some Krispy Kreme shops just to take a look. They were immediately impressed.

"I have had doughnuts from all over the world," Maria Bruckman shares. "I literally inhaled four [Krispy Kreme] doughnuts. It was totally unbelievable."[11]

Bruckman immediately began courting potential investors and Krispy Kreme executives. Although he hoped to gain franchise rights for New England, the company instead offered him a chance to establish a joint venture for northern California, stretching from Visalia to Monterey to the Oregon border. Krispy Kreme offered to invest $2 million in return for a 59 percent ownership stake in a company to be called Golden Gate Doughnuts. The 38-year-old Bruckman would be the company's managing partner.

The Bruckmans spent three months learning all about the doughnut business at Krispy Kreme's Winston-Salem headquarters. They then moved to Sacramento in November 1998 and spent more than a year planning for the opening of their first Krispy Kreme in the Bay Area. Today, Golden Gate Doughnuts runs more than one dozen stores and ultimately plans to have 30 outlets throughout northern California.

DO WHAT IT TAKES

Then there's Roly Morris, who had to be both ambitious and persuasive in his quest to become a Krispy Kreme franchisee. The native of Toronto, Canada, is a former Starbucks executive who convinced the company to put him in charge of expanding its Canadian presence. Under Morris's leadership, Starbucks went from having 15 stores, all in the Vancouver area, to 155 throughout Canada. Before Morris left Starbucks in 1997, he oversaw a total of 350 outlets in Canada and three U.S. states.

In early 2001, Krispy Kreme granted Morris and investment banker Robert Fisher the right to develop Krispy Kreme stores in eastern Canada. There was a heated bidding war to get the rights to build the first Krispy Kreme stores outside the United States. Despite his proven success with Starbucks, Morris had to work hard to prove he was the right man for the job. Among other things, he spent six weeks in a California Krispy Kreme store making glaze and washing rest rooms to demonstrate his commitment.

The first Canadian stores opened in mid-2002, six months ahead of schedule. Despite heated competition from rival doughnut chain Tim Hortons, which had a lock on the Canadian doughnut market, Morris is amazed with how well Krispy Kreme has done.

"The response is overwhelming, and we've been very fortunate in having high-quality real estate become available to us sooner than we thought, virtually in all market places," Morris says.[12]

Morris is president and chief executive of what's known as KremeKo, the venture that holds Krispy Kreme development rights for Ontario, Quebec, Western Canada, and Atlantic Canada. The company plans to open about 40 stores in Canada over the next five years. Morris admits he was a bit skeptical that the doughnut chain would prosper as it has, because Canada has more doughnut shops per capita than any other country. "One of [the refrains we heard] . . . from the get-go two years ago was Canadians don't typically buy doughnuts by the dozen," Morris remembers. "Well, take a look around at all those dozens going out that door. They're buying doughnuts by the dozens because they're not just doughnuts, they're Krispy Kremes. That's the explanation."[13]

Morris believes that, like his former employer Starbucks, Krispy Kreme will actually be able to expand the market for its products rather than simply taking market share away from rivals such as Tim Hortons. "What very likely will happen is more people will consume doughnuts [in Canada] than have ever consumed doughnuts before," he predicts.[14]

MAKE THEM WORK FOR IT

Most Krispy Kreme franchisees have similar stories: They come from illustrious backgrounds, yet still have to work hard to become part of the Krispy Kreme family. There's no doubt that Krispy Kreme puts its potential franchisees through some serious scrutiny. The basic qualifications for the job are daunting indeed. Franchisees must have what the company calls "an entrepreneurial spirit and desire to succeed," rounded out by real-world business experience, preferably in the food service industry. Add to that a sound reputation, strong business acumen, integrity, business values similar to Krispy Kreme's, and, of course, an understanding of the Krispy Kreme business model. Franchisees must also generally live in and know the market they choose to develop, which explains why most, though not all, hail from their assigned territories.

"Under our area developer concept, we want an entrepreneurial spirit where our franchisees rely on their local expertise to tailor the Krispy Kreme brand to their specific markets. Many times we get great marketing ideas from them, like we did in Chicago. They said, 'We're by the airport. Hey, wouldn't it be great to have our logo on the roof. Then people could see it from planes as they land at O'Hare,' "[15] marketing chief Stan Parker says.

It's no stretch to compare the search for a Krispy Kreme franchisee to the search for a NASA astronaut. Many dedicated and hopeful people apply, but few possess the talent to survive the selection process. "We [work with] really bright folks who understand what a brand is about and who are trying to do what's right for the business,"[16] CEO Scott Livengood says.

CHARGE WHAT YOU'RE WORTH

Franchising has long been a way for entrepreneurial-minded individuals to start their own businesses without facing the same risks and challenges as those who start from scratch with a new idea. "We like to use the term, 'In business for yourself, not by yourself,' " explains Don DeBolt, president of the International Franchise Association, an organization started in 1960 by the founder of Krispy Kreme rival Dunkin' Donuts. The types of business opportunities available vary: A franchisee could own a nail salon, a bail bonds office, a cookie shop, or a burger joint. In the majority of cases, a normal person with a little bit of a nest egg, some business sense, and a dream can buy and open a franchise. About two-thirds of the franchises in America, DeBolt says, require an initial investment of less than $250,000, and probably half of them take less than $100,000 to get started.

But not Krispy Kreme. These doughnut shops may feel simple and homey, but no mom-and-pop operation could meet the high standards that Krispy Kreme requires of its franchisees. The company refers to them as *area developers* because they sign up to open many stores. "The little growth we've done outside the South has been with area developers. These people are all local operators who have proven themselves in those areas," Parker explains.[17]

"They've got a long line of people that would love to get a Krispy Kreme franchise," says the International Franchise Association's DeBolt. "And there is going to be a long line of disappointed people. The very strategic growth approach they've taken is designed to give franchisees the best possible opportunity for profitability.

"It's a carefully managed and crafted expansion strategy. They're doing it market by market. They're being so very selective about the franchisees that are chosen. You're basically trying to do a manufacturing job in a retail store under the same roof, and that's pretty complicated. The franchisees Krispy Kreme selects are good business people that are very sophisticated and that have the financial resources to develop a market's potential."

Though it once granted franchises on a store-by-store basis, Krispy Kreme is now interested only in partnerships with area developers who commit to open multiple stores—usually at least 10—in a set geographic region. These partners must have significant skill, experience, and money to join the Krispy Kreme franchise family. "You're talking about very high volume levels, which would overwhelm most mom-and-pop fast-food franchisees," explains Chicago-based consultant Don Boroian, chief executive officer of Francorp. "If the operators aren't strong, it's a big problem."[18]

That's why, even though the company now boasts around 300 locations worldwide, it only has around 30 franchisees among its ranks.

The requirements for owning a Krispy Kreme shop are clearly spelled out in the company's Uniform Franchise Offering Circular (UFOC), a thick stack of footnoted and appendixed legal documents that the Federal Trade Commission requires the company to give to any serious potential franchisee. This hard-to-get publication is released only to those individuals who have already passed muster with the company as a potential partner.

At Krispy Kreme, the UFOC is handed over during the first face-to-face meeting with Waugh or someone else from the company's franchise department. As current Krispy Kreme franchisees—and plenty of wanna-bes—can attest, that first meeting is hard to score. The company is generally interested in talking only to people with proven industry experience and a record of success. But even they aren't immediately accepted.

James Cosentino of Dynamic Doughnuts Inc., whose Krispy Kreme territory includes the New York cities of Buffalo, Syracuse, and Rochester, campaigned for two years and visited corporate headquarters three times before winning area developer rights. Cosentino, owner of 19 T.G.I. Friday's restaurants and six Denny's, has 30 years of experience in the restaurant industry. Kevin Gordon is a former banker who spent his career lending money to franchisees. Still, he had to work the phones for six months, calling every business day, before convincing Krispy Kreme to let him open nine restaurants through his Lone Star Doughnuts Ltd. in Houston, Texas.[19] Illinois-based Glazed Investments, which is opening Krispy Kreme stores in Wisconsin, Minnesota, and Colorado, is part of AmeriKing, which operates hundreds of Burger King restaurants throughout the country. Nick Valenti, of New York's Restaurant Associates, heads up KKNY, the developer for New York City and New Jersey. Restaurant Associates, which is credited with inventing the theme-restaurant concept in 1950, now includes more than 130 restaurants. And the maestros behind the Chuy's Tex-Mex restaurant chain run Glazing Saddles, the Krispy Kreme area developer for the Texas cities of Austin and San Antonio.

Yet even when it's pairing with such veterans in the restaurant business,

Krispy Kreme doesn't take anything for granted—not even experience or past success in building and running restaurants. All applicants are subjected to the same grueling process.

Of course, there's another reason so many potential franchisees are immediately disqualified from realizing their goal of owning a Krispy Kreme store: lack of cash. Franchisees must have the financial resources necessary to develop the store, and that goes far beyond the initial minimum up-front, out-of-pocket cash investment of $175,000.

In 2002, *Fortune Small Business* writer Carlye Adler compared Krispy Kreme's franchising practices with those of other chains in the food service industry. Adler found that Krispy Kreme is the most expensive food franchise out there. It costs about twice as much as a McDonald's restaurant, and potential franchisees must have a net worth of at least $5 million to even apply for a franchise. The $250,000 to $350,000 Krispy Kreme charges for its proprietary doughnut equipment, which is made only at a factory in High Point, North Carolina, could in itself buy a Dunkin' Donuts or Cinnabon franchise or two stores from the Manhattan Bagel chain.[20]

The Uniform Franchise Offering Circular provides a glimpse into just how much franchisees must put up to build and open a Krispy Kreme store. Consider these figures:

- Each operator pays a $40,000 initial franchisee fee for the privilege of being selected by Krispy Kreme.

- On top of the franchise fee, area developers are charged a $15,000 development fee for each additional store they open.

- Franchisees must spend between $5,000 and $10,000 to buy doughnut mix, napkins, coffee, hairnets, milk, paper towels, soap for the bathroom, and other inventory for the new store.

- The stainless steel doughnut cooking and glazing machine costs $250,000 to $350,000, depending on the size of the store and the anticipated production volume.

- For at least one month before a new store opens and for its first three months of operations, franchisees must earmark another

$5,000 to $10,000 to advertise locally and promote their new location.

- The Krispy Kreme store itself, following strict guidelines from the corporate headquarters, costs about $400,000 to $500,000 to build.

- Franchisees spend $100,000 to $125,000 for various other in-store equipment, signs, furniture, and fixtures. This figure includes the $20,000 to $25,000 cost of a 16-foot customized truck to make doughnut deliveries.

- Franchisees can expect to shell out $65,000 for deli/bakery equipment and displays. This expenditure will buy a franchisee the necessary supplies (displays, racks, pans, etc.) to set up Krispy Kreme sales kiosks in supermarkets, grocery stores, and other off-premise sales channels.

- Training and other preopening expenses, including initial employee wages, deposits for utilities, permits, uniforms, recruitment costs, telephone and electricity bills, paper, cleaning supplies, insurance premiums, and licenses tack on another $15,000 to $20,000.

- A high-profile piece of real estate in a busy part of town and big enough to accommodate a 3,500- to 4,500-square-foot Krispy Kreme store could cost $500,000, perhaps more.

The final tally: A new Krispy Kreme store, including real estate, costs close to $2 million to build. That price tag doesn't include recurring expenses, such as the regular royalty and brand development payments franchisees must make to corporate headquarters. Royalty fees are 4.5 percent of gross sales, while another 1 percent of gross sales must be paid into a public relations, advertising, and brand-building fund.

Is it all worth it? The answer—at least for now—is yes. Several of the newer Krispy Kreme stores, particularly those in untapped markets, have provided their owners with close to a 100 percent return on investment during the first year of operation. This means, in simple terms, that some franchisees recoup in a single year what they spent to build the entire store. Centioli, for example, posted sales of $454,000 during the opening week alone at his Issaquah, Washington, store. It was a record at the time. Few businesses can promise those kinds of results. Restaurants, in particular, are normally slow to turn a profit. Many never make it past the first year.

Profitability at a Krispy Kreme store, of course, varies depending on a number of factors. Location, as it does with most every business, plays a big role. Stores in new markets tend to sell more doughnuts to retail customers than do so-called southern heritage markets, where Krispy Kreme is deeply rooted. Operating costs and a franchisee's talent in managing and controlling the business also affect profit and loss. Yet Krispy Kreme locations across the board have strong sales. In company-owned stores, where wholesaling accounts for a large share of the business, average weekly sales have risen from $42,000 in 1998 to $76,000 in 2003, according to Krispy Kreme's most recent annual report. Franchised stores, many of which are still new and get a larger share of their revenues from retail customers, averaged weekly sales of $58,000 in 2003—amounting to about $3 million annually.

The UFOC provides an even more detailed look at sales and profitability at select Krispy Kreme stores, all of them owned and operated by the company. One store in Charlotte, North Carolina, that opened in September 1990 took in revenues of $1.23 million in fiscal 2001, including about $1.1 million from retail sales of doughnuts, coffee, drinks, and Krispy Kreme collectibles. That particular store had an annual operating profit of $549,942.

During that same year, Krispy Kreme's store on West Thirty-eighth Street in Indianapolis, Indiana, had an operating profit of $1.35 million on retail sales of $812,133 and total revenues of $3.7 million, 75 percent of which was generated by the store's wholesale business. The full-service store, opened in May 1995, was Krispy Kreme's first foray outside the Southeast. A second store in another Indianapolis neighborhood recorded retail sales of $771,945 and total revenues of $2.78 million in 2001. That location's operating profit was $1.22 million for the 2001 fiscal year.

In Krispy Kreme's hometown of Winston-Salem, its flagship store on Stratford Road, a busy restaurant and shopping thoroughfare in a relatively high-income neighborhood, took in revenues of $2.69 million in fiscal 2001, including retail sales of $1.96 million. Operating profit at the full-service Winston-Salem store was $953,111.

Such results were too much for Jim Morrissey to ignore. Morrissey is a principal of Rigel Corporation, whose Krispy Kreme territory includes Arizona and New Mexico. Morrissey sold his interest in nearly 100 franchises, among them Bruegger's Bagels, KFC, and Godfather's Pizza, when Krispy Kreme selected him as an area developer.[21]

"It was an easy decision," admits the 27-year restaurant business veteran, who claims revenues of $3.5 million to $4.5 million at each of his Krispy Kreme stores. "I still shake my head over the sales-per-unit numbers. I've never seen anything like it."[22]

Indeed, few restaurant or hospitality businesses can compare with Krispy Kreme in terms of financial performance, brand awareness, and customer loyalty. The company owes that unmatched reputation largely to the pristine partners with whom it chooses to do business.

Of course, such success sometimes breeds contempt. In February 2003, an arbitration panel awarded $7.9 million to two potential franchisees who sued Krispy Kreme, claiming they should have been given franchising rights for northern California over Brad Bruckman's company, Golden Gate Doughnuts. Kevin Boylan and Bruce Newberg accused Krispy Kreme of breach of contract and intentional interference with contract and business relations, among other things. Golden Gate Doughnuts is now 67 percent owned by Krispy Kreme. According to press reports, company CEO Scott Livengood was originally a partner in the company as well, but sold his interest in 2002 to avoid conflicts of interest and was dismissed as a defendant in the lawsuit.

Newberg and Boylan originally filed suit in March 2000. The case was later transferred to arbitration. For its part, Krispy Kreme admitted it had discussions with Newberg and Boylan, but argued that differences regarding the terms and conditions of their participation in the business were never resolved. According to Krispy Kreme, there were no written or oral agreements granting the two men rights to open Krispy Kreme stores in California. The arbitration judge obviously didn't agree.

GO FOR THE BEST

Krispy Kreme continues to scout hard for the right partners, even though most of its territories in the United States are already taken. In fact, the company is not accepting applications for franchisees in the United States at this time. It is, however, looking for partners in certain international markets. As evidenced by its stringent franchisee standards, Krispy Kreme wants only top-level players running its stores.

The company works exclusively with the best, most successful food service operators. Even industry veterans must prove they have the special mix of skill and passion necessary to run a thriving Krispy Kreme shop. That's a disappointing reality for many glazed doughnut lovers who dream of running their own Krispy Kreme shop, only to find there is likely no possible way for that to happen.

CHAPTER 3

Make Good Use of Your Time and Resources

The new Krispy Kreme store in Greensboro, North Carolina, won't open for another day, but employees are already in the kitchen, suited up in hairnets, colorful T-shirts, and plastic gloves. Busy workers make constant trips back to the stockroom and return with pallets of doughnut mix packed in brown paper bags, along with gallon-sized jugs of whole milk and other ingredients. All the while, canisters of jelly, crème filling, and lemon custard are readied and await the next batch of empty doughnuts in need of filling.

A pair of men—one a traveling trainer from corporate headquarters, the other a doughnut apprentice—feed dry and wet ingredients into a huge standing mixer. They also keep close watch on a nearby tank, where regular cane and powdered sugar are being heated and transformed into the glaze that will top a variety of confections.

Another doughnut maker stands on a stepladder and spoons gooey dough into a mixing bowl fitted with a special device called an extruder. With careful precision, the young employee moves the mixing bowl from side to side and back and forth. Through a spout at the bottom of the mixing bowl, he punches perfectly formed doughnuts through the extruder. These are cake-style doughnuts, one of the more than 20 varieties Krispy Kreme sells in addition to the signature hot original glazed that have made it famous.

The puffy rings of dough slide along a conveyor belt into a vat of hot oil, then into a cooling tunnel. A group of young women scoop up the cooked doughnuts by hand and stack them—not flat, but upright like dominoes—onto cold, gray bakery trays. They slide the full trays between the racks of rolling, stainless steel carts, then return to the doughnut-making machine to grab the next batch of fresh-cooked treats.

Krispy Kreme has the process of making doughnuts down to a science. Likewise, the company has perfected the process of selling these doughnuts to as many people through as many channels as possible. Its secret: establishing techniques that work, employing them religiously, and making good use of its available time and resources, often in unconventional ways.

RUN A WELL-OILED FACTORY

"We make 4,000 dozen doughnuts a day," says manager John Under-wood, an ordained minister who once worked at Oak Ridge National Laboratory (a Tennessee nuclear reservation) before returning to his home state to run this new Krispy Kreme shop. "It's a factory."

Some of the doughnuts Underwood and his staff make at the store will be used to fill the glass bakery-display case underneath the cash registers. But most aren't being readied for the opening-day crowds. Instead, they are destined for grocery stores, convenience stores, the cafeteria at nearby North Carolina Agricultural and Technical State University, and the other wholesale accounts that this restaurant serves.

Each Krispy Kreme store has the capacity to make between 4,000 and 10,000 dozen doughnuts daily. That's 48,000 to 120,000 dough-nuts every 24 hours at each store, much more than the company could sell from its retail counters or drive-through windows. As a result, Krispy Kreme has come up with a way to ensure that this extra capac-ity doesn't go to waste.

Though the red light signifying that fresh hot original glazed dough-nuts are available burns only twice a day, most Krispy Kreme shops run at full steam around the clock. At virtually all hours, you'll find the fac-tory behind the glass wall churning out some variety of doughnut. Krispy Kreme's unique strategy for selling excess inventory means the company's employees and equipment are rarely idle, even when busi-ness is slow at the retail counter. That's because Krispy Kreme, though perhaps most famous for the hot and fresh sweets it serves at its retail doughnut shops, isn't just a food retailer. It also has a thriving, money-making wholesale business that is expected to grow significantly as Krispy Kreme executes its growth plan.

GET IT FOR THEM WHOLESALE

In some cities, wholesale demand for Krispy Kreme doughnuts is so high the company has built what it calls commissaries to fill all the orders. These commissaries are true factories, designed to make dough-nuts exclusively for wholesale accounts. They have no windows for cus-tomers to peek inside, and no retail counters from which to serve those lured in by the strong smell of cooking pastries. At the commissaries, all of the action takes place out of public view, and all of the goods go out the back door. Krispy Kreme trucks arrive at the loading dock hourly to pick up the latest production run of doughnuts, which are quickly delivered to the company's many retail customers.

Nevertheless, every Krispy Kreme doughnut shop is indeed a factory. The massive cookers that are the centerpieces of most stores aren't there simply to entertain retail customers. Like sewing machines in textile mills and steel shapers in automobile plants, these cookers are vital, expensive pieces of industrial equipment. The cookers are engineered to make thousands of doughnuts an hour, sufficient to meet demand during peak retail sales times without creating lengthy waits for customers. Each machine costs about $350,000. The company and its franchisees have a strong financial incentive to recoup this expense by using the cooker as often as possible.

"What that means is that during non-peak hours we have excess capacity, so we're just like any manufacturer at that point. Idle capacity becomes a cost,"[1] Krispy Kreme's chief executive officer Scott Livengood explains.

At stores that have been open at least a year, Krispy Kreme utilizes what would otherwise be idle time to make doughnuts that will be sold through its off-premises sales channels—namely, grocery stores, coffee shops, airports, coliseums, convenience stores, and other retailers.

MAKE EVERY MINUTE MATTER

John Underwood's store is a little different from most new Krispy Kreme locations. It's in the heart of Krispy Kreme's home state of North Carolina, which is one of the company's heritage markets. Krispy Kreme doughnuts have been around these parts for decades. Unlike most places where the company puts down new roots, Underwood was making doughnuts for both retail and wholesale customers from his first day in business.

Normally, when Krispy Kreme enters a new market, the initial focus is on cultivating and building retail business and on delivering the hot doughnut experience to a new group of customers. In such cases,

Krispy Kreme waits until excitement over its doughnuts has cooled, generally a year or 18 months, before beginning to ship boxes of fresh-made doughnuts to other vendors.

"As the retail excitement becomes more routine, sales out the back door become possible,"[2] says Richard Reinis, chief executive officer of Great Circle Family Foods. Reinis's company owns and operates Krispy Kreme shops throughout southern California. It plans to open a total of 40 in the region by 2005. Reinis has also developed a significant wholesale business that keeps his stores churning out the goods almost nonstop, day and night.

"We've taken the opportunity to sell doughnuts to college campuses, casinos, movie theaters, supermarkets, convenience stores, and elsewhere," said Reinis, whose first doughnut shops opened to huge crowds and broke all opening-week sales records at the time. "Krispy Kreme doughnuts can be found at Dodger Stadium, Staples Center [both in Los Angeles] . . . the Rose Bowl [in Pasadena] . . . and at Qualcomm Stadium in San Diego. And don't be surprised if you find our incredible original glazed or other variety at the Hollywood Bowl or Legoland."[3]

SELL TO MULTIPLE CUSTOMERS

Back in 1994, when Krispy Kreme was still a privately held company with only about 100 stores, wholesaling represented about half of all sales. Retail, direct-to-customer sales accounted for about 40 percent of the total, with fund-raising initiatives through scout troops, schools, and churches making up the remaining 10 percent.[4] These days, as a publicly traded company on the New York Stock Exchange, Krispy Kreme doesn't reveal what portion of its revenue comes specifically from doughnuts sold to its wholesale accounts, which include Kroger, Target, Exxon, Giant, Starbucks, and Au Bon Pain. But there's no question it's a meaningful amount.

The company's past three annual reports show that off-premises sales helped to fuel comparable sales growth in its company-owned stores: Off-premises sales increased by $31.5 million in fiscal 2001, by $27.1 million in fiscal 2002, and by $32 million in 2003. In-store retail sales during those same years improved by $18 million in 2001, by $25.4 million in 2002, and by $21.4 million in 2003.

As you'll recall, Krispy Kreme began as a wholesale business. It didn't open its doors to the public until customers began showing up at the bakery asking to buy the fresh product directly from founder Vernon Rudolph. Rudolph borrowed ingredients for his first batch of dough-nuts from a local grocery store and sold his finished goods through that same store. It didn't take long for Krispy Kreme to take off, and the company slowly began opening locations throughout the South. These shops all functioned as factories, making doughnuts for wholesale cus-tomers. It wasn't until the 1940s, after World War II, that Krispy Kreme began building stores with retail customers in mind by installing coffee bars and doughnut showcases.[5]

In the mid-1990s, under the leadership of Mac McAleer and Scott Livengood, Krispy Kreme started looking for ways to increase its retail business by creating a unique experience for customers who came inside its stores and ordered hot glazed doughnuts. Yet the company never completely abandoned its wholesale operations, which have always been a significant source of revenue and an important contribu-tor to the bottom line.

Krispy Kreme, however, has changed the way it sells doughnuts out-side of its retail storefronts, most notably by searching for distribution locations beyond grocery stores and by strongly branding its products in those off-premises sites. It has also gone beyond the traditional way of selling prepackaged Krispy Kreme doughnuts in boxes of a dozen.

REPLICATE THE EXPERIENCE

Several years ago, the company began setting up self-service, in-store bakeries in grocery and convenience stores. "Instead of serving them [the doughnuts] prepackaged," chief executive officer Scott Livengood explains, "we were serving them in trays, just like we did in our stores. We developed a system to support that."[6]

These in-store bakeries resemble the display cases in Krispy Kreme's own restaurants. Truck drivers bring the doughnuts in daily on large trays. Some stores even announce the arrival of fresh doughnuts over

the public address system. "Mr. Krispy Kreme is here," at least one grocery store manager proclaims. The trays of fresh doughnuts are placed
into large, well-lit glass cases that in many ways resemble the upright
freezers that grocers use for such items as ice cream, pizza, French fries,
and vegetables. The cases, usually positioned prominently near a store's
own bakery section, are emblazoned with the red-and-green Krispy
Kreme logo and the promise, "Delivered Fresh Daily." These bakeries
are self-serve. Customers simply open the door and grab a single
doughnut or a dozen. Shoppers get to serve their treats up the same way
Krispy Kreme employees do in stores, using squares of sanitary parch-
ment paper to ladle them into paper boxes.

Sharon Gorman, a national account manager for Krispy Kreme, is
responsible for working with one of the company's large grocery store
partners in Atlanta, Georgia. This account includes more than 200
locations, each of which Gorman must monitor to make sure doughnuts are being sold according to Krispy Kreme's freshness and branding
standards.

"These points of distribution, these Krispy Kreme off-premises
channels of sales, are essentially extensions of our factory stores," says
Gorman, an animated redhead. "Therefore, they must mirror the quality, cleanliness, and consistency of the Krispy Kreme store experience.
This is what our customers expect and deserve.

"We have to maintain our brand. Our brand, our image, is very
important to us, so we look for partners who have great respect for
Krispy Kreme and demonstrate that they have a great respect for their
own brand, too."[7] Currently, 24 percent of packaged doughnuts sold in
grocery and convenience stores nationwide are Krispy Kremes, compared with 6.4 percent in 2002.

As a logical extension of its product line, Krispy Kreme is now in the
process of introducing three new drip coffee brews, frozen drinks, and
other espresso-based beverages to its stores around the world. Once the
company completes this rollout and has seen it succeed with customers,
executives may consider selling their brand alongside Folgers, Maxwell
House, and Seattle's Best on grocery shelves.

It's still too soon to consider a move like that, according to D. J.
McKie, senior vice president and general manager of Krispy Kreme

Coffee and Beverages. Just as Krispy Kreme focuses on its retail operation when it first opens a doughnut shop in a new market, McKie notes
that the initial goal with the new coffee program is to introduce the
drinks to customers in stores. That way, Krispy Kreme can control how
the coffee is brewed and served.

"Over time, we may start looking at ways to make it even more convenient," he says. "I think we've seen so many similarities between
doughnuts and coffee that it makes sense . . . that maybe eventually
we'll look at other channels."

DON'T GIVE TOO MUCH OF A GOOD THING

Krispy Kreme officials insist these off-premises sales do not hurt business, either by eroding retail sales, weakening the brand, or saturating
the market with its unique doughnuts.

Stan Parker, Krispy Kreme's marketing mastermind, focuses much of
his effort on getting Krispy Kreme doughnuts into the mouths of as
many people as possible. Krispy Kreme employees firmly believe that
all it takes is one bite to snare a customer for life, and off-premises sales
help introduce more and more people to the brand. "It's a great trial
vehicle for us," Parker contends. "The more doughnuts we sell in those
channels, [the more] it helps the retail channels."

But these off-premises sales channels do more than assist Krispy
Kreme in recruiting new customers. They also remind existing customers to come back to the chain's retail factory stores for hot doughnuts and coffee, as chief governance officer Randy Casstevens
emphasized to the audience at a consumer-brand growth conference
sponsored by CIBC World Markets.

"It's trial and awareness. It's really our form of advertising,"
Casstevens said, noting that Krispy Kreme spends almost nothing on
traditional television, radio, and print advertising. "As customers see
our products in these grocery and convenience stores and other outlets,
they buy them there, or it reminds them to go back to our factory stores
that we build." Only there can customers experience a Krispy Kreme
doughnut as it's meant to be eaten—hot and fresh.

No matter how available Krispy Kreme doughnuts become in

grocery stores, there are plenty who agree with the company that out-side sales channels will never usurp business from the factory restaurants. Bakery trade industry reporter Dan Malovany and Gayle Anderson, president of the chamber of commerce in Winston-Salem, North Carolina, where Krispy Kreme is based, are among them.

Malovany's belief in Krispy Kreme's business model is based on an in-depth study of the company and his years of covering the snack food business on both the retail and wholesale levels. Anderson's reason is more visceral. Both have to do with differences in the way a glazed doughnut tastes—and is experienced—when it's served at a location other than a Krispy Kreme store.

"I don't think they're in any danger of oversaturation," says Anderson, a 52-year-old Ohio native who claims to eat Krispy Kreme doughnuts weekly. "There's no comparison to hot and cold. I've tried warming them for five seconds in the microwave. It's okay. It ain't great. So you can't get it everywhere."

And that's the key, maintains Malovany. No matter how ubiquitous cold Krispy Kreme doughnuts become at grocery stores and mass retailers, people who crave a hot one will always prefer to seek out a Krispy Kreme shop. And those will never be located on every street corner.

"It's the fact that you have to go there and get them hot and fresh," he says. "There's a difference between a Krispy Kreme that is really hot out of a fryer and glazer and one that is on the grocery store shelf."

Malovany interviewed Scott Livengood for a 2002 article when the trade magazine *Snack Food & Wholesale Bakery* selected the Krispy Kreme chief as its executive of the year. Malovany and Livengood talked at length about Krispy Kreme's hybrid retail-wholesale business model. The reporter quizzed the chief executive about saturation and sales cannibalization. Livengood told Malovany that grocery stores were good for the company's bottom line and that they helped fuel comparable sales growth in stores. (Comparable-store figures are generally considered the best measure of a retailer's health because they compare sales at stores open at least a year.) Livengood also dismissed the idea that selling Krispy Kreme doughnuts at places other than its own stores might make the treats too common and therefore cause them to lose some of the mystique and rarity that makes them so popular with customers.

"Saturation? I don't believe in the S-word," Livengood told Malovany. "The S-word that I would use is that I don't believe we have scratched the surface even yet as we continue to explore new ways that are refining and improving and elevating the customer experience."[8]

Despite these passionate assurances from Livengood, Parker, Casstevens, and other company officials, those who study consumer marketing and brand building worry that Krispy Kreme may indeed sacrifice its uniqueness in the marketplace to increase sales. And that could cost the company some of its brand cachet.

After all, at one time Krispy Kremes were a rare commodity. One had to travel potentially hundreds, if not thousands, of miles to get a hot original glazed, or any other flavor of doughnut, be it hot or cold. If Krispy Kremes become so common that they're found in virtually every supermarket, will that detract from the allure and mystique that has traditionally drawn fans into Krispy Kreme stores like flies to honey? It's too soon to tell, although Starbucks has implemented a similar successful wholesale strategy on a much larger scale by extending its brand to items from prepackaged ground coffee to ice cream, seemingly without putting a damper on sales at its retail locations. Then again, coffee doesn't pack the calories that a doughnut does.

Ultimately, such overwhelming saturation might hurt Krispy Kreme's sales, earnings, and stock price—things a public company is obligated to protect. "Part of the problem of being a publicly listed company is that the financial pressures to do short-term things are far greater than they were before," says Neil Morgan, a former faculty member at the University of Cambridge in England who now teaches graduate-level branding classes at the University of North Carolina at Chapel Hill. Each year, he assigns students to study Krispy Kreme and to place an estimated dollar value on the brand.

"If you look at the stock price, built into the stock price is an expectation of future growth. That expectation means an expectation of profitability," Morgan points out. "The easy way to get greater profits is to sell through more grocery channels."

But the easy solution, Morgan believes, may not be the best one for Krispy Kreme. Morgan views Krispy Kreme as a strong brand and praises management for the successful company and unusual marketing relationships it has built. Still, he's not convinced the company is immune to making missteps and worries that some of its business decisions could hurt both the company's brand and its future.

"People can create things and unintentionally screw them up," Morgan maintains. "Krispy Kreme's problem is going to be resisting the temptation to do that [to] itself rather than someone else doing that to [the company]. Whenever you have a brand, you have to worry about where you're selling it and what that says about your brand. There are associations that will be picked up on the basis of the retail channels that you use."

Additionally, the company has positioned itself as a different kind of doughnut company, a place where sweets, unlike revenge, are best served hot. However, at gas stations and grocery stores, Krispy Kreme doughnuts are cold. Room temperature maybe, but never hot. This means that when purchased from outside vendors, Krispy Kreme doughnuts aren't much different from any other brand on the shelf, says Alan Siegel, another branding expert.

"I think you can hurt your brand promise, which is built around watching the product being made and getting it hot and fresh," observes Siegel, a partner at Siegelgale in New York City. "Why compromise that by putting a product in other channels of distribution against competitive products where you're not putting your best foot forward?"

The company's answer: to build sales.

CREATIVELY INCREASE SALES

Since its initial public stock offering in April 2000, Krispy Kreme has experienced a meteoric rise in popularity, awareness, sales, and earnings. Unlike most retailers, Krispy Kreme stores open to huge crowds. People camp out and wait in mile-long lines, literally, for a hot glazed doughnut. First stores in new markets have posted opening-week sales of close to $500,000, and some franchisees estimate that figure can grow larger with the right blend of preopening publicity, marketing, and promotion. Stores operated by Krispy Kreme's newest franchisees, the area developers who have been selected to expand the company into new markets like the Pacific Northwest, New England, Canada, and California, make revenues of $60,000 to $70,000 a week on average, or about $3.4 million a year.[9]

Typically, according to financial analyst Kathleen Heaney of Brean Murray Institutional Research in New York, most restaurants and specialty retailers open with lower initial sales and build momentum as the business becomes entrenched. Same-store or comparable-store sales grow over time. "Krispy Kreme is unique versus a typical retailer in that the sales are high in the beginning," she says. Because Krispy Kreme sells so many doughnuts during its opening period, retail sales may actually drop after a location has been open for a while. The opposite is true of most retailers.

Were retailing Krispy Kreme's only sales channel, this certainly wouldn't be good for business, either at the individual store level or from a corporate standpoint. But the wholesale side of the business should help to protect the company from that fate, provided Krispy Kreme is aggressive and prudent about finding other places to sell its goods. "Off-premise growth will become even more imperative as the spate of new markets that came on line over the last couple of years continue to mature and move away from their initial publicity," wrote Peter Oakes, an analyst with Merrill Lynch, in an early research report on Krispy Kreme. "This makes finding more channels of distribution increasingly important, while heightening the risk of saturation and quality control."

Heaney, who is director of institutional research at Brean Murray, still sees huge growth potential for Krispy Kreme, through its international expansion, its new line of coffee and other drinks, and wholesaling.

"It seems to make a lot of sense," she says of the off-premises sales. "Here you have a 4,000-square-foot store. By developing the wholesale [side of the business], it does enable them to run each store at close to 100 percent capacity." Selling in grocery stores, at airports, on college campuses, in office cafeterias, and in other off-premises outlets builds Krispy Kreme's brand recognition, saves idle time, and helps cover a store's fixed costs, Heaney insists. It also gives stores a way to maintain sales over the long run, as evidenced by comparable-store sales figures from company-owned Krispy Kreme stores, most of which are decades old.

"We believe the wholesale business can be a promising long-term growth opportunity for the company," Heaney advised potential investors in a lengthy research report on Krispy Kreme. "Doughnut sales in the supermarket [and] grocery store channel alone are a $1 billion a year market. Perhaps more importantly, pastry/doughnuts and pies/cakes are two product lines that are gaining more shelf space within the bakery departments of supermarkets. By utilizing off-peak capacity to bake doughnuts for sale into the supermarket, grocery, and restaurant markets, [Krispy Kreme] has built a strong wholesale business which has been instrumental in driving same-store comps (or comparable sales) at company-owned stores and should remain an important contributor to same-store sales growth."[10]

BUILD ON TRADITION

Krispy Kreme once again seems to have the magic recipe. Building on a tradition that began with its founder, Vernon Rudolph, the company has found a way to make good use of its time and resources, which include expensive equipment as well as dozens of employees at each store. Unlike so many other retailers, manufacturers, and companies that simply accept costly production downtime as a reality of doing business, Krispy Kreme doesn't. Its solution—selling thousands of doughnuts made during these idle hours to other restaurants and retailers—brings millions of additional dollars into the corporate coffers each year.

These sales, according to the company, appear to have little negative effect on Krispy Kreme's stellar reputation with customers and investors. The company is strict about whom it allows to sell its doughnuts, and the rules governing these sales are even tighter. That's how Krispy Kreme is able to maintain its strong brand presence well beyond the borders of its stores. In fact, Krispy Kreme store operators actually embrace wholesaling because they know the practice has historically helped—not hurt—sales. In addition to the extra business from the hundreds of grocery stores that buy tens of thousands of doughnuts each day, the practice also brings in more retail customers eager to taste a hot Krispy Kreme doughnut.

Krispy Kreme has built drive-throughs at many of its stores, most of which serve customers around the clock, even when the rest of the store has closed its doors for the night.

All of these sales channels allow the company to sell more product. In this business, that's what it's all about.

CHAPTER 4

Expand and Protect Your Brand

On padded bulletin board walls normally papered with sketches and snapshots, Jay Jung tacked up letters that adoring customers wrote to Krispy Kreme. Full of praise and stories about restaurant visits and fond family memories, the letters served as the blueprint for his first big project at the company.

Jung had worked for the doughnut maker periodically for several years on contracted projects while running his own graphic design firm. Now he was a full-time employee, ready for his first big assignment.

Krispy Kreme executives knew Jung understood the company's brand, which is less about doughnuts and more about creating pleasant, memorable experiences. It's also about the company bonding with its customers. That's why Jung was tapped for the project of updating and redesigning Krispy Kreme stores while maintaining the company's distinct flavor and brand. "We like the way you create spaces and you incorporate brand into physical environments," executives told him. "Will you come help us?" He decided to answer their call for assistance.

When Krispy Kreme hired Jung, the company was preparing for its initial public stock offering. It was still at the beginning of its evolution from a little-known regional chain to one with a national presence and solid brand awareness. At the time, Krispy Kreme had deals in the works with several partners to open doughnut shops in most major markets across the United States. Jung's job was to create a distinct look and feel for those new stores. In addition to a restaurant that was comfortable, inviting, family-friendly, and efficient, executives wanted a structure that effectively conveyed the essence of the brand.

Jung, who was raised in the Midwest but migrated to the South after college, looked at his bulletin board, at the words used by customers to describe the company. He and his coworkers in the concept development department highlighted passages, circled words, and underlined phrases that defined Krispy Kreme in the minds of its customers. "We really listened to what people said and what they wrote," recalls Jung, who is now the company's creative director for concept development. "If they took time out once they left a Krispy Kreme shop to write us a letter, how meaningful must that be to them? So, the words that they used were very important."

From those letters, Jung and his colleagues extracted ideas that really struck at the heart of the brand: *Warm. An inviting place. Americana. Fun. A reminder of a simpler time. Like a factory. Comfortable. Familiar. Genuine. Memories.*

With these words in hand, they began the design process.

PAY ATTENTION TO YOUR CUSTOMERS

Listening to customers brought Krispy Kreme its early successes. Such conversations and customer surveys have also set the stage for future growth, according to chief executive officer Scott Livengood. Customer influence and impressions will guide how Krispy Kreme plans and opens its new stores throughout the United States as well as in Canada, Australia, the United Kingdom, Asia, and other international markets. "The real key to Krispy Kreme's success . . . was the fundamental decision we made to really understand the relationship we had with the customer and become more of what the customer wanted us to be," Livengood said. "And it was the right decision."[1]

Though still a relatively small company with only a few hundred restaurants, Krispy Kreme is a consumer brand powerhouse. Because of Krispy Kreme's strong word-of-mouth appeal, *Advertising Age* magazine named it one of the "21 Brands to Watch in the 21st Century." Other brands on the list include Amazon.com, ESPN, Palm, Microsoft, Wal-Mart, and musician Sean "Puffy" Combs. Krispy Kreme has high name recognition, along with customers who are cultishly loyal ambassadors for the brand.

"The power of the brand is such that when a new store is opening, otherwise 'rational' individuals have been known to get up at the crack of dawn and wait on line for several hours to purchase doughnuts. This new store opening frenzy has generated widespread media attention, which in turn further strengthens the brand," wrote analyst Kathleen Heaney of Brean Murray Research in a stock research report on the company.

Krispy Kreme recognizes that the brand is perhaps its most valuable asset, Jung says. The brand distinguishes the company from such competitors as Dunkin' Donuts and Tim Hortons. It is meaningful to customers. The brand, not the doughnuts, connects them to the company and keeps them coming back again and again.

"I don't mean to belittle the doughnut," notes Jung, who speaks excitedly about his job and his employer. "The product is so great. Somebody else could go out and make a good doughnut, but they couldn't be Krispy Kreme."

"When people write in to Krispy Kreme about how they love us, it's not always, 'I love your doughnuts' or 'I love your coffee,' " he adds. "It's, 'Let me tell you my story about how my mom used to take me there.' And, 'Boy, am I glad you're in California now because it just brings back great memories.' "

Krispy Kreme's goal—and part of its mission statement—is to become the best-loved brand in the world. Everything the company does is built around making that happen. Management is constantly trying to strengthen the brand's personality and increase customers' allegiance to it. This commitment shows at the company's stores, at its web site, even in the T-shirts and sweatshirts Krispy Kreme sells. The tags on these items don't list cotton content or washing instructions. Instead, they talk about remembering the good times you've had with Krispy Kreme doughnuts.

MAKE THE RIGHT IMPRESSION

To fully comprehend and appreciate why Krispy Kreme's brand is so strong, you must first understand exactly what the company represents. The outside marketing experts, public relations firms, designers, and architects that Krispy Kreme hires to help out on various projects nearly always get it wrong on the first try. They constantly want to cast Krispy Kreme as a retro business. The company has a heritage dating to the 1930s and a simple, from-another-time store design that includes primary colors and an old-fashioned red neon sign. But unlike most retro companies, Krispy Kreme is not stuck in the past. The company is always moving forward and branching into new product categories such as coffee, while at the same time making technological improvements to its doughnut-making machines to get more hot treats into the hands of more people.

"I think I started there [with the retro theme in mind]," Jung admits. But retro somehow connotes an intentional theme, an attempt to be something you're not. And that's just not Krispy Kreme, which prides itself on being genuine and connecting with customers through its truthfulness and personal experiences, Jung insists.

"I think that Krispy Kreme represents a time when things were simpler and slower and maybe a little more real and a little less ubiquitous," he says. "I don't really think that I'm going to Australia when I go into an Outback Steakhouse. But I do feel like I'm going into a simpler time of Americana going into a Krispy Kreme. It's not because it's a theme. I think it's because our doughnut has stayed the same, and it feels a little retro. Yet our coffee's changed because coffee tastes have changed.

"The thing about this brand that amazes me even today—and I think always amazes people wherever we open up—is that it's real. There's something that connects with the human spirit about Krispy Kreme that's much more than a doughnut. There's something that happens around the doughnut. The experiences that happen around the doughnut are impossible for us to create, manipulate, re-create, control, or turn into a business formula. And I think that once you try to do that, people are going to fight back. . . . This brand is so real. People accept it because it's real. It's genuine. We know who we are."

Mystique is also a big part of Krispy Kreme's brand personality. Because the company still has relatively few stores—mostly concentrated in the South and in bigger cities elsewhere in the United States—the doughnuts remain an often-talked-about but oh-so-hard-to-get treat. Many people are familiar with Krispy Kreme, even those who have never tasted one of its doughnuts. There's a feeling of exclusivity, of experiencing something rare when you bite into a just-cooked glazed Krispy Kreme.

"I think, to their credit, they've got this well-known, yet best-kept secret," says Sheri Bridges, a professor at Wake Forest University in Winston-Salem, near Krispy Kreme's home base. "It's very cool and chic to be associated with Krispy Kreme doughnuts. I don't think Krispy Kreme would have the same cachet if there was a Krispy Kreme on every corner."

Krispy Kreme is a long way from achieving that kind of market penetration and saturation. The company plans to open hundreds of additional stores worldwide over the next decade. New doughnut-making technology gives the company the chance to open in more small markets than executives first anticipated when they took Krispy Kreme public. But they don't intend to grow Krispy Kreme to the size of McDonald's, for example, which in some cities seems to literally be on every street corner. Still, Krispy Kreme deals with the specter of its own ubiquity every day.

"We have to grow," CEO Scott Livengood insists. "But we have to be vigilant to make sure we don't disappoint anyone."[2]

Jung, the designer, even now occasionally brainstorms brand-saving solutions for that time in the future when Krispy Kreme stores are no longer destinations, but seem to be everywhere. He has no clear solution—only the outside pieces of a still emerging puzzle.

"Krispy Kreme has a really, really rich past, but I think we have even greater potential in the future," Jung believes. "When we get to be in every market . . . I personally think that will be a problem. But I think we've got a long way to go before we get there. And on the way to that maybe we can find a way to create new kinds of experiences and show people that we can do other kinds of products in the same Krispy Kreme way. Or maybe it's not even products. Maybe we can do other things in the same Krispy Kreme way."

Or perhaps, he posits, the way to fight ubiquity in the future is to make every Krispy Kreme store just a little unique. Maybe in the future it won't be so important for every doughnut shop to look the same. "I want to make as big a difference as I can and keep the brand on point, but I don't want to force it to be and look the same everywhere."

KNOW WHAT YOU STAND FOR

Unlike so many other retail and food service companies, Krispy Kreme's employees and executives seem to have a clear understanding of the company's uniqueness and what attracts customers. They are careful to never lose sight of that as they move the company forward, expanding into new markets and product categories, such as coffee and other hot and frozen beverages. This, in turn, makes for a strong brand, says New York brand consultant Alan Siegel, whose clients include Harley-Davidson, another company that connects well with its customers and has achieved a cultlike status of its own.

"I think a strong brand really comes out of a clear, relevant, and differentiating brand promise—a projection to the marketplace of what the company is, what it stands for, what value it provides, and what's distinctive about it," Siegel observes. "These people [at Krispy Kreme] have built their brand around this proposition of going into stores, smelling the product, watching the product being made, and getting a hot product."

Krispy Kreme markets itself as a purveyor of magical moments and special memories—not just doughnuts—and therein lies the company's brand strength. "Pretty much everything this company does seems to flow out of their commitment to create a distinctive experience in buying doughnuts and creating an emotional connection to the company and having the product stand out as the hero," Siegel says.

Sheri Bridges, the Wake Forest professor who is also a marketing and branding expert, says Krispy Kreme never fails to keep its promise to deliver a rewarding eating experience to customers. That's what makes the brand such an integral part of many people's lives.

"It's not just that we know them. We know what they stand for. We know what the brand means," Bridges points out.

Krispy Kreme strives to never disappoint anyone, be it customers, civic groups seeking donations, or members of the media looking to do a story on the company. That feeling tends to rub off on you, according to Gayle Anderson, who is president of the Winston-Salem Chamber of Commerce. Anderson's job is to promote the businesses in her city, so it's no surprise she's high on Krispy Kreme. It's not the biggest company in town. R.J. Reynolds Tobacco Company and Sara Lee are among the city's much larger employers. But she feels a special connection with Krispy Kreme and always mentions that company first when meeting someone new.

"I'm from Winston-Salem. That's the headquarters of Krispy Kreme doughnuts," Anderson begins every introduction of herself to the potential business prospects she is trying to lure to the area.

"And then I just shut up and I hear a Krispy Kreme story," she says. "Either they have a store in their own town, one's going to open, or they ask how they can get one. Every single time. As soon as you say Krispy Kreme, you can hear the smile in their voice."

As her city's biggest business booster, Anderson is willing to do a lot of things to cast Winston-Salem and its companies in a good light. But she is a busy executive, with too much on her plate to run errands for out-of-towners seeking Krispy Kreme doughnuts.

At least that's what Anderson thought when a woman from a tiny chamber of commerce in Ohio called and asked for help buying some Krispy Kreme doughnuts. The woman's son was a student at the North Carolina School of the Arts in Winston-Salem and had an upcoming theatrical performance. His mother wanted several boxes of Krispy Kreme doughnuts delivered backstage on opening night.

"Have you lost your mind? We don't have time to do this," Anderson thought.

"But we did it," she remembers, laughing at the incident. "I think a lot of it had to do with the fact that it was Krispy Kreme and we wouldn't want to disappoint them, and I really didn't want to disappoint this woman. So, there I was one morning getting the Krispy Kreme doughnuts."

BUILD A MEMORABLE BRAND

Helping the company connect with customers emotionally, in their memories, and in their hearts is a challenge that Jung and his colleagues at Krispy Kreme struggle with every day. They're always trying to root out why people like Anderson and the mother from Ohio feel so strongly about the company. "We continue to ask ourselves, 'What is it that makes Krispy Kreme special? What do people connect with?' " Jung observes.

The answer to that question is fairly simple. Krispy Kreme customers love the company's doughnuts, but the hot glazed treats alone don't keep them coming back. Customers return to Krispy Kreme because the product and place often trigger fond memories. A visit to a Krispy Kreme store is generally guaranteed to be a pleasant experience, whether you're an adult or a child.

"It makes you feel good," explains Bridges, the Wake Forest University professor. "When you need a pat on the back and there's no one to give it to you, you go to Krispy Kreme and you feel comforted. You have to go to a place that feels like you've been there before."

Neil Morgan, who teaches master's and doctoral level branding classes at the University of North Carolina at Chapel Hill, tells his students that to be in the brand management business is to be in the memory management business on an individual-by-individual basis. Krispy Kreme, he believes, has a leg up on most of the competition because its brand is already a part of so many people's memories. Longtime customers remember Krispy Kreme as a Sunday after-church tradition, or as the place they were taken after receiving a good grade in school.

"If you're starting with people's preexisting memories and tying them to your brand rather than trying to create new memories that are associated with your brand, you have a huge advantage," he says. "One of the strong things that you can do if you are in the brand business is to link your brand with things that already exist in a consumer's memories, because then you don't have to pay to get them there."

Krispy Kreme, with its emphasis on providing customers with good experiences, as well as tasty, hot, fresh doughnuts, has done that better than most. "One of the things that these guys have managed to do well is to link their brand image with a whole kind of Americana in better times," Morgan says. By creating an image that makes people think about their own past as soon as they hear the name Krispy Kreme, the company has etched itself forever in its customers' minds. Those memories make for positive brand associations that are unlikely to change or fade. "One of the nice things they have going for them is that they're tapping into existing pleasant memories," Morgan adds.

Despite this built-in advantage, Krispy Kreme continues to strive daily to make its brand stronger, particularly as the company grows and targets more markets outside its base in the United States. In other countries, customers don't have these strong personal connections to the brand. In most cases, it's a totally new experience for them. There-fore, Krispy Kreme will have to trade on being an American company, at least in its early stages of growth, according to Morgan.

"In international marketplaces, you are literally selling Americana. In marketplaces where Americana sells, you will do well. But there will be lots of marketplaces in which that won't sell," he cautions. "There are marketplaces overseas where just being American and tapping into American heritage will still cause Krispy Kreme to do well. But it's a dif-ferent proposition. It ain't going to work in France." At least it hasn't worked well there historically for many American companies.

CONTROL AND PROTECT YOUR BRAND

Although Krispy Kreme has dozens of franchisees and area developers—each an independent operator with his or her own ideas of how the business should be run—the corporate office maintains tight control over how the brand is portrayed, both in the United States and abroad. New managers and area developers go through brand stewardship classes as part of their lengthy doughnut university training to become Krispy Kreme employees. The 1 percent of total sales that franchisees contribute to the brand development fund fuels the work that's done by Jung and his creative development team.

"The more we roll out stores through area developers, the more it's important for them and their marketing partners to understand the way that we portray the brand," Jung says. "The people in Montana who are going to buy a doughnut, the people in the United Kingdom who are going to buy a doughnut, they all need to see us represented in the right way."

The small concept development staff, which includes Jung and Krispy Kreme vice president Jack McAleer, works in a bright, open space that you might expect to find at an Internet company. They toil in glass-walled offices and at modern-style conference tables strewn with paperwork in an unmarked building next door to company head-quarters. They are also often found at a prototype doughnut and coffee store in a posh Winston-Salem neighborhood and business district. Every idea for something new at Krispy Kreme passes through one of these locations to make sure it aligns with the company's brand image. The concept development staff works on big projects, such as how new restaurants will look. It also monitors the smaller details and oversees every item bearing the Krispy Kreme name, including the replica miniature Pontiac delivery trucks that most stores sell, the T-shirts servers wear, and the zippered plastic bags in which coffee is packaged.

"We design our own furniture, our own booths, our own wall graphics, our own tile patterns," says Jung, surrounded by a laboratory full of ideas that didn't pass brand muster. Most of the current design flotsam scattered around Jung's office now has to do with Krispy Kreme's new brand of coffee. There's a prototype coffee bag adorned with the familiar green Krispy Kreme polka dots. It was rejected in favor of a chocolate-brown bag with a boldly colored logo that is slightly different for each coffee blend. Sketches and printouts hanging on the wall show how many incarnations the coffee logo went through before Jung's team settled on the final design. "I'm really responsible for how our brand ends up in store environments. I also oversee packaging, marketing, uniforms, how we talk to customers, and signage—everything that has to do with the brand."

Good ideas are often tested—and then dismissed—because they don't fit with the Krispy Kreme brand.

When the creative development staff was designing a new store prototype—the first of which opened in Issaquah, Washington, in October 2001—they made thousands of sketches of what they deemed to be the perfect Krispy Kreme store. They were striving, Jung says, for the practical iteration of one consultant's suggestion that the perfect Krispy Kreme store would have glass walls with a doughnut-making machine in the middle.

"With these new stores, we are incorporating new approaches that are getting Krispy Kreme ever closer to the essence of the brand," which is the experience of enjoying a hot doughnut, says CEO Scott Livengood. "That ranges from the design itself; the interior of the store; additional product lines, primarily beverages; new packaging design that's supporting the store; and new technology that's smaller and less expensive and allows us to take the real signature product—the hot original glazed doughnut—deeper and deeper into the market."[3]

Some design sketches were rejected outright, wadded up, and thrown in the trash. Others were made into cardboard models that were reconfigured thousands of times. The best of those were used to create a life-size plywood model, which was installed in the empty office space next door to the creative development workshop. Then, employees, executives, board members, and customer focus groups were invited inside to test how the prototype store worked and to judge whether it fit Krispy Kreme's image. The working prototype was changed many times. Some features were added; others were taken away in the quest to build the perfect Krispy Kreme store.

"We could probably assemble four or five restaurants from the things that we've discarded," Jung says.

Beautiful tables and booths in glowing, warm wood tones—the kind of you might find in a cozy pub or a boutique bread restaurant—were rejected because they didn't feel like Krispy Kreme. They simply didn't look right in a place designed for families, where children are encouraged to explore and play. Cozy, padded booths, simple Formica tables, and frosted plastic and metal chairs were a better fit.

The designers also dismissed the idea of installing fake conveyor belts throughout the kitchen area to make the store look more like a factory. That didn't mesh with Krispy Kreme's brand, either, or with its reputation for being genuine. There are things you try—things you even love—that must be rejected because they don't fit with the brand, Jung contends.

"All of a sudden someone asks, 'Is that us?' " he says. "You hold them up to the lamp and you ask, 'Do they match with who we are?' "

No matter how good the idea, if the answer is no, Krispy Kreme won't pursue it, because its brand is that important. Such diligent shepherding of the brand extends to other departments within the company, too.

HOLD FIRM TO YOUR PRINCIPLES

In the summer of 2002, the marketing director at Candie's shoes called Stan Parker with an interesting proposition. The company was shooting an advertisement featuring rhythm and blues singer Ashanti, who loves Krispy Kreme doughnuts. Candie's wanted permission to use a box of assorted doughnuts in the ad, which appeared in the September 2002 issue of *Jane* magazine. But Candie's marketing director also wanted to talk with Parker, who is Krispy Kreme's senior vice president of marketing, about some joint promotions.

Maybe, the shoe company executive suggested, *Jane* readers could trade the ad in for a free doughnut at a Krispy Kreme store. Candie's would even pay for all the free doughnuts and any advertising costs.

Parker considered the proposal and eventually allowed Candie's to use the doughnuts in its ad. But he rejected the coupon idea because it's not the kind of thing that Krispy Kreme does. The company gives away plenty of doughnuts. In fact, that's a cornerstone of its marketing strategy. But Krispy Kreme never appears in traditional advertising. To publish a magazine coupon would be like foisting the company on people, Parker rationalized, and that's not what Krispy Kreme is all about.

Most companies must advertise to achieve the level of brand recognition that Krispy Kreme enjoys. But Siegel, the branding expert from New York, thinks the company's low-key strategies help to endear Krispy Kreme to its customers. "By avoiding this flashy kind of advertising, I think they've helped their brand by instead using viral marketing [which involves friends spreading the word to friends]," he says. "They have a real folksy, grassroots, neighborhood kind of feeling. Their small-town southern origins and the values of the company come through."

But Siegel and other branding experts worry that even with its high brand consciousness, Krispy Kreme could make mistakes in the future that will hurt the business and the brand. For example, they believe that a key part of the company's sales strategy, one that is popular with analysts because it helps revenues, could actually damage Krispy Kreme's reputation and its brand, especially in new markets.

For years, Krispy Kreme has been packaging its doughnuts and selling them through other outlets, primarily grocery and convenience stores. Krispy Kreme doughnuts are also now available in Target stores and at some coffeehouses, including select Starbucks locations. Krispy Kreme has strict rules for vendors that sell its doughnuts and often requires them to purchase signage and bakery display cases directly from the company. There are also careful controls to ensure that the doughnuts are as fresh as they can be. Despite that, experts say the company may be harming itself by selling doughnuts this way instead of sticking to its trademark hot-off-the-fryer method found in the retail environment. The big problem with this off-premises sales strategy is that, though it may boost revenues, it doesn't help Krispy Kreme fulfill its brand promise. It also forces the company to give up some control of its brand, which is always a risky proposition.

"If you're going to build your brand around this experience of seeing the product being made and buying it hot and getting it fresh, anything you do to compromise that in the interest of building sales through other channels compromises your proposition," Siegel says. "I think the most important thing is to protect the brand."

Krispy Kreme executives contend that selling the product in grocery and convenience stores, which has been part of the company's business model since it began in 1937, doesn't drive people away. Instead, they claim, these distribution channels actually fuel sales at retail stores. People who taste a Krispy Kreme doughnut that they've bought at a grocery store or from a Boy Scout trying to raise money for his troop are even more likely to come into a Krispy Kreme restaurant for a hot doughnut.

"We spend a lot to understand everything relating to the brand, including where we [should] sell off premises,"[4] Livengood says. "You think if your product is in other channels of the market there might be some cannibalization, but in reality you create greater top-of-mind awareness and you get a vicarious store experience. You have a Krispy Kreme doughnut, but all it does is make people want to go back to the store for the hot doughnut experience."[5]

Without question, Krispy Kreme's brand is highly popular with consumers, investors, and most Wall Street analysts right now. But the company will be challenged to maintain this success in the future.

"Brands don't commit suicide. They're murdered by the people who manage them every day," insists Sheri Bridges, who has watched brands rise and fall in popularity during her years of teaching and working in the industry.

As Krispy Kreme opens more stores around the world and sells its doughnuts through a greater number of channels, the company is in danger of diluting its powerful brand, which is a key sales driver and its strongest weapon against competitors. As franchises are granted to more area development groups, Krispy Kreme, if it's not careful in choosing partners and deliberate in its growth, could lose some of the branding control it now enjoys.

"If they're careful to preserve the values, and if they maintain the integrity of the brand by rolling out slowly and carefully, I think they'll be fine," says Alan Siegel. "Sometimes when you get big and you have too many franchises, you lose control of your brand values and you get into trouble. I think it depends on how carefully they do it."

Growth is dangerous for other reasons. As its doughnuts become more widely available, Krispy Kreme may lose some of its mystique, just as Coors beer did when it shifted from a coveted regional product to just another brew available in every grocery store cooler. If Krispy Kreme doughnuts reach such dime-a-dozen availability, fewer people may crave them unless the company can give those customers a compelling reason to keep buying the treats.

Concept development director Jung is forever focused on that. While taking cues from the past to define Krispy Kreme, he is always preparing for the company's future as it evolves from a regional restaurant to whatever it's destined to become.

"We have to be creating heritage every day," Jung says. "It took me a long time—possibly several years—before I was really able to understand this thing. But as I got involved in more and more of what Krispy Kreme was doing, I understood why it wasn't just about yesterday and why what we created in a doughnut we can create in other things. Why would you ever want to get stuck in the past?"

CHAPTER 5

Think Big, but Grow Carefully

Dark days knocked on Krispy Kreme's door with a vengeance in May 1976. Founder Vernon Rudolph had died about three years earlier, just 17 days after his fifty-eighth birthday. The business he had built was held in trust and run by a bank until Rudolph's family located what it deemed to be a suitable buyer for the company. On May 28, 1976, they decided to sell Krispy Kreme to Chicago-based Beatrice Foods, which was once the world's largest food company.

Beatrice, a diversified corporation with sales in the billions, purchased Krispy Kreme for an undisclosed sum and added the regional doughnut maker to its conglomerate of dairy, grocery, soft drink, meat, candy, and bakery companies. But being part of such a large powerhouse ultimately had a devastating impact on Krispy Kreme. As a unit of Beatrice, Krispy Kreme couldn't behave like the small-town, homegrown enterprise it had always been. Instead, it had to operate like so many big businesses of the time, driven primarily by the pursuit of profits for its new parent company.

Under Beatrice management, Krispy Kreme grew from fewer than 100 stores to 116 by 1980. Yet you have to look beneath those numbers to find the real story of the effect Beatrice's corporate politics and goals had on the doughnut maker. Even today, Krispy Kreme officials speak bitterly of the six years that Beatrice owned and controlled the company.

The conglomerate was focused on getting the most out of its investment. It wanted to build a company that sold lots of products and made plenty of money. Beatrice officials, therefore, weren't committed to hot original glazed doughnuts in the same way that founder Rudolph had been and that the current management team is. "Our soul is in the doughnut business, and Beatrice just didn't get that," contends chief executive officer Scott Livengood.[1]

For example, Beatrice executives, who were expert at running food companies, fiddled with ways to bring in more business during the middle of the day, when Krispy Kreme stores typically aren't very busy. Doughnut sales then, as now, peaked in the morning and evening. Stores were relatively empty during lunchtime hours. Beatrice decided that synergy was the answer. It began importing products made by its other business units into Krispy Kreme. That led to sausage biscuits, ice cream, soup, and sandwiches joining the menu. Such changes raised operating costs at stores, but didn't bring in new customers. Beatrice, in its drive to modernize Krispy Kreme, also redesigned the company's familiar script logo that was likely designed by founder Vernon Rudolph's father, Plumie Harrison Rudolph.

Those close to the company contend that Beatrice's biggest mistake—the legacy that no one at the company will ever forget or forgive—was changing the recipe for Krispy Kreme doughnuts. Forgetting, or perhaps ignoring, that people had lined up for these doughnuts when Vernon Rudolph first made them, Beatrice altered the recipe and removed some of the secret ingredients that for 40 years had given the sweet treats their unique, special taste. Beatrice's justification: The changes would cut costs and improve Krispy Kreme's profit margin.

But Beatrice, in one money-minded move, had abandoned the primary promise that Vernon Rudolph always made to his customers and his employees. "We believe," he once wrote in a letter outlining Krispy Kreme's philosophy, "that our prime opportunity for continuing success and growth is to deliver to our customers the best value in fine, palatable, and nutritious pastry at all times."[2] Forgotten was Rudolph's promise that Krispy Kreme would always focus first on its customers, whom he called "the lifeblood of our business," and the founder's commitment to always delivering "Krispy Kreme quality," and never settling for second best.[3]

"They [Beatrice] sucked it dry is what they did,"[4] maintains J. A. "Mac" McAleer, a Krispy Kreme board member who was the company's leader for eight years beginning in 1988. Current CEO Livengood, who took over from Mac McAleer in 1997, joined Krispy Kreme's personnel department in 1977, around the time of the sale to Beatrice. Those years were pure turmoil, Livengood contends, with Beatrice's business goals at odds with Krispy Kreme's business model. The new owners were focused on short-term results that Krispy Kreme, then primarily a wholesale company, simply couldn't deliver. "Krispy Kreme was more of a low-margin wholesale business, and Beatrice had internal financial objectives. With heavy wholesale as our base concept, we were a lot slower to reach the level of profitability they expected."[5]

Many of Krispy Kreme's original franchisees were disgusted and distraught by the way their company was being run. They were fearful that Beatrice, with its singular goal of profit making without regard to the core product, would run what had once been a thriving, growing business with great potential into the ground. Joseph A. McAleer, Mac McAleer's father, was among the disenchanted. Though he was an apprentice of Vernon Rudolph, and had been with the company since 1951, Joseph McAleer considered leaving Krispy Kreme to start his own doughnut business with his family.[6] But before things got bad enough to make Joseph McAleer leave, Beatrice Foods put Krispy Kreme up for sale in 1981.

Joseph McAleer, who started his career with Krispy Kreme earning $1 an hour and working 120 hours a week, didn't have the cash to buy Krispy Kreme himself. So he rallied together about 20 other devoted franchisees, and they staged a leveraged buyout of the doughnut maker. The franchisees, or *associates,* as they were called, paid about $22 million to buy Krispy Kreme from Beatrice. Much of that amount was financed with funds provided by both Beatrice Foods and Wachovia Bank in Winston-Salem, North Carolina.

The former dollar-an-hour apprentice from Mobile, Alabama, was suddenly at the helm of Krispy Kreme. As president, Joseph McAleer's job was to correct all of those things he had long complained that Beatrice messed up. The first changes were easy. Joseph McAleer, noting that Krispy Kreme had been sidetracked under the leadership of Beatrice Foods, resurrected the recipe that Vernon Rudolph had locked in a vault at Krispy Kreme headquarters. "We reverted to our 1967 mix formula, putting all the basic ingredients back in,"[7] McAleer said in early 1983, about a year after leading the leveraged buyout. "We're going to try to concentrate on what we do best. We are going to try to get back to where we feel we ought to be."[8]

LEARN FROM HISTORY

The Beatrice Foods experience had a colossal impact on Krispy Kreme's future, particularly over the way the company planned and executed its growth. Much of this carries over to today. Legacies and lessons from the Beatrice years, some still relatively fresh, have forced the company to take a slow and deliberate approach to expansion. By learning from its own storied history, Krispy Kreme may be able to protect itself from a fate that has stricken many companies that have grown too fast and fallen hard—sometimes into financial difficulties and bankruptcy, sometimes completely out of existence.

No one in Krispy Kreme's current executive suite would tell you the break from Beatrice Foods via the leveraged buyout was a mistake. In fact, at Joseph McAleer's funeral after his death from lung cancer in 1998, he was eulogized as a visionary and as the doughnut king. "The Beatrice folks deviated from the original recipe. It was still Krispy Kreme, but the quality diminished and it made it difficult to make a high-quality product," Scott Livengood said at the time. "Joe reinstituted the original recipe. What's happened . . . since then proves it was the right decision."[9]

But the right decision came with consequences.

Krispy Kreme franchisees staged their leveraged buyout in the 1980s, a decade characterized by high inflation and double-digit interest rates that kept many well-paid Americans from buying homes. Businesses, including Krispy Kreme, also struggled with the financial burden wrought by high lending rates. Initially, Krispy Kreme's buyout debt was five times greater than the company's equity.[10] As a result, Joseph McAleer and Krispy Kreme's other new leaders focused on paying that debt off and making money through proven channels, specifically by selling more doughnuts to wholesale outlets. The store base shrank to fewer than 100 outlets, about what it was before Beatrice Foods took over. For nearly a decade, Krispy Kreme eschewed growth.

It wasn't until Joseph McAleer retired from his day-to-day work at Krispy Kreme in May 1988 and handed the business over to his son, Mac McAleer, that there was any talk of growth. For 15 years, beginning when Beatrice Foods took control, Krispy Kreme didn't actively pursue any new franchisees. But Mac McAleer, not even 40 at the time he became president of the company, had new goals for the company. McAleer, who studied marketing at the University of South Alabama for two years but dropped out to work in the family business, did what his father, who had been hamstrung by corporate debt, couldn't. He put his focus on company growth, while shifting Krispy Kreme's business model from wholesaling doughnuts to retailing them. He finally answered queries from people around the country who wanted to become Krispy Kreme franchisees. "For fifteen years, that phone has been ringing off the hook . . . and all we said was no," Mac McAleer noted when he debuted his growth and franchising plan to the local media. "And now I'm the man who said yes."[11]

GROW AT A MEASURED PACE

Even so, Krispy Kreme's growth was slow and continues to be done at a measured, carefully scripted pace. Company directors and executives, some of whom worked at Krispy Kreme for decades and who witnessed the Beatrice Foods fiasco, know the consequences of rash ambition. Therefore, they move the company forward more at a tortoise's pace than a hare's, believing that steady consistency and well-studied growth is the key to success. Krispy Kreme's current executives, unlike their predecessors at Beatrice Foods, have a carefully drafted plan for the company, which takes into account both current and future goals, challenges, and prospects. They have found a way to build retail sales, without sacrificing the soul of the company.

"They seem to be approaching things in a very thoughtful, long-term way. They have a clear vision. They don't get distracted," says RBC Capital Markets stock analyst David Geraty, who is bullish on Krispy Kreme. "That's a potential risk of all brands. Do they try to do too much too soon? They need to make sure that they continue to act like a private company even though they're public. What does that mean? They still follow their own vision. They don't get distracted by Wall Street. They invest for the long term. They're interested in creating social and economic profit, not just economic profit."

History is filled with plenty of companies that tried to get too big too fast, to grow beyond their means, beyond their brands, beyond their executives' abilities to manage them. Think of all the dot-com businesses that came and went in a flash during the 1990s: Pets.com, Etoys, Garden.com, and others that were even more fleeting. Most were ill-formed ideas to begin with that were poorly executed. What's more, the often inexperienced founders and managers of these companies tried to grow these businesses as fast as possible, only to watch them tumble to the ground.

In Krispy Kreme's arena—the food industry—there was Boston Chicken. Like Krispy Kreme, Boston Chicken began as a regional chain of well-loved quick-service restaurants that offered roasted chicken and home-style side dishes. Customers loved the food and investors adored the stock, saddling it with a premium valuation similar to the one Krispy Kreme carries today. Boston Chicken, which later became Boston Market, went public and quickly expanded beyond its regional base. The company endowed many franchisees with the financing they needed to open Boston Market restaurants. Following this ill-advised strategy, the chicken chain amassed a huge pile of corporate debt that was too large to be paid off using sales generated by the new stores. Eventually, the company became so mired in debt that it filed for bankruptcy and closed many of the restaurants that had opened during its aggressive expansion push. McDonald's eventually bought Boston Market, but with plans to raid the corporation's real estate, not to resurrect its failed restaurants.[12]

In its measured approach to growth, Krispy Kreme has avoided the trap that befell Boston Market and other overly ambitious companies. Through careful stewardship by management and smart growth, Krispy Kreme has shaken off the initial comparisons with other tarnished cult brands like Boston Market and Coors beer. It now keeps company with strong, proven, well-managed, and well-loved consumer brands such as Starbucks coffee, Apple computers, and Harley-Davidson motorcycles.

All companies, particularly those with publicly traded stocks, face the risk of growing too big too fast. It's a question of growth versus execution, of vision versus planning, asserts Geraty, the stock analyst. Just like children, businesses grapple with getting too big for their britches. Yet Krispy Kreme is successfully facing that challenge of balancing growth and execution. And its secret to success is really taken right out of Business 101.

"The big danger is diluting the brand through growing too rapidly, growing beyond your abilities to manage your growth and maintain your

standards," Geraty says, laying out the basics of good business stewardship as if he were teaching a class on the topic. "That's a barometer. If your
standards start to slip, you know you need to slow down the growth."

KNOW WHERE YOU'RE GOING

Krispy Kreme executives have a clear plan for their company's future.
They can tell you how many full-sized stores they would like to have in
the United States and which international markets they'd like to con-
quer. But executives have never rushed to make their plans a reality
before the time was right. Whether domestically or internationally,
Krispy Kreme officials study potential locations to make sure that each
one already has a strong market for doughnuts and the population to
support a full-scale doughnut theater. They also spend considerable
time scouting for the right real estate for stores and maintain rigorous
standards for their franchisees. Such strategies take time, but they have
served Krispy Kreme well in the two decades since the company sepa-
rated from Beatrice Foods.

By the end of Mac McAleer's tenure as chief executive officer in
1997, evidence of this slow, yet carefully planned, growth was clear.
The company, which had 100 stores in 1989, added only about two
dozen more during what was, for Krispy Kreme, an aggressive growth
phase. This deliberateness had proven to be a smart move for Krispy
Kreme, which was finally beginning to stretch across the boundaries of
the Mason-Dixon line and into less familiar territory.

On May 9, 1995, Krispy Kreme opened its first store outside the
Southeast, in Indianapolis, Indiana. This market, where only 2 percent of
the population was familiar with the name Krispy Kreme, would be the
first test of the brand's popularity in places where people didn't speak with
a twang or a drawl. "It took about 10 years to get into a position where
they could begin aggressively expanding. We didn't really know what the
acceptance would be,"[13] said Scott Carpenter, who works for Ralph
Simpson & Associates, a public relations agency that Krispy Kreme hired
to promote the company in its home city of Winston-Salem.

Southerners living near Indianapolis came to the store opening and
brought their friends. Customers, starting a trend that has yet to fade,

lined up to get their first taste of a hot Krispy Kreme, packing the streets and the store with impassable traffic. "It was a hallmark day for Krispy Kreme,"[14] Carpenter reflects.

"We knew then that we could grow the franchise program,"[15] adds Jack McAleer, Mac's younger brother and a major shareholder, director, and vice president at Krispy Kreme.

The company's experience when it opened its first store in New York in June 1996 underscored this belief. The turnout for the store opening was phenomenal, and so was the publicity. The national media latched onto the story, catapulting Krispy Kreme into the spotlight and prompting doughnut connoisseurs around the country to ask, "When is my town getting a Krispy Kreme?"

"In every market, we've gotten a lot of attention," Jack McAleer says. "But New York translated beyond local media to national media and we never had that before. All of a sudden, we were being recognized, and we started getting phone calls from all over the country."[16]

But Krispy Kreme prevented itself from falling into the trap that so many in-demand companies succumb to. It didn't diminish cash reserves or operating funds by rushing to open more company-owned stores, which can cost millions to build. It didn't answer every call to franchise or jump at every mom-and-pop's dream to run a Krispy Kreme. It didn't loan money to people who wanted to own a Krispy Kreme store. Nor did the company trifle with franchisees of limited financial means who could afford to open only a store or two.

Krispy Kreme remembered the lesson it learned from Beatrice Foods: Be prudent and careful about change and growth.

The company instead selected a small group of area developers to open and operate Krispy Kreme stores in various geographic regions throughout the country. The original area developers selected by Krispy Kreme combined experience in the restaurant or specialty retail industries, along with a love of Krispy Kreme, an understanding of the powerful consumer brand, and the money and commitment to open multiple locations over a long period of time. "They [the chosen area developers] already know how to run restaurants and food service places," says Tom Ogburn, a marketing professor who is familiar with Krispy Kreme's business model. Area developers generally sign two types of agreements with Krispy

Kreme: one that establishes how many stores they'll build in an area and a second franchise contract in which they commit to follow the corporation's high standards at every store they open.

When it became clear that there was a nationwide market for Krispy Kreme—and a ready pool of experienced restaurateurs to run the new shops—the company embarked on perhaps the biggest change and growth of its history. In April 2000, Krispy Kreme abandoned its private, regional past to become a public company. It earmarked the $65.7 million raised through its initial public stock offering to improve its existing stores and to fund the infrastructure that would be needed to support its domestic growth through new franchises. Among the goals of the IPO: raise enough capital to build another doughnut mix manufacturing plant to support the new stores outside the South and provide money for joint ventures with franchisees.

In the years since Krispy Kreme first left the South to open that store in Indianapolis in 1995, the company has doubled in size, with most of the growth occurring since the IPO. Krispy Kreme, through its franchise partners, now has stores in such states as New York, California, Washington, Oregon, Massachusetts, Colorado, Ohio, and Minnesota. Fueled by new store openings, during the last three years the company has posted average annual sales gains of 14 percent, net revenue growth of 20 percent, and earnings growth of 22 percent.

But the existing base of roughly 300 stores represents only about one-third of Krispy Kreme's growth potential in the United States—and a much smaller fraction of its anticipated international scope. The company is, as executives like to say, still in the infancy of its growth in terms of stores and sales.

"The long-term prospects are outstanding," says stock analyst John S. Glass, who has covered Krispy Kreme for the brokerages Deutsche Bank Alex. Brown and CIBC World Markets. "We call it a new old brand or an old brand in the early stages of growth."

FIND NEW WAYS TO EXPAND

Though a nationally recognized brand, Krispy Kreme has yet to venture into every state in the United States, and the majority of its stores remain concentrated in the Southeast. "There are still a lot of places in the country that don't have a store," says Kathleen Heaney, who studies branded consumer companies as director of research at Brean Murray Institutional Research in New York City. "These guys just have a lot of room to take the basic business and move it into other markets."

Krispy Kreme, when it first filed registration papers with the U.S. Securities and Exchange Commission to become a public company, estimated it could have about 750 large stores throughout the United States. That would put the company in most urban markets with populations of 250,000 or more. The company is about one-third of the way there. It will take Krispy Kreme several years to reach that goal at its current pace of development.

But Krispy Kreme's business prospects have changed significantly since the April 2000 initial public offering. Following years of research and consumer testing, the company's equipment department recently pioneered a new doughnut-making machine. The smaller, less expensive cooker provides Krispy Kreme with the opportunity to open a different class of store, which is cheaper to build and more suited to suburbs, small towns, malls, airports, and other places where real estate is expensive and scarce.

This development, the result of years of planning and experimentation, multiples Krispy Kreme's potential, according to Heaney, who says she became more enamored of the company's growth story in late 2002 after traveling with management to visit investors. "Krispy Kreme will now be able to open smaller factory stores in smaller suburban areas. These smaller stores will target towns with populations of 30,000 to 40,000 versus 250,000 for the current larger format, significantly expanding the potential store base for the company," Heaney wrote in a report for investors. "Given its small retail base and limited geographic reach, Krispy Kreme Doughnuts, in our view, has many years of robust growth ahead of it."

Analyst David Geraty, who attended college at Wake Forest University, just miles from Krispy Kreme's first store and headquarters, says the company seems to have everything investors want in a restaurant stock: a solid, established brand; a good business model; and plenty of room to grow. "Clearly, with only about 200 units and room to probably have well in excess of 1,000 units nationwide in both big and small markets, it is just virtually a very early-stage growth company even though the brand is 60 years old," insists Geraty. "It is the best of both worlds. You have a proven brand that works. Consumers are very loyal. Unit returns are good, and so are financial returns and growth prospects."

Though it's nowhere close to reaching its growth limit in America, Krispy Kreme has smartly begun exploring international growth opportunities. "They're moving internationally now slowly when they don't have to, while U.S. stores are still strong," Heaney observes. This will allow Krispy Kreme to proceed cautiously in choosing the best international locations and business partners while also giving the company time to craft a marketing and branding strategy that will work well outside of the United States.

Krispy Kreme's first international store opened on December 11, 2001, in the Toronto suburb of Mississauga, Ontario. A second Canadian location opened in Richmond Hill, Ontario in the fall of 2002. The area developers for Canada have plans to open a total of 40 stores over six years in eastern and western Canada. New Zealand and Australia are also on tap to get about 30 Krispy Kreme stores over the next five years. And American entertainer Dick Clark, famous for hosting the music show *American Bandstand* and ABC's annual New Year's Eve celebration, joined with a group of partners in 2003 to obtain the rights to open 25 Krispy Kreme shops throughout the United Kingdom and Ireland by 2008. Other potential international markets for the company include Japan, South Korea, Spain, and Mexico. "Their strategy in the U.S. and in international markets has been to target cities with high doughnut consumption," Heaney notes. "And they're doing it slowly."

When Beatrice Foods took over Krispy Kreme, it could have meant the end for a much-loved growing company. But savvy franchisees, who were passionate about the business and the brand, stepped in to rescue Krispy Kreme from its corporate controllers. Granted, the leveraged buyout, which was financed during the high-interest-rate 1980s, saddled the company with millions in debt and stalled growth for nearly a decade. But it also taught the company an important lesson about managing expansion.

Krispy Kreme officials have big plans for the future of the company. Judging from the excitement that accompanies each new store opening, doughnut lovers around the world are anxious to see Krispy Kreme stores on street corners and in shopping malls at nearby locales. However, having learned a painful lesson during the Beatrice years, the company isn't allowing this excitement to cloud its good business sense. Krispy Kreme is committed to growing slowly and smartly, expanding only when and where it makes sense. Krispy Kreme is a company that acts on knowledge, not faith. And this has helped to make it a premium brand that still carries an amazing degree of allure.

CHAPTER 6

Be a Guerrilla Marketer with a Soft Touch

It's the last Tuesday of October 2001, the day before Halloween. It's the kind of morning that feeds stereotypes about Seattle. The wind is blowing hard and bitter cold. No amount of polar fleece or Gore-Tex can keep out the chill. The forecast calls for a likely chance of rain—not intermittent drops, but hard, stinging pellets of water. If the sun were up, the sky would surely be gray. But it's too early for that.

It's only 5:30 A.M. The one light in the sky that matters most to many in Issaquah, Washington, is not that of the moon or stars, but rather the glow from a circular, red neon sign blazing out the words: "Hot Doughnuts Now." The headlights from hundreds of cars, queued in the drive-through lane and in snaking lines throughout the East Lake Sammamish Center parking lot next door, burn like constellations around a sun.

People in Issaquah have been waiting a long time for Krispy Kreme to come to their town of 14,000, which is about 18 miles from downtown Seattle. This is the doughnut chain's first location in the Pacific Northwest, and its opening is much anticipated. Franchisee Gerard Centioli used to get e-mail messages from anxious Krispy Kreme fans. "I don't know how long we can wait for a Washington location to open up," wrote one. "Our mouths are watering, and we're jealous. Jealous of everyone who has a store they can walk, run, or drive to and sink their teeth into just one. Any time one of our co-workers leaves town and there is a Krispy Kreme nearby, they bring back a box or two . . . but it's never enough!!"[1]

To them, the wait seems like forever. To be told that a coveted treat will soon be sold in your neighborhood is wonderful news. But to learn that it will be months before you can taste that treat seems like a cruel irony. Anticipation is high. People here have watched as the restaurant rose from a muddy construction site with little more to show than an old-fashioned scoreboard sign counting down the days to the opening. It's the same kind of sign NASA uses to count down for its space shuttle launches. Folks here have listened to television talk show hosts and celebrities prattle on about how delicious a hot Krispy Kreme doughnut is. Now they're about to taste one for themselves. Sure, it's cold, cloudy, and very early. But that won't keep these masses from pursuing their collective goal: being among the first to devour one of these hot and tasty treats.

WAIT FOR THE PRIZE

Twenty-five-year-old Nate Frickel, who lives a half hour away in Kirkland, Washington, arrived at about 5:30 P.M. the previous night. He's number one in line. Twelve hours of waiting is nothing to him, not when he's been planning this camp-out for eight months, ever since he heard Krispy Kreme was coming to Issaquah.

"Have you ever had this kind of doughnut before?" Frickel asked a reporter from the *Seattle Times*. "They literally melt in your mouth. You don't even have to chew."[2]

Fourteen students from Seattle Pacific University are here, too. They're wearing hand-decorated T-shirts and tank tops that they painted the night before. Inky black and blue arrows point to their mouths above the phrase "Insert Donut Here."[3]

Once open, thousands of equally passionate doughnut fans push into the store on its first day of business, some waiting as long as four hours to hand over $5.59 for one dozen glazed treats. The conveyor belts that carry the yeast-raised doughnuts to the fryer and through a torrent of glaze never stop running, while the cash register rings up a continuous stream of sales. Every few seconds, a new face steps up to the counter or pulls up to the drive-through window and everyone has a different story to tell about why they love this company and these doughnuts.

Outside, reporters from various local radio and television stations interview satisfied customers while singing praises of their own about Krispy Kreme doughnuts to their live, at-home audiences. At the same time, several of the city's leading newspapers, both large and small, have reporters on hand collecting quotes, facts, and details for what will become one of tomorrow's top stories.

Franchisee Centioli and his business partner, Rich Melman, expected to be in demand on opening day. They figured that reporters from newspapers and television stations would have questions for the two restaurant visionaries responsible for bringing Krispy Kreme to the Pacific Northwest. At the very least, they would be needed as doughnut ambassadors, to run through the waiting crowd passing out free hot samples.

As it turned out, Melman and Centioli had little time to bask in the glorious glow of the Krispy Kreme hot light. From 4:30 Tuesday morning and for the next 24 hours, they were in the thick of the buying and selling binge. "We were busy. We were rolling that whole time," Centioli recalls. "That's the shortest 24-hour day I ever worked. Rich and I were everywhere. We were on our feet, picking doughnuts off the assembly line, serving doughnuts, ringing up orders, picking up papers. Anything that needed to be done, we did it."

SET RECORDS

Centioli, Melman, and their other franchise partner, attorney Michael Fox, made Krispy Kreme legend with their Issaquah store, the first of many they plan to develop in Washington, Oregon, Alaska, Hawaii, and the Canadian province of British Columbia. People told the partners it would be hard to sell many doughnuts in health-conscious Seattle, where people watch what they eat and routinely bike and walk to work. But in the first week the restaurant sold $454,125 worth of Krispy Kremes, crushing the previous opening week sales record of $369,000 set by developer Dan Stahurski in Lone Tree, Colorado. On Lone Tree's opening day, two blocks of people waited outside the door for doughnuts, and the drive-through line stretched for five blocks.[4]

It's more than Centioli ever expected. "I underestimated the power of the brand," he says. He knew the store would be popular and would draw crowds, but he didn't realize just how many people would come or how much they would spend. Nor did he fully appreciate the power of Krispy Kreme's incredible guerrilla marketing machine.

HAVE AN OPENING LIKE NO OTHER

Centioli is a successful veteran restaurateur whose father, Gil, brought Kentucky Fried Chicken and fast-food hamburgers to Seattle. He's been to many busy restaurant openings before. Colonel Harland Sanders, Kentucky Fried Chicken's founder, used to stay with the Centiolis whenever he visited their part of the country. "It made me pretty popular in the neighborhood," recalls this native of Seattle, who is a principal with ICON restaurants and Lettuce Entertain You Enterprises, both in Chicago.

Centioli is used to seeing both adults and kids go bonkers for restaurant icons. During his decades in the business, he has developed the concepts for 40 different eateries and supervised hundreds of grand openings.

Yet Centioli knew that his Krispy Kreme opening would be different from any other. Though the company sells a simple product, it has an amazing grassroots appeal among its customers. People are passionate—some would say crazy—about a hot Krispy Kreme doughnut. "The closest thing I ever saw in my business experience to a Krispy Kreme opening was in the early days of Kentucky Fried Chicken. On opening day, we had to bring in traffic police to direct traffic. But it was never at the level it was at our Krispy Kreme opening in Issaquah."

Centioli knew of the brand's drawing power. He'd heard about other grand openings, such as the one in Colorado. But until you've lived it, Centioli says, such tales seem like puffed-up fables. Surely, stories of mile-long lines at the drive-through and parking lots filled with pup tents are exaggerations, fish tales franchisees tell one another to seem more successful than they really are. But when you work for Krispy Kreme, there's no need for puffery. What seems unbelievable is real.

USE EXCITEMENT MARKETING

How do you explain why adults with jobs, families, and responsibilities would drag themselves out of bed before dawn in crummy weather for a doughnut?

The answer has a lot to do with Krispy Kreme's product, which many call the best doughnut in the world. But it has even more to do with the company's savvy marketing machine, which is designed to get a big bang for as few bucks as possible. And it works like magic.

"They know how to create . . . excitement. I can't think of a better word," says Dan Malovany, editor of the trade magazine *Snack Food & Wholesale Bakery.* "They know how to get people fired up over a hot fresh doughnut."

Since 1994, Krispy Kreme has worked with GSD&M, the largest advertising agency in Austin, Texas. The two companies formalized their partnership in the summer of 2001, but theirs is no typical agency-client relationship. Stan Parker, Krispy Kreme's vice president of marketing, made that clear when the partnership was announced. Krispy Kreme, he said then, had no intention of starting a corporate advertising campaign. Instead, GSD&M would help the doughnut maker craft its marketing message and strengthen its relationship with customers during its expansion phase. Getting products to customers and other key people is all the advertising Krispy Kreme has ever had to do.

Krispy Kreme has never paid a fee to place its doughnuts in movies and televisions shows. Still, in 2002, the company tallied more than 2 billion media impressions, making appearances on such shows as *Sex and the City, Will & Grace,* and CNBC's *Squawk Box.* Krispy Kreme's annual advertising budget is less than $100,000, amazing considering that the company has the third-best-known brand in the nation, according to a survey by BrandChannel.com. Only Target and Apple Computer have stronger brands, and these companies spend tens of millions of dollars on high-concept magazine and newspaper advertisements, inserts, Internet sites, and catchy television and radio commercials, according to BrandChannel.com.

Krispy Kreme's marketing strategies are subtler—and sometimes incredibly simple.

LET THEM TASTE THE GOODS

Ask anyone at Krispy Kreme why the company is so popular—from chief executive officer Scott Livengood to the counter clerks at your local store—and they are likely to answer with a question. "Have you tried the doughnuts?" plays like a recording from the mouths of most Krispy Kreme employees. "We have the best doughnuts in the world."

To try a Krispy Kreme doughnut, it seems, is to love it.

"Many consumers think that a bite of a Krispy Kreme doughnut is a bit of heaven on the tongue," observes Sheri Bridges, a marketing professor at Wake Forest University in the company's hometown of Winston-Salem.

"What is all this about? What is the big deal? When I get those questions from somebody, I know they haven't had a hot original glazed," Centioli insists. "It's all about the doughnut and people's passion for the doughnut."

When you walk into a Krispy Kreme store and step up to the counter, the clerk will likely greet you by handing you a hot original glazed, right off the cooling tray, to savor as you decide what you want to order. Not a small taste on a toothpick, like most restaurants hand out, but a whole doughnut. This small gesture often encourages people to buy more than they intended in the first place. Their taste buds scream out, "This is delicious! I want a lot more of that!"

Bakers have long known that the way to curry business is to let people taste your product. It's a cheap form of advertising, one not as easily ignored as a television commercial or an insert in the Sunday newspaper. People rarely refuse a free taste, and in offering it, a company makes a potent one-on-one contact with a potential customer in a way unlike any other form of marketing.

"Once someone's had a hot Krispy Kreme, it's done the job for us,"[5] company marketing representative Steve Bumgarner contends.

Krispy Kreme gives away thousands of doughnuts every year, not only to introduce new people to the airy confection, but to reward the legions of loyal customers who buy from the company on a regular basis.

SEEK GOOD (AND FREE) WORD OF MOUTH

Krispy Kreme benefits greatly from what most companies would love to have: strong and free word-of-mouth eulogistic endorsements from its customers, the media, and those celebrities who have tried its doughnuts.

Free publicity was so pervasive after the company's initial public offering in April 2000 that sales grew by double digits and earnings soared four cents per share above financial analysts' expectations. In its first quarter as a public company, Krispy Kreme's net income rose 61.2 percent, from $1.9 million to $3.1 million. For the same quarterly period, sales increased 41.3 percent to $103.3 million. "I'm not sure it's just a trendy thing. It's a new group of people being exposed to a new taste [in glazed doughnuts]," said Togo West, a former Clinton cabinet member and Krispy Kreme director, at the company's first annual meeting as a public firm. "This reminds us of just how unique an experience it is."

When the first New York Krispy Kreme store opened in 1996, southern humorist Roy Blount Jr. and filmmaker Nora Ephron wrote dueling essays for the *New York Times Magazine* and the *New Yorker* on the goodness of Krispy Kreme doughnuts, all because they like the product, not because they were pitched the idea by the company's hired public relations staff.

"The whole operation is visible from the street and you can stand there and hold your children up to the window to watch as an automatic gadget turns the doughnuts over, and another automatic gadget gives them a little push and finally, gloriously, they're hosed down with a gusher of powdered-sugar glaze that coats them and turns them gently crispy as they move along, just as regular as a clock can tick," penned Ephron, who wrote *When Harry Met Sally* and *Heartburn* and was briefly married to Pulitzer Prize–winning Watergate reporter Carl Bernstein. "The sight of all those doughnuts marching solemnly to their fate makes me proud to be an American. Sue me. That's how I feel."[6]

Blount, a sturdy man with a quick, if sometimes acerbic, wit and a Georgia drawl grew up in towns where Krispy Kreme was part of the culture, as common as church on a Sunday morning. Not surprisingly, he was compelled to weigh in on the phenomenon when the company migrated north.

"You owe it to yourself to eat two . . . while they're hot. And I don't mean while they're fashionable," Blount wrote in the *New York Times Magazine*. "Even after they've cooled down, Krispy Kremes are the best doughnuts in creation. When Krispy Kremes are hot, they are to other doughnuts what angels are to people. They're not crispy-creamy so much as right on the cusp between chewy and molten, kind of like fried nectar puffed up with yeast."[7]

As Pulitzer Prize–winning, Alabama-born reporter Rick Bragg wrote in his memoir, *All Over but the Shoutin'*, "Trying to explain how good they are to someone who has never had one is like telling a celibate priest about young love."

To many observers, including some within the company, the national Krispy Kreme frenzy and the birth of the brand's cult status began with the opening of its first New York store. It gained momentum when the company went west to California and celebrities became customers and unpaid publicists. Suddenly, thin, pouty-lipped movie star Julia Roberts was on late-night talk shows chatting, not about her latest movie, but of her love affair with Krispy Kreme doughnuts. Rosie O'Donnell had a doughnut fryer installed on the set of her talk show and mentioned the glazed treats nearly as much as she talked about her idol Tom Cruise or trying to slim down with Weight Watchers. And Clint Eastwood used a clearly labeled box of Krispy Kreme doughnuts to convince a pair of uncooperative cops to help him out in the 2001 film *Bloodwork*.

"We keep waiting for this [incredible media attention] to level off, and it hasn't so far. We're grateful for it," said chief operating officer John Tate during an investor conference at which 2,000 doughnuts were consumed in two days. "As you might imagine, we spend a lot of time trying to understand our brand and the connection that seems to exist between our customers and our brand. Still, I can't claim that we fully understand it." Tate went on to concede, "We are somewhat intentional about it [attracting positive press coverage]. Again, we don't completely understand the passion of that connection, but we do things to try to stimulate it."

STAGE CLEVER STUNTS

In May 2001, Krispy Kreme detoured one of its doughnut fryers on its way to a new store. The stainless steel cooker was set up in front of the New York Stock Exchange, and a busy sidewalk was transformed into a Krispy Kreme factory. A crew led by Fred Mitchell, senior vice president of Krispy Kreme's manufacturing and distribution division, made it happen. His team squeezed 18-wheeler trucks onto tiny, crowded downtown streets and assembled the cooker on the sidewalk. They began at 10 P.M. and worked straight through sunrise, accomplishing in 10 hours what normally takes three days.

The next morning, Scott Livengood, civil rights leader Jesse Jackson, and New York Stock Exchange chairman Richard Grasso accessorized their expensive, expertly pressed suits with paper cook's hats. They helped pass out 40,000 hot doughnuts and 70,000 cups of coffee to traders and anyone else who stopped by.

"We often use the words 'magic moments' to describe elements within the Krispy Kreme experience. Maybe we say it too much, but that May 17th day on Broad Street right in front of the NYSE was truly the most magical moment I can ever recall seeing since I've worked here," Mitchell remembers. "We made the doughnuts. The magic happened on its own."[8]

The impromptu show was designed to celebrate Krispy Kreme's switch from the Nasdaq to the NYSE. It generated much more press attention than a normal turn-of-the-screw financial event, all for the price of 40,000 free doughnuts.

"That was a nice one,"[9] Krispy Kreme marketing chief Stan Parker told *PR Week,* reflecting on the company's media-attracting endeavors.

Months before Krispy Kreme's first Australian store opened in 2003, the company constructed what it called a *commissary* in Sydney. The doughnut-making factory was built so Krispy Kreme would have a convenient place to train its new Aussie employees how to cook doughnuts; how to fill them with jelly, custard, and creamy icing; how to brew coffee; and how to behave in its theater-like stores. But the commissary also played an important marketing role. It enabled Krispy Kreme to give customers, community officials, and reporters an early taste of its signature product.

GET THE WORD OUT

Without question, Krispy Kreme knows how to use the media. In advance of every new store opening, Krispy Kreme dispatches public relations workers to newspapers, television stations, radio stations, and magazines with deliveries of fresh—and preferably hot—doughnuts. Interviews begin with the offer of a doughnut and either a glass of cold milk or a mug of hot coffee. Every press kit comes with a coupon for a dozen free glazed doughnuts. Some employees' business cards can be turned in at stores for free doughnuts as well.

"We work hard with the media, but not in the sense of trying to buy favoritism," contends Donald Henshall, former vice president of international development. "We do supply them with as many free doughnuts as they want."[10] And experience proves that few reporters can turn down the temptation to savor these tasty treats. Krispy Kreme doughnuts are like pizzas in a newsroom; they disappear almost as soon as the box is opened.

While Krispy Kreme doesn't pay for placement on television or in the movies, the company often provides its doughnuts free to production companies. Erik Martin, a young independent filmmaker, found that out firsthand when he asked for permission to use Krispy Kreme doughnuts in his low-budget movie *Dog Nights.* Martin, who lives in Chapel Hill, North Carolina, where Livengood went to college, called the CEO at home one night. He introduced himself and nervously pitched his movie to Livengood. Martin told the executive how the doughnuts fit into his movie, and Livengood agreed to let the young filmmaker use them. Livengood also arranged for free doughnuts to be delivered to the set for the crew.

"No Dunkin' Donut will ever touch my lip," said Martin, who advertises Krispy Kreme's generosity on his web site.

In 1998, Krispy Kreme helped another movie producer, this one with a much bigger audience. At the request of Universal Pictures, the company set up a mock Krispy Kreme store to be used for a scene in the political lampoon *Primary Colors,* which follows the presidential campaign of a Bill Clinton–like character played by John Travolta. In the movie, the politician pigs out on doughnuts and has the heft to prove it. But Krispy Kreme wasn't bothered by the portrayal, which it paid for with free doughnuts for the film crew. "The character eats a lot of other things, too," Mike Cecil, former head of marketing and so-called minister of culture at Krispy Kreme, told *Forbes* at the time. "He is constantly eating pizza and soft drinks. Anyone can overdo it."[11]

A few times a year, studios in New York and Los Angeles receive surprise doughnut deliveries for writers, camera operators, grips, actors, directors, and other employees. They're meant, in part, to encourage the inclusion of Krispy Kreme pastries in big-time productions. And any star who mentions Krispy Kreme during an interview gets what Tate describes as "substantial portions" of free doughnuts. Madonna, for example, gets a complimentary supply of doughnuts backstage at her concerts because she has been such a vocal fan of the company.

CREATE GOODWILL

Not all of Krispy Kreme's giveaways are so well scripted. Many times they are spontaneous.

As previously mentioned, when customers walk into a store while doughnuts are being made, they're often offered a free sample before ordering. The company also gave away free cups of its new coffee blends and frozen espresso drinks when these products were first introduced. Kids can always get a free sweet treat of their choice if they bring in a report card with at least one A on it.

Weeks before a new store opens, employees are encouraged to take doughnuts home to share with neighbors and friends. Free preopening samples are also often delivered to nearby businesses. Anxious onlookers who stop by stores still being readied can sometimes get free samples just for stopping by and asking. And preopening VIP parties make certain that community bigwigs get their fill a little before everyone else.

Krispy Kreme vice chairman Jack McAleer, whose father led the leveraged buyout from Beatrice Foods in the early 1980s, loves nothing better than going to new store openings and pretending he's the Santa Claus of the doughnut world. McAleer runs down the line of waiting customers, passing out samples from a tray of hot doughnuts. "I love to see trails of sugar on everything," McAleer once told a friend.

When nine Pennsylvania men were trapped in an underground mine in 2002 and rescue workers were trying to save them, the manager of the local Krispy Kreme store carted dozens of doughnuts and coffee to the emergency scene. The doughnuts were free for paramedics, police officers, mine diggers, firefighters, and families standing vigil. That giveaway didn't happen because Krispy Kreme wanted publicity. In fact, the company rarely mentions it. Instead, it was Krispy Kreme's way of being a good neighbor in a stressful time. Store managers are empowered to respond whenever and however they are needed.

BE LOCAL WHEREVER YOU ARE

Though it has nearly 300 outlets in the United States and is planning an aggressive international expansion, Krispy Kreme always wants to be considered a hometown company. That's another essential part of its overall marketing strategy. The company began in 1937 as a modest local business that attracted customers because people had either heard about the delicious doughnuts from friends or smelled the sweet aroma as they cooked. Krispy Kreme remains focused on making sure that, like its doughnut recipe, this local feeling never changes.

"Being a true and relevant global brand, I think, means being a neighborhood brand as well," CEO Livengood says.

That's why, according to company marketing chief Stan Parker, store managers are encouraged to become involved in their communities and help out as best they can. They don't need corporate office approval to provide free doughnuts at a blood drive, a rescue site, a football game, or a county fair. They just do it. And all employees are told to do whatever they can to make customers feel happy, special, and well served. For example, Patrick Gallagher, Krispy Kreme's area developer for the Pittsburgh area, once delivered doughnuts to a Pennsylvania woman whose husband wanted to surprise her with a special anniversary gift.[12] Yes, it attracted media coverage, but that was merely a by-product of the good marketing deed.

Corporate chef Ron Rupocinski, whose office is a test kitchen at Krispy Kreme's mix manufacturing plant on the outskirts of Winston-Salem, even gives couples advice on how to build wedding cakes out of doughnuts. He won't make the cake for the doughnut-loving brides and grooms. But Chef Ron, as he's called, will tell them exactly how to stack tier upon tier of doughnuts into cake form without crushing them. And you'd be surprised how many couples do this. Scott Livengood himself had a doughnut cake at his wedding to former Krispy Kreme executive Michelle Parman in the summer of 2002.

MAKE SURE THE TROOPS KNOW YOUR MESSAGE

Stan Parker oversees a marketing staff of fewer than a dozen people. He and his employees craft a centralized marketing strategy for the company. But Parker's primary duty is to infuse the Krispy Kreme spirit throughout the company, to explain what the brand means, and to model how all employees should shepherd it.

Parker is a soft-spoken, friendly man in his forties with thick, dark hair and a fit build. He still wears his college class ring and prefers blazers and open-collared shirts to suits and ties. He joined Krispy Kreme in 1998 after an early, brief career as an oil trader in Singapore and 10 years with Winston-Salem-based Sara Lee Corporation, a global manufacturer and marketer of brand-name consumer products, from cakes to underwear. Parker initially accepted the Krispy Kreme job interview as a courtesy to a friend who worked there. The whole thing started on a golf course near Winston-Salem after a celebrity fund-raising tournament named for singer Bing Crosby. The friend told Parker that Krispy Kreme was looking for someone to head its marketing department. "How about me?" Parker joked.

Parker grew up in the South and attended college at the University of North Carolina at Chapel Hill, also the alma mater of Livengood. He thought Krispy Kreme doughnuts were ubiquitous until someone showed him a map with 130 dots on it during his interview. Each dot represented an existing store. In that map, Parker saw the opportunity to join a good, small company at the beginning of its growth. But that didn't convince him to leave his job at Sara Lee.

Katie Couric did.

Krispy Kreme had offered Parker a job, but he was still mulling over the decision. Should he leave a 10-year career with a big, established company to go to work for what was then a small, privately held doughnut maker? He made his decision in front of the television. One day Parker, who normally arrives at work by 6:30 A.M., was enjoying a leisurely morning at home with his wife, Karen. They were talking, half listening to *Today* on NBC, when Katie Couric came on the screen and started raving about Krispy Kreme.

Turning to Karen, Parker said, "I'm taking it." He couldn't ignore such a spontaneous, public endorsement.

Years later, Parker said he has often thought about writing a thank-you note to Couric. He never has. But like any other celebrity, Couric receives dozens of free doughnuts whenever she mentions Krispy Kreme on the air. That's probably thanks enough.

Parker, who puts in long days and works most weekends, is as modest about his role at Krispy Kreme as he is about the company's appeal. Krispy Kreme is just a local doughnut company. It grows bigger every month, but remains married to simple ideals, like treating customers well, creating events that get people excited, selling only the freshest products, and giving back to the community whenever it can. Such strategies, in turn, pay dividends for Krispy Kreme in the form of customer endorsements and prolific media coverage.

BECOME NEWSWORTHY

Whenever a Krispy Kreme store opens, particularly in a town that's never had one before, the company strives to make the event the biggest and most anticipated of the year. The company encourages its franchisees to hire a local public relations firm to promote the opening. Franchisees also are required to spend between $5,000 and $10,000 to publicize the new location at least a month before opening and during the first three months of operation.

Sometimes, store openings are tied to a local celebrity or a cultural institution, as was the case when Krispy Kreme began selling its goods in Austin, Texas. George W. Bush's presidential campaign staff was given an unusual campaign donation: dozens of doughnuts.

"Our whole local store [grand opening] marketing program really started sort of off the cuff," claims Jennifer Gardner, a marketing manager who works for Parker. "We had a store in a new market, so we made several hundred dozen doughnuts and started delivering them all over town to the police and fire departments, banks and businesses, hospitals, gas stations—just everywhere—and we told everyone we were opening next week, so be sure to drop by. The waiting line on opening day was an hour and a half."[13]

Krispy Kreme has mastered event marketing, and in doing so guarantees big crowds and press coverage for its store openings. Sometimes several months before a grand opening, construction crews put up the big green Krispy Kreme logo with a huge countdown sign. Such things get people excited and talking, planning for the day as they would for a wedding or a vacation.

It was summertime when Krispy Kreme put up a sign that read "Opening in 21 Days" in front of its store in Cameron Godwin's hometown of Greensboro, North Carolina. On vacation from middle school, the 12-year-old rode his skateboard to the construction site for each of those 21 days. He talked to construction workers, watched them move dirt and steel, and dreamed about doughnuts. Then, on opening day, he convinced his parents to drop him off at the store at 2:45 A.M. so he could be among the first to taste a hot original glazed fresh from the new fryer. He would be safe, Cameron convinced his parents, because he was at Krispy Kreme. Nothing bad can happen to you there, he surmised. Plus, Cameron explained, you're surrounded and protected by dozens of other eager fans.

"We now go to the store about every weekend," says Cameron's mother, Loui Young, who maintains that being part of the opening-day celebration was one of the most exciting things her son has ever participated in. "We are definitely Krispy Kreme fans."

Dynamic Doughnuts, the Krispy Kreme developer in upstate New York, hired the marketing firm Buck & Pulleyn to spread the word about its new store in Rochester. Working with a limited budget, the agency in Pittsford, New York, had to spread the gospel of Krispy Kreme to a broad audience to ensure that as many people as possible would show up for the December 2000 opening. Buck & Pulleyn invited customers, local officials, and reporters to a groundbreaking celebration and served Krispy Kreme doughnuts that had been trucked in fresh that morning from a store 200 miles away. Just before the grand opening, the marketing agency gave away more than 700 dozen doughnuts and hosted an invitation-only sneak preview party for VIPs. The company advertised the opening on a few billboards around Rochester and in several publications.

The results from the low-budget advertising and marketing campaign were phenomenal. During its grand-opening week, the Rochester store served more than 16,000 doughnuts each day. People waited in 90-minute lines for the doughnuts, and the drive-through lane was routinely clogged with 75 cars or more. To top it all off, media outlets in the region ran a total of 130 stories on the new store; 75 of them appeared during the store's first 24 hours in business.[14]

Plenty of Krispy Kreme customers show up on opening day of their own accord, as did Cameron Godwin, Nate Frickel, and the masses in Rochester, New York. But Krispy Kreme sometimes brings in its own crowds, too, encouraging college students and scout troops to camp out by offering free doughnuts for fund-raising purposes. The first New York franchisees, for example, invited alumni from southern universities to their grand-opening party. Occasionally the company identifies diehard fans in a market and gives them incentives to come to an opening. The more people, the better, especially to make a scene on TV.

"They don't just cultivate people who say Krispy Kreme is a better doughnut. They cultivate people who eulogize over it," according to Neil Morgan, a marketing professor at the University of North Carolina at Chapel Hill. "They target these consumers and turn them into what they call 'Krispy Kreme ambassadors' through Web sites, chat rooms, and regular mail. Before they enter a market, they'll send packets of memorabilia to these people—T-shirts, hats, and such—and they form an unpaid loyalty base."[15]

Morgan explains, "Krispy Kreme is not trying to create these people. These people already exist. What Krispy Kreme does is give them the ammunition to be effective in what they do. They are enabling [these ambassadors] to spread the message that they want to spread. The problem for most other companies is that there aren't enough people who feel like that about their brand for them to organize the fans in a sensible way."

In North Carolina, a Krispy Kreme opening is not nearly the big deal it is in places such as New England or southern California. North Carolina, after all, is the state where the company was born. Hot glazed doughnuts have been sold in North Carolina since 1937. Fresh Krispy Kreme treats are available at nearly every grocery store and gas station in the state. As a result, new store openings aren't expected to draw the big crowds they do in markets where people have only *heard* about Krispy Kreme doughnuts, but never tasted them. Still, the company manages to create excitement around its North Carolina store openings, too, attracting campers and good-sized hungry crowds while dragging sleep-loving reporters out of bed early to write about the company's newest location.

How? By using the same strategy that has proven effective in other markets time and time again: Give people and the media a reason to come—and they will. And if each opening has a new twist of its own, all the better.

In September 2002, Krispy Kreme partnered with Project Homestead in Greensboro, North Carolina, to open its second black-owned franchise and the first one partly owned by a nonprofit organization. Project Homestead aims to revitalize the mostly minority eastern section of Greensboro, which is about 30 miles from Krispy Kreme's corporate headquarters. The community development group also builds affordable homes for low-income people.

After years of weekly, persistent phone calls to Scott Livengood, Project Homestead's loquacious and enigmatic leader, the Reverend Michael King, finally convinced Krispy Kreme to sell him a franchise. "My shortest five-minute conversation with Michael lasted 30 minutes," Livengood jokes.

Project Homestead uses its profits from doughnut sales to fund its home-building and economic development mission. Because of that unique partnership, the local media felt obligated to write about the deal. Reporters also covered the groundbreaking ceremony several months earlier because economic development in east Greensboro is a touchstone issue in the community.

Few people expected much of an opening-day crowd beyond the politicians who had to be there and the Boy Scout troops that had been invited to camp in the parking lot overnight. After all, North Carolina had seen its share of new Krispy Kreme openings many times in the past. But the company, with the help of its new franchisees, made the opening a community event, just as it does in markets where Krispy Kreme doughnuts are a much rarer commodity. Close to 1,000 people attended the event, which lasted almost six hours from the time the first doughnuts rolled off the conveyor to the end of the formal opening ceremony.

Johnnetta Cole, president of the nearby all-female Bennett College, sent out an e-mail message to the student body a few days before the opening. Cole, formerly head of Spelman College, another historically black women's college in Atlanta, Georgia, had been persuaded by the franchisees to lend her support to their venture. Project Homestead pledged to help with some much-needed cleanup and renovations at Bennett College, using profits from doughnut sales to support the work. Cole reciprocated by bringing in hungry customers.

"My sugar high came from watching my students seriously connect with a neighborhood business," she said.

At around 4:30 A.M., Cole and about 100 Bennett College students (Belles, as they're called) met on a campus corner. The women, about a quarter of Bennett's student body, power-walked through the morning darkness and arrived just in time to see the new Krispy Kreme neon "Hot Doughnuts Now" light flicker on. They were rewarded with as many goodies as they could eat.

Student Danielle Hatcher ate hers immediately, devouring her first ever hot Krispy Kreme doughnut almost as soon as she put it in her mouth. "It was worth it," said the freshman from Boston.

College president Cole walked back to campus carrying her glazed doughnuts in a waxed-paper bag. She ate them for breakfast, slowly savoring every bite, making each doughnut last as long as possible. "I don't know that the power walk got rid of the calories from the doughnuts," Cole chuckled.

Five hours later, Cole was back at Krispy Kreme, this time made up and dressed in a tailored pantsuit instead. An equally large number of Bennett College students, some of them returning walkers, and hundreds more from the surrounding community gathered around the store to watch Livengood, King, and other dignitaries cut a ribbon strung with glazed doughnuts to officially open the store. The mayor pro tempore and two county commissioners showed up, as did a few campaigning politicians and at least a half-dozen press to witness the festivities orchestrated by Krispy Kreme and its franchisees. As an added treat, this opening also gave fans a chance to see and hear a local literary star.

Cole's friend, Maya Angelou, the renowned author, poet, and professor who wrote a poem for Bill Clinton's presidential inauguration and counts Oprah Winfrey as one of her closest friends, presided over the grand opening. Angelou, who lives in Winston-Salem and teaches at Wake Forest University, arrived in a limousine that parked in the drive-through lane. The audience of hundreds clapped and cheered as she was introduced, then parted like the Red Sea as she made her way to a microphone near the store entrance. In her speech, Angelou praised Krispy Kreme for building a store in an economically depressed neighborhood and for being the first national company willing to serve as anchor for the revitalization efforts to bring commerce back to an area where minority-owned companies had once thrived before being pushed out by urban renewal projects in the 1960s.

"One hundred businesses gone and one starting up to replace 1,000 dreams," Angelou said, peppering the speech with stanzas from her poem, "Still I Rise." As she spoke, Angelou's rough-hewn voice took on the cadence of a gospel singer, then a preacher.

"Look where we've all come from," she sang to applause from the audience, before switching into more sermonizing language. "I thank, of course, Krispy Kreme for having faith. Nobody thought that Krispy Kreme would occupy this corner and start the revival of this corridor."

Angelou's speech and the Krispy Kreme opening garnered coverage by several newspapers in the area, along with a number of TV and radio stations. One reporter called the opening "a significant event for the black community."

It could have been another routine North Carolina grand opening. Instead, Krispy Kreme turned it into a newsworthy event unlike any other the area had ever seen. And the media ate it up.

MAKE IT EASY FOR THE MEDIA

Krispy Kreme knows better than most companies how to court the press, observes Tom Ogburn, a southern-born professor at Wake Forest University who left a marketing position at R.J. Reynolds Tobacco Company to begin teaching.

Krispy Kreme recognizes that big crowds attract reporters. In turn, media coverage gives it a no-cost way to connect with thousands of potential customers. The company invites radio announcers and television morning-show hosts to broadcast live from the site of a new store. Krispy Kreme also generally donates opening day profits to local civic groups, particularly those that help children. Those donations lead to even more follow-up media reports about the company's generosity.

"What they do is create situations that generate lots of consumer interest," says Ogburn. "If you open a store and you have three lanes of cars lined up, that's a news story."

When most companies call the media to announce their grand openings, they receive little or no coverage. After all, dozens of businesses open their doors in large towns each day, and often few people care, especially the media. But with Krispy Kreme, every opening is a major event.

Some newspapers, including the *Chicago Tribune* and the Minneapolis *Star Tribune,* have dispatched multiple reporters and photographers to cover the first-day frenzy at a new Krispy Kreme shop. These are the kinds of resources usually reserved for high-profile political events or major crimes. Ask why a business opening merits such heavyduty coverage and the consistent answer is, "It's newsworthy." Krispy Kreme *makes* it newsworthy. The company knows that's the difference between gaining coverage and being ignored, as most grand-opening ceremonies are by all but the smallest neighborhood publications.

Delma Francis certainly expected to find news when she was assigned to cover yet another record-breaking Krispy Kreme opening in Minneapolis, Minnesota. "When people wait in line 15 hours for something, that's news,"[16] she told another reporter who was writing a newspaper article about the coverage Krispy Kreme receives.

Krispy Kreme is also notoriously easy to work with. Its marketing and public relations staff, as well as employees from the small public relations firms it hires to help with new store openings, normally return reporters' telephone calls promptly to set up interviews and arrange behind-the-scenes tours. They understand and respect tight deadlines.

Dan Malovany, reporter and editor for the trade magazine *Snack Food & Wholesale Bakery,* expected he would have to wait for some lull in the corporate schedule to interview Stan Parker and Scott Livengood for his magazine cover story. But a public relations handler quickly sent him an e-mail response: "You can interview Stan Parker next week." An interview with Scott Livengood was just as easy to secure.

"Why do they get a lot of media coverage? Because they're public relations savvy. They don't make the job difficult," Malovany says. "When we wrote the story, we found them just very easy to work with. They're very forthright. I was scheduled for an hour interview; it ended up lasting an hour and a half."

Area developer Richard Reinis was just as accommodating when a local TV host asked to broadcast live from his new Krispy Kreme store in southern California. Reinis, the chief executive officer of Los Angeles–based Great Circle Family Foods, in turn discovered just how fruitful a genuine media endorsement could be for business. Huell Howser, a local television personality who is from the South, showed up hungry and fawning. His program wasn't an unbiased report at all, but something of an unsolicited infomercial for hot Krispy Kreme doughnuts. Within minutes of Howser's broadcast, Reinis said, more than 60 cars were waiting in the drive-through lane. And that was just the beginning of a phenomenal year for Great Circle Family Foods, which has the right to develop other West Coast locations. In its first year of operations, the company's store in La Habra, California hosted more people than the Anaheim Angels did at Edison Field.[17]

"Somehow, it never stopped after that," Reinis says, harkening to Howser's important broadcast. "The experience of opening that store changed my life. This was not 'Field of Dreams' for any of us. We built it, but frankly, we didn't know if they would come. They came in droves. Great Circle Family Foods' success in this business is everything for which I could have hoped. It also helps to have one of best products in the category—Krispy Kreme doughnuts."[18]

By being good to the media, creating newsworthy events and grand openings, and sticking to its roots of creating strong community goodwill, Krispy Kreme has managed to create a premier brand that has become the envy of veteran marketing pros everywhere. Unlike most companies, Krispy Kreme has done it by spending next to nothing on traditional advertising. Instead, the company uses guerrilla marketing. By enlisting both the media and enthusiastic customers to spread the word and create a mystique about a product as simple as doughnuts, the company has made Krispy Kreme a name recognized and renowned around the world.

CHAPTER 7

Maintain High Standards

Fred Mitchell has only been working at Krispy Kreme for 10 years, but he talks about company founder Vernon Rudolph as if they were personal friends.

Old Rudolph was a visionary, says Mitchell, who works in an office that once belonged to the founder himself. Sure, Rudolph was smart because he had the good sense to bring his uncle's secret doughnut recipe to Winston-Salem and start using it. But that's only part of the story, Mitchell insists. Sitting behind a neatly kept wooden desk, Mitchell rocks back in his big executive chair like an old southern gentleman, ready to entertain you with a good tale.

Mitchell is Krispy Kreme's senior vice president of manufacturing and distribution. He likes to reflect on how far the company has come without having to sacrifice the high standards set by Rudolph in its earliest days of growth.

When Rudolph first started Krispy Kreme in 1937, he made each batch of doughnuts from scratch, measuring and mixing together the right amounts of sugar, flour, milk, yeast, eggs, and other ingredients. Within 10 years, Rudolph's business had grown from one tiny sweetshop in Winston-Salem, North Carolina to bakeries in seven southern states. There, as at the flagship restaurant, cooks made doughnuts the hard way—from scratch—following Rudolph's secret recipe, which is locked in a fireproof safe in a storage room just a few steps away from Mitchell's office. Quaint and a bit old fashioned, the process certainly fit with Krispy Kreme's reputation as a company steeped in heritage. But it didn't do much for efficiency or consistency in the taste and appearance of the doughnuts, Mitchell says.

That lack of consistency concerned Rudolph. He knew that to build a successful business and to keep customers coming back for his doughnuts he had to build a process that ensured the same high-quality taste, bite after bite. So, in 1948, the founder created Krispy Kreme's mix department, opening a plant on Ivy Avenue in Winston-Salem, where all ingredients would be premeasured and premixed, then sent to each

4

individual store to be turned into doughnuts. The stores then simply had to open the bag and add just a few extras. The process was as simple as opening a box of Betty Crocker cake mix and making the finished product merely by following detailed instructions and adding a few precalculated measures of water and oil.

By providing all of the ingredients himself, Rudolph had an instant solution to his consistency problem, notes Mitchell in his friendly and distinctive southern accent. "He immediately had more mix than he could use." That's when Rudolph began looking for people who would open Krispy Kreme franchises and buy the doughnut mix from him. In turn, Rudolph had created a new revenue stream for the company—one that has become increasingly lucrative as Krispy Kreme signs on new franchisees and opens stores all over the world.

"The mix that we sell to our stores is much like syrup is to Coca-Cola," observes chief governance officer Randy Casstevens. Krispy Kreme franchisees can't run a doughnut shop without it, and the corporate office is the only source of this essential ingredient.

CONTROL DISTRIBUTION

The creation of the mix department decades ago was just the first step in Krispy Kreme's vertical integration. The company, like many of its peers in the earlier part of the twentieth century, was part of an industrial revolution pioneered by Andrew Carnegie, who discovered that there could be a substantial advantage to controlling all aspects of the design, manufacturing, and distribution of a product. It worked for Carnegie's steel plants, and it also worked for Rudolph's doughnut shops.

Shortly after opening the mix department, Rudolph created a laboratory—which is still in operation today. There, every batch of doughnut mix is carefully tested, and chefs work diligently to create new doughnut varieties. By 1949, Rudolph had hired engineers and machinists to work at Krispy Kreme in the newly created equipment department. It was here that the Ring King Jr., Krispy Kreme's first doughnut-making machine, was invented. Its introduction meant that in-store bakers no longer had to cut each doughnut by hand. The machine, which is now in the Smithsonian Institution as an example of American invention and heritage, took up only seven square feet of space. But it cut, fried, turned, and cooked as many as 75 dozen doughnuts an hour.[1]

Turning Krispy Kreme into a vertically integrated business with many revenue streams was Rudolph's real genius, Mitchell maintains. Through the years, he did what was necessary to keep the business successful and growing. Today, Rudolph's early vision lives on in a Krispy Kreme that is truly vertically integrated. The company makes all of its doughnut mix at both the original plant on Ivy Avenue and at a second location in Effingham, Illinois. The company plans to build a third mixing plant in the western United States. Krispy Kreme also roasts and bags its own coffee at Ivy Avenue. And its entire line of doughnut-making equipment—including the huge stainless steel fryer and conveyor belt contraptions found in every Krispy Kreme restaurant—is assembled at a plant in High Point, North Carolina, a town just east of Winston-Salem that is best known as a center of furniture manufacturing and wholesaling. Just about everything else found in a Krispy Kreme store (napkins, cups, uniforms, raspberry jelly, packets of sugar and Equal, lemon custard, juices, signs, and display cases) comes from the corporate office by way of distribution centers in North Carolina, Illinois, and California.

This vertically integrated business model affords Krispy Kreme many benefits. By making and delivering the ingredients and equipment for its stores, Krispy Kreme is able to keep tight control over its products and therefore maintain the high standards customers expect. By using volume buying power, Krispy Kreme saves on the cost of supplies, a strategy that makes good economic sense. Because of these factors, the mix and manufacturing department that Mitchell oversees adds to the company's overall profitability. Its share of total Krispy Kreme revenues—close to 31 percent in fiscal 2003—is projected to grow further as more stores open around the world. "We estimate that for every dollar of franchise sales, [Krispy Kreme] realizes 25 cents to 30 cents of support operations revenue and generates approximately 10 cents of operating profit," according to Kathleen Heaney, an analyst at Brean Murray Research in New York. "As a result of its vertical

integration, the company makes excellent returns in the support operations business."

Because Krispy Kreme manufactures its own doughnut cookers, the
company has the opportunity to continually improve the equipment
and innovate, as it did in 2001 with the creation of a new so-called hot
doughnut machine. This strategy also gives the company tight control
over store openings because Krispy Kreme doesn't have to count on a
supplier to finish making a doughnut machine before it enters a new
market.

KEEP AN EYE ON QUALITY

Ivy Avenue, the location of Krispy Kreme's mix and coffee roasting
plant, is in an industrial part of Winston-Salem, about a 10-minute
drive from the company's headquarters in a much tonier neighborhood. Raw ingredients arrive daily by truck and railcar. But before
Krispy Kreme accepts any of them for its doughnuts, an employee
climbs into the truck and takes a large sample. Scientists in a glassed-in
analytical laboratory test the ingredients. "It's not just taste," a Krispy
Kreme food technologist once told a reporter. "It's chemistry."[2] Ingredients must meet Krispy Kreme's strict standards. Consistency is crucial, after all. Batches of flour, shortening, or sugar that don't measure
up are rejected and sent back to the supplier.

Acceptable ingredients are transferred to big hoppers inside the mix
plant, which is a mostly automated facility that roars with activity
through two shifts, 24 hours a day, seven days a week. Doughnut mix
is made daily through a complicated, computerized process that takes
both wet and dry raw ingredients, mixes them together, then drops the
finished product down a chute to be bagged for shipment to stores.
Every 50-pound bag of mix is stamped with a serial number, a date, and
a packaging time, just in case a flaw is discovered in the batch. Each
brown paper bag also goes through a metal detector so sensitive that it
can detect a metal sliver as small as half a staple.

Before a single bag from any batch of mix is shipped out to a Krispy
Kreme store, a cook from the test kitchen slits open a bag and fries up
a sample serving of doughnuts. If the sample doughnuts don't taste

exactly right, and if they don't have that gooey airiness unique to Krispy Kremes, that batch of mix never leaves the warehouse. Krispy Kreme, at its Ivy Avenue plant and at a new one in Effingham, Illinois, has the ability to make 9 million bags of mix annually. With a modest capital investment, capacity can easily be increased to 12 million bags, an amount that should serve the company for years to come, according to Casstevens. In fiscal 2002, the company used slightly less than 4 million bags of mix.

"It took 65 years to build a process that pays that much attention to consistency and quality," says Krispy Kreme spokeswoman Brooke Smith.

PERCOLATE NEW OPPORTUNITIES

Recognizing its own success, the company emulated its mix-making process when it launched its own brand of drip-brew coffee, which is now sold both by the cup and by the bag at many of its stores.

Krispy Kreme once bought its coffee from outside vendors. However, in February 2001, the company took yet another step toward complete vertical integration with the purchase of Digital Java, a small coffee company based in Chicago, Illinois. "After more than 60 years making a doughnut that people actually line up for, we decided it was time to challenge ourselves to make a coffee that tasted just as good," Krispy Kreme said at the time. "It wouldn't be easy. It would take passion, commitment, and time, not to mention people who know coffee like we know doughnuts." The key to good coffee, Krispy Kreme determined, is the same as the key to good doughnuts: Don't trust your success to anyone else. Build a system so you can make the product yourself and monitor the quality through each step.

D. J. McKie was part of the package when Krispy Kreme bought Digital Java. McKie, a stocky young man with thick, spiky dark hair and a neatly trimmed mustache and beard, started fiddling with roasting coffee while working as an investment banker in Chicago. His research, done primarily in bookstores, taught him that most coffee roasters were probably burning their beans and distorting the flavor of the coffee. McKie decided to buy a crank-turned popcorn popper and start roasting his own coffee beans in what he considered to be the right way. He would do it by employing various unconventional techniques that he had read about. McKie's passion for good coffee soon turned into a small business—Digital Java, a roaster and seller of imported espresso machines that he initially ran out of his home. "When we'd fire up our roaster in our small retail store," McKie recalls, "people would start coming in and buying our coffee. Looking back on that, it had the same effect that turning on Krispy Kreme's 'Hot Doughnuts Now' sign does. People are drawn in."[3]

After Krispy Kreme bought Digital Java, McKie moved to Winston-Salem and set about building a coffee roasting facility that followed the same principles as the mix plant of creating and delivering a consistent product.

Beans, carefully selected from only the top 5 percent of the world's growers, arrive in huge 2,000-pound bags called *supersacks*. The beans are still green at this point, and they smell fresh and earthy, like grass on a summer day. To test the quality of the beans in these supersacks, employees roast a half-pound sample and taste the coffee at a *cupping ceremony*, an elaborate ritual that involves slurping fresh brew from a spoon, swishing it around in the mouth, then spitting it into a carafe. This is the traditional way that coffee experts and connoisseurs taste the beverage. Unlike many regular coffee drinkers, they don't drink it served in a mug or diluted with copious portions of cream and sweetener. If the sample beans pass that test, the bags are hoisted by forklift into one of 12 storage silos.

"We're a doughnut company, so we have a dozen silos," jokes McKie. Actually, each silo represents a different coffee-growing region from which Krispy Kreme buys its beans. Each silo sits on a giant scale. This helps the company keep precise track of how much coffee is roasted in each batch. As with the doughnuts, everything must be exact and in the same proportions every time. A cup of Krispy Kreme coffee served in Myrtle Beach, South Carolina, must taste the same as a cup served in Toronto, Canada. Therefore, nothing is left to chance. You don't trust that each supersack weighs exactly a ton; you weigh it precisely.

Unlike many companies, Krispy Kreme roasts each type of raw bean separately, then mixes them into three different coffee blends—smooth, rich, and bold. It's a little bit like making stew, McKie says. You don't throw the meat, carrots, onions, and potatoes in the pot at the same time or you'd have an unevenly cooked, bad-tasting dinner. Coffee beans, like food, require different cooking times.

Krispy Kreme prepares its beans in barrel roasters that have been retrofitted to suit the company's needs. The beans grow dark and pungent as they tumble above a fire in the barrel roaster's drum. The machines are computerized to roast and then cool each type of bean for a set amount of time for optimum flavor—not too weak, not too bitter. But with consistency and Krispy Kreme's reputation with customers on the line, automation isn't good enough for McKie. Coffee experts again taste a sample from each batch of roasted beans. They taste-test for quality once more after the beans have been blended into one of Krispy Kreme's three signature brews.

"We'll taste each individual component of it," McKie says, recognizing that such step-by-step shepherding is the key to a finished product that is the best it can be.

Once roasted and blended, the finished whole-bean coffee is packaged by machine into bags that are also made at the roasting plant. Each finished bag is marked with a sell-by date for shipment to Krispy Kreme's nearly 300 stores. Coffee roasted at the Ivy Avenue plant doesn't sit around on pallets for long. It is sent to stores weekly to ensure that it is used within 28 days of roasting for optimal flavor. The company is committed to not serving coffee that is more than 28 days old. That's a promise Krispy Kreme couldn't make to customers before its acquisition of Digital Java because the company bought its coffee from a third-party supplier.

"Now we ask [our franchisees and employees] to think about coffee like it's milk or eggs. It's perishable," asserts McKie, who drinks his coffee black.

"This," he says while gesturing to the vast warehouse that houses the roastery, "was really driven toward . . . always giving the customer a consistent cup of coffee."

Through vertical integration and by taking control of the production process itself, Krispy Kreme has created "truly the coffee we should have had all along," according to chief executive officer Scott Livengood.

Krispy Kreme, while improving the taste and consistency of the coffee it serves, has also opened up a new revenue stream for itself. Coffee is a huge business around the world, as the success of Starbucks and other coffeehouses, large and small, has demonstrated. Coffee consumption is on the rise, according to analyst Kathleen Heaney of Brean Murray Research, with 3 million new drinkers since 2000. About 80 percent of the world's 164 million coffee drinkers have a cup daily, she notes, making coffee quite an attractive addition to Krispy Kreme's product offering.

The coffee business has profit margins that are about 75 percent higher than the doughnut business, providing Krispy Kreme with a great vehicle to increase its sales. Before the acquisition of Digital Java, beverages accounted for about 10 percent of Krispy Kreme's sales. With the new coffee and the addition of espresso and frozen drinks, beverage sales have risen 40 percent and should go higher, says chief operating officer John Tate, formerly an executive with catalog and retail giant Williams-Sonoma and Dole Foods. Other analysts agree with Heaney that coffee could be a key growth area for Krispy Kreme in the future, especially if it is able to continue to maintain its high standards for this product.

FOSTER CONTINUOUS INNOVATION

About a half hour's drive southeast of the mix plant, another example of Vernon Rudolph's business genius is still going strong. The equipment department, which for decades was housed next door to the mix plant, recently moved to High Point, North Carolina, to make room for the roasting facility. In the equipment department, workers build the proprietary doughnut cooking and glazing machines that franchisees must install in every store. Krispy Kreme's corporate office is the only source of this crucial equipment. It charges about $350,000 for each of these machines—a figure that will become even more significant as the company hastens its expansion. The company made about 75 doughnut cookers in 2002 and an estimated 100 in 2003.

This part of the business has allowed Krispy Kreme to experiment with the way its famous doughnuts are prepared—a task that would have been more difficult and costly were the company forced to rely on outside vendors to do the work.

In 2001, the company started testing a new automated hot dough-nut machine that could greatly enhance its ability to expand, particu-larly into congested urban areas and cities with smaller populations. Engineers spent three years developing this hybrid doughnut cooker that began as a set of drawings by Garcie McCall, the company's man-ager of research and development.

Management knew its existing store model could stifle the com-pany's growth. That's why executives charged McCall's department with creating a way to make authentic hot glazed Krispy Kreme dough-nuts in a much smaller space.

The average Krispy Kreme store is about 4,200 square feet and costs close to $2 million to build, including real estate. One reason the tra-ditional stores have to be so big is because they need plenty of space to fit the huge machine that turns raw dough into cooked, glazed pastries in a process that's entirely visible to Krispy Kreme customers through a large plate-glass wall.

Such size and cost demands limited Krispy Kreme's potential for expansion. At the time of Krispy Kreme's initial public stock offering in April 2000, executives told potential investors that the company could grow to about 750 stores in the United States and that those stores would have to be built in populous markets with more than 250,000 people to be profitable.

McCall and his colleagues in the research and development depart-ment had two huge challenges as they worked on this new management-inspired project. The doughnuts coming out of the smaller machine had to look, smell, and taste like those produced in Krispy Kreme's full-scale stores by the gigantic, costly cookers. And the new machine also had to fit with Krispy Kreme's brand promise—to deliver hot, fresh doughnuts to customers in a theater-like atmosphere. Customers, whether they bought their doughnuts from a full-scale store or a smaller doughnut and coffee shop, needed to be able to watch their food being made. They had to see the doughnuts marching down the conveyor belt, then slid-ing under a rain of glaze.

"We looked at so many different oven systems, but nothing worked the way we wanted it to,"[4] said James Murray, a technical services specialist who helped develop the hot doughnut machine. Then McCall walked into a meeting with his drawings, and a prototype was soon built, tweaked, tested, and tweaked again.

"In the beginning, when we thought we were getting close to having the hot doughnut right, we would run taste tests and find out that we were off a little," Murray recalls. "The hot doughnut out of this machine had to match exactly the look, taste, and texture of the factory-produced doughnut. There has been no shortcutting on this three-year project."[5]

The new hot doughnut machine, still being tested in just a few stores, could turn the company's initial expansion estimate to investors on its head. It gives Krispy Kreme the ability to serve hot doughnuts from much cheaper and smaller storefronts, as tiny as 900 square feet. Financial analysts view this move as a huge growth driver for Krispy Kreme, especially as the company matures and excitement over its grand openings and comparable-store sales begins to slow.

Here's how the hot doughnut machine works: Doughnuts are cooked, but not glazed, at one of Krispy Kreme's full-scale factory stores. Then they are transported as far as an hour away to doughnut and coffee shops equipped with the hot doughnut machines. There, the confections are loaded into the hot doughnut machine. The machine warms the doughnuts in a convection-style oven, then douses them with sugary glaze in a matter of minutes. Customers shouldn't be able to tell any difference in the taste. So far, they haven't. The response to the warmed-up doughnuts has been favorable in the three North Carolina cities—Winston-Salem, Greensboro, and Charlotte—where Krispy Kreme installed the first of these hot doughnut machines. More tests will continue through 2003, with additional implementation planned for 2004.

James Murray was at the third test store when it opened in Charlotte, North Carolina's largest city.

"I was amazed," he remembers. "Just amazed and proud. Every customer who came through picked up a hot doughnut, ate the doughnut, and was happy. They never noticed the piece of missing equipment, the fryer."[6]

This accomplishment provides Krispy Kreme with great potential. With the new technology developed in its own equipment-making factory, Krispy Kreme has the chance to open in places executives never thought possible—congested urban areas, shopping malls, airports, coliseums, and towns with populations as small as 30,000 people.

"This actually creates the opportunity for thousands of stores," senior vice president of marketing Stan Parker said, sitting in a booth at the second hot doughnut machine test store in Greensboro, North Carolina, on the day before it opened in November 2001.

"We haven't had to invent a new system," he said, nibbling on a doughnut, still sticky and hot off the conveyor. "We've been able to use the system we had to make this happen. The new machines have the added benefit of giving hot doughnuts to customers whenever they crave them, not just twice a day as at most existing Krispy Kreme restaurants. And because the hot doughnut machine can heat up a doughnut within minutes, customers can sample other Krispy Kreme varieties while they are hot, not just the original glazed. Take the chocolate devil's food cake, Parker says. Served cold, it's tasty, but dense. Served hot, it's moist and smooth and disappears quickly, like a brownie scooped out of a hot pan.

"Within five minutes, you can have a hot doughnut" that tastes exactly like one prepared by Krispy Kreme's traditional in-store cooker, Parker says. "We did side-by-side taste tests. We're confident we can replicate the experience. We've gone to great measures to make sure the experience is the same."

QUALITY + CONTROL = PROFITS

Vernon Rudolph's pioneering idea to vertically integrate Krispy Kreme in 1947 as a means of safeguarding quality has served the company well in the decades since. The manufacturing and distribution division brings in one-third of the company's annual revenues, which reached $491.5 million in fiscal 2003. This division stands to be an ever-growing part of the business for years to come because stores will continue to open worldwide at a brisk pace, fueling demand for the proprietary cookers and the new hot doughnut machines. Demand for doughnut mix and coffee will grow, too, as these stores open and draw in more customers anxious to enjoy the unique Krispy Kreme taste and experience.

By mixing up the ingredients that go into these doughnuts and beverages itself, Krispy Kreme can be certain that customers are fed only the best. That's the type of quality control that can be accomplished only through vertical integration. Few food service companies, which rely on ingredients from multiple outside sources, can guarantee this kind of quality and consistency. That helps to make this Southern company a premium brand, with high name recognition and customer satisfaction.

Because Krispy Kreme has decades of experience making the ingredients and equipment necessary to run its business, it isn't hamstrung to innovate. The coffee roasting plant and the hot doughnut machine exemplify this. Executives realized that Krispy Kreme needed to make changes to its coffee and its doughnut-making capabilities to grow. The company accomplished these changes internally, using homegrown talent and expertise, instead of farming out the development business to third-party vendors. This saved both time and money, while keeping plans for these products secret until Krispy Kreme was ready to reveal them to the public, creating a significant competitive advantage. It also kept all of the potential profit from these ventures in-house, a point that wins praise and favor for the company from shareholders and Wall Street investors.

CHAPTER 8

Harness the Power of Technology

Krispy Kreme made its stock market debut on April 5, 2000, amid much excitement and fanfare from financial analysts and commentators anxious to taste the free doughnuts the company handed out with every interview and media appearance. But many market pundits were somewhat skeptical about the six-decade-old company's long-term prospects and growth potential.

In addition, it wasn't a very exciting offering at the time compared to some of the other companies entering the public marketplace. Many had amazing stories to tell about how they were going to revolutionize the world and be at the forefront of the so-called new economy.

The Winston-Salem doughnut maker scheduled its initial public offering at the height of the high-tech boom, at a time when dot-com companies were sexy investments and considered surefire routes to wealth. During 2000, 382 technology and biotechnology companies completed IPOs.[1] Among them were personal digital assistant manufacturers Palm and Handspring; mobile phone provider AT&T Wireless Services; integrated circuit maker Stanford Microdevices; mobile software developer AvantGo; pharmaceutical makers Keryk, Rigel, and Arena; and chemical and agricultural products provider Monsanto Company. No one ever dreamed that Krispy Kreme, a simple doughnut chain founded in 1937, could compete with that ilk.

Yet Krispy Kreme, a company more likely to buy chocolate chips than microchips, had the second-best performance of all new stock issues in 2000. Its stock rose from its $21 offering price to $83 a share by the end of the year, a 295.3 percent increase. Only Embarcadero Technologies, which designs database management software, bested the doughnut maker, rising 376.5 percent from its $10 offering price.

Krispy Kreme also stayed fresher in investors' minds than any of these other companies. Paul Rogers, president of CIBC World Markets, asserted at the second annual Consumer Growth Conference in the summer of 2002 that Krispy Kreme has "made more money for investors than any IPO in any industry in the past three years. . . . The stock is up over five-fold since April 2000." By contrast, many of the technology companies that went public that same year are now either operating in bankruptcy, trading for pennies, or completely out of business.

Stock forecasters who bet against the doughnut maker's long-term potential missed an important fact: Krispy Kreme is a high-tech company, though not in the traditional sense. By reputation, Krispy Kreme represents a more innocent, less complicated time in America. But the company has never been afraid of innovation. Executives have long embraced technology as a vehicle for growth and better efficiency. As Jay Jung, the creative director of concept development, likes to say: "Krispy Kreme is nuts about two things—technology and consistency."

BE TECH-SAVVY, NO MATTER HOW OLD YOU ARE

Krispy Kreme is old-fashioned and traditional in many ways. Its stores have the look and feel of a 1950s diner, and its doughnuts are cooked according to a recipe from the 1930s. But the doughnut chain uses computers as any aggressive technology company would, whether to connect with customers and investors through its data-rich web site or to outfit employees with gadgets that help them monitor sales statistics and inventory levels.

Although it aggressively pursues innovations that will improve business, Krispy Kreme is frugal in its spending on such things. While the average company in the restaurant industry spends 0.78 percent of revenues on information technology, Krispy Kreme spends just 0.5 percent of its revenues on IT.[2] The company's information technology department is relatively small—only about 20 people—and it plans to stay that way. Krispy Kreme wants to use technology and computer networks that will grow with the company, but that won't require hiring a lot more people to maintain those systems.

"The battle is to grow but not add too much expense," chief governance officer Randy Casstevens said. "If we are considering an infrastructure that can support 2,000 stores, we can't add a person to IT every time we add 20 stores."[3]

Chief information officer Frank Hood joined Krispy Kreme in June

1997, after spending most of his career working for textile companies in the Southeast. When recruiters from the doughnut company called, Hood thought they wanted his opinion on a software package Krispy Kreme was considering buying. Such requests are common among information technology professionals, who seek references on computer programs the way businesses seek references for potential employees.

But Krispy Kreme wanted Hood himself, not merely his opinion. The job offer immediately enticed Hood, who at the mention of Krispy Kreme was reminded of a pleasant childhood experience. The company name brought to mind a visit he made with his father to a Krispy Kreme shop in Myrtle Beach, South Carolina, for hot doughnuts and a glass of cold milk.

"It was a product that invoked a memory and a feeling that transcended the experience," says Hood, who longed to work at a place where he would be challenged as a computer expert and working on a product that resonated with customers. "The product has a unique ability to evoke an experience—a feeling, a moment in time. It's like a song or a smell."

Hood left Dan River Mills, a Virginia company that makes fabric for sheets, upholstery, and clothing, for a job as vice president of information systems at Krispy Kreme. As the company's first chief technology officer, Hood was hired as a change maker. His position was crucial to the regional company's plans to expand nationwide and to go public.

"We needed an [information technology] strategy that would position the corporation for growth," remembers Hood, a tall, thin southerner with dark hair and a salt-and-pepper moustache.

Hood came on board at Krispy Kreme three years before the company began publicly selling its stock and pushing into markets that had long been dominated by the much larger king of doughnut chains, Dunkin' Donuts. He also began work just as the company, like so many others around the world, fretted about potential problems to its computer systems that might be caused by the so-called Year 2000 Bug. Because of the way in which Krispy Kreme's fiscal calendar is set up, Hood and his information technology staff had to make the corporate computer systems Y2K-compliant by February 1999.

That alone was a huge job. At the same time, Krispy Kreme's relatively small computer systems staff was busy revamping the company's entire information technology infrastructure. "We literally replaced everything,"[4] remembers Hood, who even had to do some employee recruiting after a few members of his staff quit the company.

Hood's assignment at Krispy Kreme was unlike that faced by most chief information officers taking a new job. He wasn't hired simply to keep the company's computers working well or to troubleshoot software. Instead, Krispy Kreme wanted him to create a technology infrastructure that would make the entire organization run better. "The most difficult part was getting people to spell out our concrete business strategy and then translating that business strategy into an IT strategy," Hood recalls.

When the information technology staff began its task of revamping the computer infrastructure, Hood discovered that a number of Krispy Kreme employees were already using the computer systems and software available to them. However, with no corporate mandate to use computers, other employees were tracking performance with pencil and paper, the way Vernon Rudolph did when he founded Krispy Kreme just after the Great Depression. Hood sometimes regrets that he didn't film some home movies at Krispy Kreme's headquarters and stores in 1997 to show how things were done then versus now.

Soon after being hired, Hood asked employees to return the old laptop computers they were using so that they could be replaced with newer, better models. Some of the machines arrived back at the corporate office unused. "They were still in the (original) plastic with the silica packs on them," Hood says. "People . . . never had a reason to use technology."

But piecemeal usage and pencil-and-paper record keeping wouldn't be acceptable for much longer if Krispy Kreme was to accomplish its goal of national and international expansion as a public company. Executives would soon be required to provide all manner of past financial data and sales projections in the company's bid to go public. Therefore, they wanted a better, more secure way to communicate and share information among stores and the corporate office. The solution had to be quicker than a fax machine, and it had to limit the information people could access, based on their position in the company. Krispy Kreme's initial computer sharing network didn't have such security controls. Any authorized user could access everything in the database.

Krispy Kreme executives also wanted a system that would quickly and coherently show sales and cost figures for a particular store so that they could easily gauge the performance of each of the company's outlets, which at the time numbered about 150 stores.

MAKE INFORMATION MEANINGFUL

Krispy Kreme, throughout its store base and at its corporate offices, had a slew of information and empirical data about financial performance, sales, ingredient usage, and its supply chain. All those crumbs of data could have been a wonderful resource for a company thinking of expanding and going public. But there was a problem. A big one. That information wasn't at anyone's fingertips. Instead, it was scattered in what Hood describes as "disorganized places" throughout the company (in a computer over there, scribbled in some store manager's day planner, etc.). It was difficult to aggregate and extract any meaningful business guidance and lessons from the batches of numbers and reports because everything was so disjointed, with no uniform organizational plan in place.

"With our original [system], we ran the risk of overwhelming users with content, making the information they needed difficult to locate," says Nathan Mucher, who as manager of client-server systems development worked with Hood on the IT project. "And we couldn't segregate confidential data for executives and other appropriate users. We needed a way to securely manage our content and resources, and we needed a system that would let us add new users, stores, content, and applications on the fly and allow us to bring new stores on line without straining our IT staff."

Krispy Kreme had to put some order to its corporate junk drawer. Executives and store managers needed digestible sales data, "broken down into crumb-size pieces—everything from drive-through sales per hour to most popular merchandise per store to comparisons of glazed to jelly-filled sales at different times of the day."[5] Hood and his staff realized that to organize this mess and help the corporation run better they needed software that would corral the data, analyze it, and present it in understandable, usable nuggets. This system should be accessible to counter clerks, store managers, distribution center employees, area developers of new Krispy Kreme restaurants, and corporate executives from any computer with Internet access. And each employee group needed different types of information, depending on their duties and responsibilities at Krispy Kreme.

To answer the need, Krispy Kreme's information technology staff built a new intranet system, called Krispy Kreme Information Exchange. It allowed franchisees to easily generate specific reports for their stores—reports that detailed weekly sales, the popularity of a particular doughnut, a location's most commonly used ingredients, and a wealth of other customized crucial data.

"It wasn't hard to see that what we were doing was the right thing to do," says Hood, a licensed pilot who is as comfortable in an airplane's cockpit as he is at a computer keyboard.

"We automated as many processes as possible . . . and built ways to poll stores automatically [for sales data]," he adds. "It took a lot of time and commitment, but without these systems and the data they provide, we couldn't have gone public." That's because precise sales data often requested by underwriters and stock analysts for use in preparing performance forecasts was not easily and quickly accessible in the past.[6]

As is common in all departments at Krispy Kreme, Hood and most of his staff have spent at least some time working directly with doughnuts, whether in a store or helping to make deliveries to wholesale customers. That gives the computer hardware and software specialists a better understanding of how the core business works and offers them a unique view into how the systems they develop at corporate headquarters are actually used. Hood, for example, traveled to Alexandria, Virginia, the site of Krispy Kreme's only store near the nation's capital. He worked in the shop for half a day, serving customers and making doughnuts. Later, Hood arose at 3 A.M. to accompany a Krispy Kreme wholesale delivery driver on his 12-hour route to grocery and convenience stores throughout the region.

Now that it has systems in place to turn raw data into business guidance, Krispy Kreme feverishly collects information from its stores. Computers log customer counts, peak sales days and times, customer preferences in doughnuts and coffee, even how the weather affects sales.

Computers are pervasive at Krispy Kreme restaurants, from the back room to the dining room. Employees arriving for their shifts swipe a plastic identification badge through a card reader to clock in for work. No more punching in using paper time cards. Employees use these same ID cards to log into cash registers, all of which have picture-coded touch screens that make it easy for them to ring up orders.

Check your receipt the next time you order a mixed dozen at Krispy Kreme. The cash registers allow employees to enter the specifics of that order—two original glazed, two plain cake, one lemon-filled, one pumpkin spice, one blueberry cake, one chocolate cream-filled, two chocolate-covered, one devil's food cake, and one cinnamon spice. They don't just report that the customer ordered a dozen assorted variety doughnuts. Such information guides everything from marketing promotions to the purchase of raw ingredients.

CREATE CUSTOMIZED APPLICATIONS

Krispy Kreme Information Exchange, the company's original corporate intranet, eventually evolved into MyKrispyKreme, a Web-based portal accessible only to Krispy Kreme employees. The system is secure and gives employees access only to specific information needed to perform their jobs. Krispy Kreme used software developed by Corechange, a vendor in Boston, Massachusetts, to build this dynamic gateway to the company's operations.

When employees access MyKrispyKreme, they get a personalized, customized screen similar to the ones customers see at an online shopping site. The new system was designed with both function and usability in mind. Krispy Kreme followed the examples of such companies as IBM, Wal-Mart, Amazon.com, and BarnesandNoble.com in designing its own intranet. The two booksellers, for example, had been successful in building web sites that were not only visually appealing, but also easy to navigate and use. Wal-Mart, as a major retailer with thousands of stores worldwide, has long used computers to successfully manage its supply chain. As a result, when an item sells out, it is quickly reordered from the nearest warehouse and restocked.

Krispy Kreme wanted to offer these same inventory guarantees to its network of franchisees and store managers in an easy-to-use format. MyKrispyKreme made that possible. The system paid for itself in about a year.

"Every time I log in," Hood explains, "it knows who I am." All the information he wants or needs to see—be it the company's stock performance, store sales data, or a weather forecast—appears on his screen. Tabs that users click on lead them deeper into the site and allow them to access a variety of functions. MySales, for example, shows a store manager the performance for a particular location—nuggets as specific as drive-through sales per hour and customer counts. The eFinancial tab allows managers to look at more detailed information about weekly profits and losses and cash flow. "Rather than sift through data aggregated for all our stores, our managers now quickly access only their store numbers," Hood offers. "MyKrispyKreme puts all the information they need to evaluate at their fingertips. Based on a store's sales history, for example, managers can anticipate busy periods, ensuring optimal staffing and inventory. With MyKrispyKreme, our stores operate much more efficiently and intelligently."[7]

Another tab lets managers access Krispy Kreme's Web-based ingredient and supply ordering system. This links users to those distribution centers in North Carolina, California, and Illinois that are stocked with everything needed to run a Krispy Kreme shop, from doughnut mix to coffee stirrers. The system keeps track of the ingredients managers have ordered and what they've used in the past, so stores are unlikely to run out of necessary supplies. "It will remind you that you've forgotten to order doughnut mix,"[8] Hood adds.

Actually, what the computer program does is much more complicated than that. Each night, the system performs complex mathematical algorithms that can project what type of ingredients a Krispy Kreme store will need based on previous usage patterns. The computer quickly does what the human brain never could, Hood claims. "It's hard for a person to really look at six weeks of data times 16,000 customers," he observes. But the computer performs this function in a snap.

ENTER THE SPACE AGE

Before the new employee computer network was created, franchisees and store managers faxed orders for ingredients and other supplies to the corporate office. Another set of employees entered these orders into the computer system for the distribution centers, which created the potential for mistakes. Now managers are able to place their orders at any time and from any place they have Internet access, including their homes. And there's less chance for error because the order goes directly from the store to the distribution center, not through a third-party data-entry clerk.

Computers are also dominant at the Krispy Kreme warehouses where these orders are filled. Most companies that supply goods for internal and external customers have at one point relied on paper packing slips to fill orders. Under that old system, warehouse workers, called *pickers,* would carry a customer's order form through the warehouse, checking off items as they grabbed them from the shelves. It was a little bit like grocery shopping from a handwritten list.

Now Krispy Kreme's distribution centers are virtually paperless. Pickers carry or ride around on forklifts equipped with radio frequency laser guns programmed with a customer's order. They use the guns to zap an item's bar code as they fill orders. As soon as an item is scanned, the computer determines whether it is precisely what the store manager ordered in the exact quantity. This high-tech system, Hood says, has significantly cut down on mistakes in the distribution centers and helps Krispy Kreme keep its promise to deliver fresh ingredients to stores each week.

"There are virtually no errors now as far as correct orders coming to us," Martin Hendrix, a Krispy Kreme manager in Fayetteville, North Carolina, told a trade industry reporter in an interview about the company's technological revolution. "Before, there were probably three or four mistakes a week. It could be off by as much as 10 or 15 bags of mix, usually not enough of it instead of too much."[9]

MyKrispyKreme is used in other ways, too. Employees send expense reports to their managers over the intranet. They are reimbursed electronically—the money is quickly deposited directly into their bank accounts. Human resources manuals, those heavy tomes of rules and benefits that companies must distribute to employees, are available electronically through MyKrispyKreme. The intranet is also a vehicle for Krispy Kreme to convey news about the company to its employees, be it in the corporate newsletter, newspaper articles, or news reports filmed live at store openings.

Especially important for Krispy Kreme, which has a carefully crafted marketing strategy and brand image, is the ability for employees and the public relations agencies that the company hires to log into its electronic Brand Book. This section of the intranet contains answers to all sorts of questions about how Krispy Kreme should be portrayed and marketed: "How should the trademark green bowtie [logo] look? What should a 'no smoking' sign look like? What fonts and colors should be used?"[10]

Krispy Kreme also uses technology to reach out and touch its loyal customers. It created an extensive web site at www.krispykreme.com, which was redesigned in 2002. The site offers a treasure trove of information about the company, including details on upcoming new store openings and nutritional information about its doughnuts.

In addition, fans can sign up to receive a monthly e-mail newsletter, which is normally signed by someone from the company's Customer Experience Department. The newsletter is primarily a tool for advertising the company's new products and featured doughnuts, and it provides links to recent articles about Krispy Kreme that may be of interest to customers.

Krispy Kreme makes further use of its coveted e-mail list by sending newsletter recipients occasional customer surveys to gain instant feedback. A survey in October 2002, for instance, included a list of several new doughnut flavors the company was considering. It asked readers to choose their favorite flavors and promised to use this information when making its final decision. The company later followed up by informing recipients which flavors were ultimately selected and thanking them for participating in the survey.

AUTOMATE EDUCATION

As an extension of its devotion to technology, Krispy Kreme has transferred most of its management training materials to the Web-based computer system. Krispy Kreme hired Handshaw & Associates, a software consulting firm in Charlotte, North Carolina, that works with restaurants, hospital companies, and customer services business, to help it develop online training procedures and tests for new employees.

Management trainees, all of whom receive 12 weeks of on-the-job training at a Krispy Kreme store, previously had been required to spend at least four weeks learning the "Krispy Kreme way" at corporate headquarters. This was a problem area for the company because employees sometimes skipped their training classes, actions that hurt consistency in how stores were run. "The challenges of being able to keep up with the store growth, having every store manager Krispy Kreme trained, having these managers spread out throughout the country, and needing to have consistency in their training led us to revise our managers' training program,"[11] recalls consultant Barbara Thornton, who at the time was vice president of human resources and corporate services at Krispy Kreme.

Thornton's team and the contractors at Handshaw & Associates had only a few months to build a new training system that taught new employees the practical skills they would need to run the doughnut shop while also indoctrinating them in Krispy Kreme's unique corporate culture. Krispy Kreme, which hired Handshaw & Associates in late 1999, wanted the training system completed by the time of its IPO, in April 2000. "The challenge put to them by Wall Street was, 'What are you going to do with all this money we give you?' " recalls Dick Handshaw, president and managing director of the training company. Investors asked, "What makes you think you can add 50 to 100 new stores a year and maintain consistency?" Handshaw says. Krispy Kreme's answer: We can do it by building a technology-based system to ensure that every new manager learns the same skills and gets the same indoctrination in Krispy Kreme culture.

Thornton and representatives from Handshaw's company worked with a team of about 20 experts throughout the company to determine both the technical and soft skills these new managers needed. Handshaw & Associates joined forces with senior Krispy Kreme management to develop a series of 12 interactive, multimedia lessons that can be completed over the intranet. All management trainees are tested on what they've learned. If employees don't pass the tests, they're automatically sent to computer-based refresher courses. Employee test results are also delivered electronically to the corporate human resources department.

Krispy Kreme's new managers are still required to work alongside an experienced veteran for at least three months and attend traditional classroom training at corporate headquarters. But the new system has allowed the company to shave two weeks from its management training program. It has also produced the results that Krispy Kreme wanted: the ability to easily and quickly train enough managers to run the hundreds of stores Krispy Kreme plans to eventually have around the world.

During its first year in operation, Krispy Kreme trained 149 new managers using the online Management 101 course. The previous year, under the old program, only 60 new managers graduated from Krispy Kreme's management training course.[12] "Folks are coming [to class] with consistent knowledge, and when they graduate they're walking out with consistent experience,"[13] says Sherry Luper, who replaced Thornton as senior vice president of human resources.

The Web-based training system, implemented in 2000, worked so well for managers that Krispy Kreme now teaches its production workers in the same manner. As with the managers, employees who make the doughnuts at Krispy Kreme's factory are taught, tested, and retested online until they master a particular skill. According to Handshaw, as hourly workers are promoted, the software creates a custom curriculum, giving employees credit for courses they have already mastered and identifying areas for improvement. "That really helps us ensure consistency in the people that we have working in our stores," Hood adds.

Krispy Kreme, which is constantly looking for ways to integrate technology into its business model, is now working to make even more resources available to employees through its MyKrispyKreme Web portal. The company will place all of its videotaped material, including archived footage of its store openings and an employee orientation speech by chief executive officer Scott Livengood, online so these messages can be easily distributed throughout the workforce.

Although at its core Krispy Kreme is a simple bakery, the company has proved that technology significantly helps every kind of business. "They've got a long history of being innovative with their technology," says Handshaw. Krispy Kreme officials, while still committed to preserving the company's heritage, understand that risk taking and innovation are essential keys to growth. Such risks have enabled Krispy Kreme to develop a technology infrastructure that supports better employee training, strong communication among departments, efficient order fulfillment, effective corporate planning, and prudent financial management and monitoring.

Without question, Krispy Kreme makes smart use of technology. This in turn helps every aspect of its business to function much more effectively.

CHAPTER 9

Give Back
to the Community

America was in a giving mood back in the fall of 2001. The September 11 terrorist attacks that killed thousands of innocent people at the World Trade Center in New York, the Pentagon in Washington, D.C., and in rural Pennsylvania had united the nation in philanthropy as well as patriotism.

Howard Heching, a student at Cornell University in Ithaca, New York, noticed that most of the money was flowing out of local communities to charities in those cities that had been directly hit. Certainly, the Red Cross, the United Way, and the September 11 Fund needed this cash to help with disaster recovery efforts and to assist the families of the dead and injured. But in the process, other worthy community groups were being forgotten, even though their needs were as great as ever.

Heching, then a junior at Cornell, set out to address this funding oversight in whatever small way he could. He rallied fellow members of the student group Human Ecology Voices, which strives to create a sense of community on campus, to raise funds for the United Way of Tompkins County, New York.

Just how would a group of poor college students, who were struggling to pay their own bills, muster enough money to make a difference? Heching found the answer during a trip with a relative to the Krispy Kreme doughnut shop in Rochester, New York. On the counter was a flyer detailing Krispy Kreme's fund-raising opportunities. Heching's nonprofit group could buy fresh glazed doughnuts from Krispy Kreme for half the retail cost, sell them to students and professors at full price, and keep the profits.

This was the perfect fund-raiser, Heching and his fellow members of Human Ecology Voices decided. Rochester—about an hour and a half from Cornell, longer in traffic—is the town closest to Ithaca with a Krispy Kreme store. "We figured people would like to get their hands on them [the doughnuts]," said Heching, a senior who has his sights set on medical school.

"There are no good doughnut places here," he laments. "We didn't feel people were getting what they deserved doughnut-wise."

Krispy Kreme made the whole process of raising money easy. All Heching had to do was fill out some paperwork at the corporate web site, submit documentation proving that Human Ecology Voices was a nonprofit, and place the order for doughnuts. Krispy Kreme then had the fresh treats made and boxed by 6:30 A.M. on the day of the sale. Store employees helped students load the polka-dot boxes into their borrowed van. Within minutes, they drove off to deliver the tasty treats.

By the time these charity-minded students arrived back on campus about two hours later, those who had ordered the doughnuts weeks earlier were eagerly awaiting them. One frantic Cornell faculty member, who serves as an adviser to the nonprofit group, met Heching and his friends as the van pulled in. She grabbed as many boxes as she could carry and dashed inside the classroom building to deliver doughnuts to several professors who were planning to enjoy a bite over coffee before beginning the morning's lectures.

It was like this all day. People were excited—and sometimes impatient—to get their hands on a Krispy Kreme. It was as if members of Human Ecology Voices had opened their own Krispy Kreme shop on Cornell's campus for the day. "As people would come in, their faces would light up," recalls Heching. Like a counter clerk at an actual doughnut store location, he listened to numerous Krispy Kreme memories that day. "Many times we heard them say that these are the best doughnuts."

That first year, Heching and his friends sold about 200 boxes of Krispy Kreme doughnuts. They charged $5 a dozen and raised close to $500 for the county's local United Way.

A year later, Human Ecology Voices resurrected the doughnut drive with the goal of "bringing one million calories to Cornell."

"We needed to sell 417 dozen to meet that goal," says Heching, who hails from Rockland County, New York. Students on the campus of 19,000 responded to the challenge by buying 6,120 doughnuts, or 510 dozen, well beyond the initial goal. In the second year, Human Ecology Voices raised $1,100 with its Krispy Kreme fund-raiser and gave the money to Loaves and Fishes, an Ithaca soup kitchen that feeds the hungry. Now, people around campus call Heching the "doughnut boy" and tell him he ought to work for Krispy Kreme. They're already asking him about the next Krispy Kreme sale. "We've gotten e-mails asking if we're running one this coming semester," he adds.

BE A GOOD CORPORATE CITIZEN

Throughout much of Krispy Kreme's history, the company has helped groups such as Human Ecology Voices at Cornell raise money for worthy causes. Good corporate citizenship and strong support of community groups are very much a part of Krispy Kreme's brand reputation. In fact, wherever Krispy Kreme has stores, the company is an active supporter of local and community organizations. Krispy Kreme can always be counted on to allow nonprofit groups to sell its doughnuts as a fund-raising activity. The company also donates doughnuts, cash, and even publicity to nonprofit organizations in need of help.

"We develop caring relationships in the communities in which we operate," the company says in a letter explaining its brand values to shareholders. "From helping nonprofit organizations raise money with our fundraising programs to supporting youth education and employee volunteerism, we strive to give back to our communities."

In fiscal 2002, Krispy Kreme donated or helped raise $27.2 million for charitable groups. With its expanded store base, the company generated $43 million in charitable gifts in fiscal 2003. New franchisees helped raise $7.6 million during that period, nearly 10 times more than new franchisees raised in the previous year.[1]

The company traditionally donates 2 percent of its pretax income, which was $54.7 million in fiscal 2003, to charities. That figure includes donated doughnuts.[2] But the charities aren't the only ones to benefit. Krispy Kreme reaps huge rewards from its philanthropy. These rewards come in the form of free, positive publicity, additional sales, and access to a wider audience of potential customers. The company also gets its own door-to-door "sales force" as a result of many fundraisers—for example, schoolkids raising money for field trips, band uniforms, or myriad other causes who go door-to-door hawking boxes of glazed treats or discount coupons for doughnuts.

"To sell a Krispy Kreme, all you have do is try it," says Wake Forest University marketing professor Tom Ogburn, repeating a line from company executives. "So what do you do? You give your doughnuts to Boy Scouts and Girl Scouts." Krispy Kreme, helped by cute kids and an irresistible sales pitch, has found an efficient and inexpensive method to get its products inside people's homes. These fund-raising sales, according to Ogburn, are a quick and easy way for Krispy Kreme to let people taste-test its fried doughnut delicacies and to lure them to local stores for more. "That's a very cheap promotion from their standpoint."

Stan Parker, Krispy Kreme's senior vice president of marketing, admits, "The program has turned out to be a huge way for us to connect to our customers emotionally. It's more of a way to be part of the community than to be in business."[3]

FIND UNIQUE WAYS TO GIVE BACK

Winston-Salem, where Krispy Kreme has maintained its headquarters since 1937, has arguably benefited from the company's philanthropy more than any other city. "I think probably every nonprofit in town has sold Krispy Kreme doughnuts at some point or another as a fundraiser," says Gayle Anderson, president of the city's chamber of commerce. "It shows the support that Krispy Kreme has for the community. They've always been very generous."

This city of about 185,000 residents is still very much an old-economy kind of place. Wake Forest University, with its medical school and strong science departments, has attracted some biotechnology companies to Winston-Salem. Such banks as Wachovia and BB&T have a strong presence downtown. But many people in Winston-Salem still make their living working for manufacturers, textile companies, and R.J. Reynolds Tobacco Company, which once practically ran the city. When groups need money, they often look to local economic institutions such as Wachovia Bank, R.J. Reynolds, and Sara Lee Corporation for donations. As it grows, Krispy Kreme is moving up that list of benefactors.

City and economic leaders in Winston-Salem decided in 1998 that public school students needed to be better prepared for the high-tech life ahead of them in college and in the working world. They responded by creating Blueprint for Technology, a plan to spend $38 million to bring computers and other technology into every school and every classroom, from kindergarten to the twelfth grade. Providing every teacher with a laptop computer is among the goals of the plan. City leaders knew that the money for this technology initiative wouldn't come from an already strapped local school district or the state of North Carolina, which was in a budget crunch. Local companies and foundations would have to foot the bill.

In the first 18 months, the school district raised $8 million dollars to fund Blueprint for Technology, with $1 million coming from Wachovia Bank, which was headquartered in Winston-Salem until its merger with First Union. By late 2002, though, the multi-million-dollar technology fund-raiser needed a boost. So the chamber of commerce turned to Krispy Kreme, which had always been a partner to the local schools.

On the day of the chamber's annual meeting, more than 1,000 people showed up to hear Scott Livengood, Krispy Kreme's CEO, give the lunchtime speech. In honor of the keynote speaker, each slice of apple pie dessert was topped with a glazed doughnut. Beside each plate was a plastic card—good for a dozen free doughnuts or another Krispy Kreme treat every month of the year. Each coupon had a retail value of $40. The cards, Anderson informed her audience, were theirs to keep for a $10 donation. "Just leave your checks or your cash on the table," she said, adding that all money would go to the school district for the technology plan. That day, the Winston-Salem Chamber of Commerce raised more than $6,000 for the technology needs of local schools.

"That was an easy $6,000 sale," said the chamber president.

But those thousand cards scattered on the banquet hall tables were just a fraction of the donation Krispy Kreme made to jump-start the ongoing technology campaign. In December 2002, the company gave an additional 20,000 freebie cards to the Winston-Salem/Forsyth County school district, and students sold them to raise more money. "They work with school systems to find ways to give and fund-raising programs that are effective in the local district," says school district spokesman Doug Hinson, praising Krispy Kreme's charitable efforts. "That's really what makes them unique."

DO GOOD BY HELPING OTHERS

Sam Fowler is one reason Krispy Kreme's fund-raising efforts work so well for so many schools and civic groups throughout the country. Fowler spent 24 years as a school principal in North Carolina before joining Krispy Kreme in the mid-1990s. A successful doughnut sale at his former school, Western Alamance High, raised $14,000 in three months. It was enough money to pay for the activities of 40 different school organizations.[4]

In Ohio, Krispy Kreme took a different approach to community involvement and giving. In October 2000, newspaper reporters, television anchors, disc jockeys, and community leaders were invited to the Krispy Kreme store in Kettering, Ohio, to meet nine-year-old D'Angelo Coleman-Boyd. D'Angelo, wearing a Krispy Kreme baseball hat that swallowed his forehead all the way down to his eyebrows, was an official doughnut shop employee that day. He just loved being the center of attention. He proudly mugged for the cameras, one moment dipping doughnuts in chocolate frosting, the next licking glaze from his fingers. But D'Angelo's life isn't always a day at the doughnut shop— and that's precisely why he was at Krispy Kreme. The boy suffers from sickle cell disease, a painful blood disorder that requires him to undergo monthly transfusions. The Community Blood Center of Dayton, Ohio, chose D'Angelo as the public face for its latest blood drive— Pints for Half Pints—and Krispy Kreme agreed to host the kickoff party. "There are a lot of children who really wouldn't be here if not for blood donation," said Sher Patrick, director of public relations for the blood center. "Their little lives depend on it."

Krispy Kreme did more than host the party for the new campaign to recruit more blood donors. The doughnut company made a long-term commitment to the center, which supplies the blood needs of 25 hospitals in 15 counties. For more than a year, Krispy Kreme sent 100 dozen doughnuts to the blood center twice a week. People who rolled up their sleeves and gave a pint on those days left the blood center with a box of doughnuts. On other days of the week, Krispy Kreme gave the blood bank free doughnuts to serve at its canteen.

"Giving blood is not always on the top of people's minds, and blood shortages have really become a national, chronic problem. It's not just in the summers. It's not just over the holidays and in the wintertime. It's becoming a problem all year long," maintains Patrick, a former television reporter. Krispy Kreme Mondays and Fridays gave people another reason to donate the much-needed blood.

"Krispy Kreme helped us get through some very difficult times," Patrick says. She estimates that Krispy Kreme donated close to $100,000 in doughnuts and other gifts during an 18-month period. "There's no doubt that having Krispy Kreme's support like that . . . brought in a lot of donors that we wouldn't otherwise have had. It got us through a lot of tight spots when the blood supply was low."

Krispy Kreme continues to support the Community Blood Bank of Dayton. On certain days of the week, donors receive coupons from the nurses who take their blood. The coupons can be redeemed for a free box of doughnuts. Krispy Kreme has similar partnerships with blood banks in other cities where it does business.

Krispy Kreme's approaches to giving back are as varied as the communities it serves. In its hometown of Winston-Salem, the company sponsors a concert series called Hot Jazz Now on the campus of the North Carolina School of the Arts, a high school and college for artistically gifted students. Krispy Kreme has also donated thousands of dollars to help graduating seniors in the college's film school promote their student films to movie moguls. In June 2001, the company spent $30,000 to send 39 students to Hollywood and New York for workshops, seminars, and interviews with famous filmmakers. Krispy Kreme used its marketing muscle to help the students put on a screening of their films for industry bigwigs.[5]

"We're both trying to reach the same audience," said Bill Porter, the school's vice chancellor for development and public relations. "It's all a concerted effort to build the profile of the School of the Arts students and the School of Filmmaking and to build the profile of Krispy Kreme."[6]

In January 2003, Krispy Kreme announced another partnership with the high school and college. The company, which had been scouting for a new corporate headquarters for close to two years, settled on a spot on the western edge of Winston-Salem's downtown. To help downtown revitalization efforts, Krispy Kreme agreed to anchor a new $87 million development, of which the North Carolina School of the Arts will be the landlord under a unique financing deal. In addition to Krispy Kreme's 100,000-square-foot headquarters, the Unity Place development will include a large performing arts center, chamber music hall, multiplex movie theater with an IMAX screen, gourmet food court, townhouses, offices, and shops. When the mixed-use development opens in the fall of 2005, it will be unlike any other office complex in the Winston-Salem. "I believe this is one of the most important projects in the history of our city,"[7] Mayor Allen Joines said.

HELP OUT WHERE YOU CAN

When the Van Eerden family in North Carolina came up with a way to honor victims of the September 11 terrorist attacks, Krispy Kreme helped them spread the word. Jim and Rachel Van Eerden and their nine children live in the tiny, rural town of Stokesdale, North Carolina, about 20 miles east of Krispy Kreme's headquarters.

The Van Eerdens were sitting around their large dinner table discussing the Independence Day holiday when they had an idea for what they dubbed "The American Tribute." They realized there was no common symbol uniting the Fourth of July celebrations held nationwide. At a time when America was still healing from the attacks, they thought there should be one.

The Van Eerdens decided that a special salute should be inserted into every Fourth of July fireworks display in America. The tribute would consist of a solitary red firework, followed by a single white firework, and ending with a single blue firework. The smoke in the sky would be allowed to clear after each explosion to give the audience a chance to reflect on the meaning of each firework: red, for the blood of many heroes shed; white, for freedom's light still shining bright; and blue, for the courage to stand tall and true.[8]

The Van Eerdens pitched their idea to President George W. Bush, and several members of Congress wrote endorsement letters on their behalf. On their own, they managed to convince some cities to insert the tribute into their holiday fireworks extravaganzas. But the Van Eerdens knew they needed more marketing muscle to spread the idea throughout the country, so they asked Krispy Kreme for help.

The company responded by assigning Steve Bumgarner from its marketing department to The American Tribute Foundation's advisory board. Krispy Kreme also asked the public relations firms it works with around the country to relay a message about the tribute to local media. In the weeks leading up to Independence Day, many of these firms delivered information kits about the tribute to reporters, along with boxes of Krispy Kreme doughnuts sprinkled with red, white, and blue candies.

In 1994, when floods devastated central Georgia and left many residents homeless, Krispy Kreme responded with money and doughnuts. To perk up the spirits of relief workers and displaced families, the company sent a truck filled with 50,000 treats to a Salvation Army warehouse in Macon, Georgia.

The mission to deliver sweets to flood victims began late on a July night. Workers from a Krispy Kreme location in Charlotte, North Carolina, stocked a truck with thousands of pastries and other products. The truck driver barreled down Interstate 85 in the darkness, arriving early the next morning at the Krispy Kreme store on Ponce de Leon Avenue in Atlanta, where workers were waiting with 8,400 freshly made doughnuts. The driver was soon on the road again, and by 8:30 A.M. he had arrived at the Macon warehouse.

But doughnuts weren't the only goodwill the driver brought. He also had the company's promise that it would donate a portion of the day's sales—15 percent—to the Salvation Army's disaster relief fund for Georgia flood victims. Eight stores in the Atlanta area participated in the fund-raiser.

"The people in central Georgia have been loyal Krispy Kreme consumers for decades, and we're pleased to do our part to help our friends during this time of crisis," Scott Livengood said, explaining the donation. "We also want to take this opportunity to commend and thank the dedicated people from the Salvation Army who have been working around the clock for two weeks to bring relief to the area."[9]

EVEN THE LITTLE THINGS HELP

Many of the company's efforts are on a much smaller scale. In Michigan, Krispy Kreme gave assistance to area homeless shelters. In one particular month, customers who dropped off three or more baby bottles, bibs, or blankets left with a dozen glazed doughnuts.[10] In Charlotte, North Carolina, students at two schools sold Krispy Kreme gift certificates to raise money for the Make-A-Wish Foundation. The students then used the money to grant the wish of a terminally ill child.

In Tower City, Pennsylvania, Krispy Kreme gave its fund-raising help to the Williams Valley Marching Band. Students needed to raise money for a trip to a national band competition, so they hit the streets with sweets, selling 750 dozen doughnuts during September 2001.[11] "This is the easiest fundraiser to do. The doughnuts sell themselves, the process is simple, and we make a good profit," said Lori Hartman, treasurer of the school's Band Boosters.

Elsewhere in Pennsylvania, the Office of Multifamily Housing Assistance Restructuring in Philadelphia needed money for its annual holiday party and toy giveaway. The group, which assists mentally retarded and emotionally disturbed children and adults by providing counseling, job training, and other social services, receives some toy donations. But in 2002, officials knew they needed to raise additional money to buy gifts for the 400 people attending the holiday party. They did so by selling 270 dozen Krispy Kreme doughnuts.

In California, franchisee Great Circle Family Foods joined with the Los Angeles Police Department to celebrate the grand opening of its new Krispy Kreme store in Van Nuys. A few days before the official opening, the store opened for a special four-hour preview to benefit the LAPD's Van Nuys Area Jeopardy Program.

The program, formed in 1990, works to keep middle school and high school students out of gangs by offering them after-school and weekend activities, field trips. and other ways to spend their free time. During the preview event, Krispy Kreme donated the proceeds from every doughnut and drink sold to the Jeopardy Program. The company often participates in such giveaways. A portion of opening-day sales for any new store traditionally goes to a local children's group. That's how Computers for Kids in Greensboro, North Carolina, scored a $10,000 donation after Krispy Kreme opened a new store in town. Another group in Greensboro also benefited when Krispy Kreme shut down a 35-year-old store to open a new one. Krispy Kreme auctioned off memorabilia from the old store, including a neon "Hot Doughnuts Now" sign that sold for $1,000 to an unnamed buyer. The auction raised $1,510 for the Children's Museum's programs. "Krispy Kreme just called us out of the blue and offered to make us the beneficiary for this silent auction," said Stephanie Skordas, the museum's director of marketing. "We just think the world of Krispy Kreme."

In Sacramento, California, Krispy Kreme marked the opening of a new store by giving 25 cents for each box of doughnuts sold to the Sacramento Children's Home. "We're proud to have an opportunity to help one of Sacramento's most effective, caring and compassionate services for children in need," explained area developer Brad Bruckman, who operates Krispy Kreme stores in northern California through the company Golden Gate Doughnuts. "My wife and I have made Sacramento our home, and it's exciting to be able to do something to give back to this wonderful community."[12]

Workers from Bruckman's store also visited the home prior to the opening and delivered the first batch of Krispy Kreme doughnuts to the young residents, all of whom have been abused or neglected. "We're thrilled they chose us," said Nancy Widby, communications coordinator for the home. "We rely heavily on private donations to help us meet the needs of thousands of children and their families."[13]

ALIGN YOUR GOALS

Philanthropy is an integral part of Krispy Kreme's business. The company long ago figured out how to structure its charitable giving to best benefit both its own business goals and the groups it strives to help.

Todd Cohen, a former newspaper business section editor, has been writing about corporate giving for about a decade as editor of the online *Philanthropy Journal.* During that period, he says, many companies have changed their approach to charitable contributions. Now, businesses want to do more than simply give money away. "Companies increasingly are putting their dollars into the sorts of projects that are directly related to what their business goals and strategies are," Cohen observes. "The key is to have philanthropy be a part of the corporate image and brand."

Microsoft, for example, has given billions in money, products, and technical expertise to nonprofit groups since 1983. This practice has provided much-needed technology to thousands of schools and community organizations. But it has also helped Microsoft, Cohen says. Among many nonprofit agencies, schools, and volunteers, Microsoft has gained a reputation as an involved, caring corporation. The company has also benefited by introducing its software products to a large audience of potential customers. "If you use something and you get to know it, you're more likely to buy it yourself," Cohen points out. The payoff for Microsoft is twofold: goodwill and guaranteed future sales.

Corporate America has plenty of other examples of such business-focused philanthropy. Pharmaceutical company GlaxoSmithKline supports science education and is also active in providing vaccines and treatment for HIV and AIDS to residents of developing countries. Progress Energy, meanwhile, contributes to math and science education, environmental causes, and economic development efforts.

Krispy Kreme was way ahead of this trend of aligning philanthropy with business goals. In turn, it has been able to sell more doughnuts and brand itself as a feel-good community company. "They've been doing it for years. Someone understood way back when that it was good business to give away doughnuts," Cohen says. "My guess is that if you analyzed the way the company's philanthropy works, it's almost a model that other companies could use."

Constant innovator that it is, Krispy Kreme continues to explore new ways to give back to the community. In 2002, it announced two new philanthropic endeavors: a charitable foundation and a Krispy Kreme store that is owned jointly by the corporation and a North Carolina nonprofit group.

Instead of fading quietly into retirement, longtime Krispy Kreme executive vice president Paul Breitbach gave up his duties managing the company's finance, administration, and support operations to run the fledgling Krispy Kreme foundation.

Plans are still developing, but Breitbach reports that Krispy Kreme will endow the foundation while also continuing to set aside a portion of pretax annual income for charitable donations. Shareholders may also be encouraged to contribute. "We obviously would like this to become a major foundation that would have an impact on a national level," said Breitbach, who worked for Krispy Kreme for 10 years and was also its chief financial officer. "We're not interested in having a small foundation."[14] The foundation, which could eventually have $10 to $20 million in assets, will fund family causes, something that Krispy Kreme has long supported.[15]

Also in 2002, Krispy Kreme agreed to partner with a nonprofit builder in Greensboro, North Carolina, to open a doughnut shop in an economically depressed part of town. By all reports, Project Homestead's leader, the Reverend Michael King, doggedly pursued Krispy Kreme to be the anchor tenant in a business development on the eastern edge of Greensboro's downtown.

The corridor had once been the site of dozens of thriving black-owned businesses. "I remember all the businesses that used to be here when I was a child," King said. But those memories were soon overshadowed by reality. Urban renewal efforts during the 1960s put most shops and restaurants out of business, and the area quickly declined.

During the 1990s, city officials and residents of Greensboro began exploring ways to revitalize the downtown's eastern edge. They determined that the key was to bring restaurants and services back to the neighborhood.[16] Project Homestead, which we first discussed in Chapter 6, has built or renovated more than 1,000 homes for low- and moderate-income families throughout central North Carolina. It has also invested $75 million in community development projects. Before long, the Reverend King, Project Homestead's loquacious and persuasive founder, became involved in the revitalization efforts and made it his goal to find business partners to fill a 30,000-square-foot retail and office complex in the area. He immediately set his sights on Krispy Kreme after meeting chief executive officer Scott Livengood during a series of statewide conferences on community development in the late 1990s.

"He has been calling me every month for the past five years,"[17] Livengood quipped during the groundbreaking for the new store, referring to King's persistence.

In 2002, Krispy Kreme agreed to award a franchise to Project Homestead, a nonprofit community development corporation. Krispy Kreme, headquartered about 30 miles west of Greensboro, took an equity-ownership stake in the Project Homestead store, as it has done with other franchises in recent years. "What impresses me most is the businesslike approach of [community development corporations] and the holistic way they look at revitalizing communities and creating opportunities for home ownership and individual advancement," Livengood said. "These people are stepping up. They're highly involved, changing people's lives for the better. When those folks say they really would love to have an opportunity to be involved in Krispy Kreme, it really resonates. I believe these people have the commitment and the passion [and] that when they make a decision they're going to get involved in something they're going to see it through."[18]

The Project Homestead store, located near several college campuses, operates like any Krispy Kreme. The hot light burns twice a day, and the drive-through window is open past midnight. Carloads of hungry customers are constantly lining up for a taste of hot glazed sweets, and fresh doughnuts are trucked daily to surrounding grocery and convenience stores. Except in this case, it's not the franchisees who are getting rich from every dozen sold. Project Homestead uses profits from the store's doughnut sales to fund its mission. The money builds houses and apartment complexes, educates residents about home ownership, and puts the economically downtrodden into nice, safe homes of their own. Krispy Kreme officials expect the Project Homestead store to eventually generate $1 million in annual sales.

"In the long term, we simply have to find more ways to generate income and decrease our reliance on grants and contributions," King says. "We believe Project Homestead can prove that corporations can make sound investments in low-resource communities with [community development corporations] as responsible partners."[19]

For Krispy Kreme, it is a perfect partnership and a great way to align philanthropy with the business of selling doughnuts.

"It feels very natural," Livengood says. "Even though we're a regional company, a national company, we still look at ourselves as a local business, and we try to operate that way and try to think of ourselves as neighbors."

By the same token, Livengood admits that Krispy Kreme, which is always very deliberate about where it builds stores and who it allows to operate them, is taking a risk with the partnership. The chain already has a commissary that makes doughnuts for wholesale customers and two other stores in Greensboro, a town with a population of about 225,000. "In a way, it's an act of faith," he says. "There's a lot less household density in this area than where we traditionally locate stores. It's the first time we've in essence carved up a market between company-owned and franchise-owned stores."

Though untraditional and a departure from standard company practices, Livengood maintains he is confident that the Project Homestead store will be successful, both in business and philanthropic terms. "This is a model for another way for Krispy Kreme to grow," he says. "I think we may have made more of an emotional commitment to this partnership than we have with any other. It's hopefully going to become a model for other partnerships."

Such commitment to what some companies would consider a risky business deal is nothing new for Krispy Kreme. The doughnut maker has been pushing the boundaries of convention, in philanthropy and in business, for most of its six decades.

This sort of generosity flows through to Krispy Kreme executives personally, including CEO Livengood. In 2003, he and his wife Michelle donated $500,000 to the private elementary school that two of their children attend. Forsyth Country Day School, which is in Lewisville, North Carolina, just outside of Winston-Salem, will use the money to build a new gymnasium and activity center for its students. The building, to be named the Scott and Michelle Livengood Center, will have a full-size basketball court, two practice courts, locker rooms, office space, a storage area, and a dance studio. "We are extremely proud of the growth of Forsyth Country Day School and its accomplishments on behalf of the students," said Scott Livengood, who served on the school's board of directors from 1997 to 2001.

GIVE AND YOU SHALL RECEIVE

Krispy Kreme found smart ways to sell more of its products while at the same time helping the community long before most big American companies ever considered linking philanthropy with business goals. Early on, Krispy Kreme earned a reputation as a company to be counted on, and it became known for its commitment to local communities. Those characteristics continue to define the brand. In addition to good doughnuts, people think of good deeds when they think of Krispy Kreme.

Through the years, as Krispy Kreme has built that reputation, the company has done much to help its neighbors across America, and now around the world. Student filmmakers have met their idols, poor children have new blankets, new charities have raised much-needed money to fill their coffers, and sick kids have been given a new lease on life thanks to the company's mission of giving back to its many diverse communities. In turn, this generosity has helped to fuel Krispy Kreme's own business, proving the adage that when you do good, the blessings really do come back to you.

CHAPTER 10

Select, Train, and Treat Your Employees Well

It's a miserable February day in central North Carolina with an icy precipitation falling. The shimmering sleet has frozen car doors shut, coating windshields with thick sheets of ice, making them look opaque. Vehicles move slowly down the ice-and-snow-dusted roads, with their lights blazing in the afternoon.

This isn't the kind of joyous wintry weather that draws neighbors together for sledding and hot chocolate. It's simply dreadful outside. No one wants to be part of this mess, much less out in it. It's about as cold as it gets in this part of the country at this time of year. The ice coating the bare tree limbs might be pretty, but people here remember what happened the last time their trees sprouted such a pretty glaze. The ice weighed down thousands of weak tree branches, and limbs cracked like rifle shots in the night, taking down power lines as they fell. Some lived without electricity—and thus without heat, hot water, and hot food—for more than a week.

Not surprisingly, on this dreary Sunday, just about everyone in North Carolina seems to be in a bad mood. That is, everyone except the folks at the local Krispy Kreme store.

Though the doughnut-making machine isn't running at the moment, a father enthralls his two young sons with an explanation about how raw dough turns into Krispy Kremes. The little boys, one wearing a Krispy Kreme hat, giddily run around the store, pointing all around as their doughnuts are being boxed up. "No, you don't need a souvenir," the father says when the boys beg him for Krispy Kreme shirts. "Not today."

Elsewhere, two women in their mid-twenties huddle over doughnuts and coffee. They are wrapped in heavy wool coats and scarves and talk animatedly, savoring this brief warm moment out of the sleet and rain. At the counter, a bedraggled woman in faded sweatpants, a baseball cap, and a ski jacket orders a cup of coffee and a doughnut to go from the smiling clerk.

"I hope you don't have to work too late," she says to the employee, wrapping one gloved hand around the hot coffee and grabbing the waxed doughnut bag with the other. The clerk doesn't take the bait to complain about the bad weather or having to work on a day when most other stores and restaurants are closed. He just shrugs and smiles, "Have a nice day," before moving on to help the next customer, a snow-plow driver on his break. It's a genuine smile that never leaves his face.

In many ways, Krispy Kreme is like any other fast-food restaurant. Its kitchen and counter employees—those on the front lines with cus-tomers—make little more than minimum wage. They're on their feet for most of their shifts, filling orders or cooking doughnuts. The work can be repetitive. There's always someone new at the counter wanting another order of doughnuts along with a carton of milk or cup of cof-fee. Watching the doughnuts being made through the large glass win-dow might be a treat for customers, but try making 3,000 doughnuts an hour, day after day, and lifting all of those hot dozens off the cooker and into boxes or onto bakery trays. The fun can't possibly last for long. It certainly sounds like a recipe for low morale and bad attitudes.

That might be true at other fast-food joints, which seem to breed surly, curt behavior. But not at Krispy Kreme. The chain enjoys a lower turnover rate, even among its lowest-paid workers, than other compa-nies in its industry. The company's employees are routinely compli-mented by consumers and business analysts for their upbeat, friendly attitudes and their attention to good customer service.

High employee morale and attention to customer service don't hap-pen by accident. They are the result of a well-crafted corporate strategy of selecting, training, and treating employees well.

USE TEAMWORK

Krispy Kreme truly is a business run by teamwork, from the executive office to its retail stores. Though plenty of companies talk about oper-ating as a team and call their employees "associates" to prove it, Krispy Kreme really walks the walk. That's a key reason for the doughnut maker's success. "They are a fabulously successful and profitable com-pany that happens to have soul and heart," says Alice Elliot, a corporate recruiter from Tarrytown, New York, who has worked with Krispy

Kreme and its franchisees. "I think the company has always been good to its people."

Krispy Kreme's workers are paid a fair wage, rewarded for performance, and given opportunities to advance within the company. Unlike their counterparts at most fast-food companies, Krispy Kreme employees are eligible for medical, dental, and vision insurance, and they may contribute to a 401(k) retirement savings plan after only one month on the job.[1] The company also has a deal with ComPsych, a Chicago-based company that provides employees with free work-life, crisis, and behavioral counseling. ComPsych claims this benefit not only attracts and retains employees, but also improves productivity and performance. In addition, Krispy Kreme workers have the opportunity to buy shares of company stock through an employee stock purchase plan. Under the plan, established in February 2002, employees can set aside from 1 to 15 percent of each paycheck to buy Krispy Kreme shares.

These benefits, and the many other programs in place for employees at both corporate headquarters and company stores around the world, help to illustrate why Krispy Kreme is so different from its fast-food rivals.

HELP EMPLOYEES MAKE A DIFFERENCE

In the summer of 2001, Krispy Kreme had to close its Louisville, Kentucky, store for three weeks for renovations. The company gave employees three options for the downtime: They could take vacation, take time off without pay, or volunteer for local Salvation Army charities while receiving their usual salary from the company.[2]

Eighteen-year-old Alex Howard, a new employee at the doughnut shop, decided to spend his time volunteering at the Salvation Army's Boys and Girls Club. "Yeah, that's something I'd like to do," Howard remembered thinking at the time. He spent three weeks refereeing basketball games, playing pool with children, and just plain hanging out with them. "It shows that Krispy Kreme loves the community and that they are there for them," Howard says of his employer.

In southern California, Krispy Kreme franchisee Great Circle Family

Foods partnered with local social service agencies to find people to work in its stores. "More than one-third of our employees graduated from a welfare-to-work program specially designed for our store needs," boasts Great Circle Family Foods president Roger Glickman. "Many of these employees have stayed on with us for more than a year."[3]

When Frank Hood began as Krispy Kreme's chief technology officer in 1997, he arrived with bad news for his employees. Not only would they have to overhaul the company's information technology infrastructure, but because of the company's fiscal calendar, they would also have to reprogram computer systems way ahead—by early 1999—to protect them from the anticipated Y2K problems. Hood immediately lost some workers—those who felt they just couldn't handle the new, frenetically paced environment. But the ones who stayed were promised the chance to work in a department without a strict hierarchy, one where employees with good ideas and a good work ethic really could make a difference. Sure, Hood told them, Krispy Kreme would challenge them, but the company would also support them in their successes and failures. "What we've tried to do is say, 'We're going to gamble a little bit. We're going to take you to what you think is the cusp of failure and then we're going to back you up,' " says Hood, who has been pleased with the resulting employee performance and attitude. "You can hardly describe it. You can see it in their eyes. They dig it."[4]

Unlike in some other companies, employees aren't treated as dispensable worker bees. Time and again, people describe Krispy Kreme as having a welcoming atmosphere, and much of it comes from the kind of people the company selects to stand behind its counters and represent it to the public.

TREAT WORKERS AS FAMILY

"They claim that their employees—and the few that we've interviewed say it, too—feel like they're family," says marketing expert Craig Conroy of Conroy Research Group in Gibsonia, Pennsylvania. "They feel like they're involved. Going home every day, each employee is encouraged to take home a dozen doughnuts. At most other places you can't take a crumb home. When you have core values like that, it's hard as hell to beat."

The small gestures Krispy Kreme makes to its employees garner big returns that improve service and the overall customer experience. Krispy Kreme employees feel invested in the company, so they smile when they take your order. They listen to your story—and everyone else's—about a special Krispy Kreme memory. When these workers spot a young child enthralled by the doughnut-making process, they offer a behind-the-scenes tour. Instead of serving you lukewarm coffee from the bottom of the carafe, they offer to brew a new pot if you're willing to wait. Simply put, they make Krispy Kreme a better company and help to build return business.

"There's something about the values, the leadership, the training, and the product itself at Krispy Kreme that creates people who live the values of the company, believe in the product, and are proud of the product," says David Geraty, a stock analyst at RBC Capital Markets in Minneapolis, Minnesota. "A lot of great service companies, first and foremost, touch the employees. That's the secret, I think. For a service company to give good service, the only way you can do that is through people who provide that service. I see it in Krispy Kreme."

Putting people first, as Krispy Kreme does, just makes good business sense, according to Joe Wheeler and Shaun Smith. These two experts, colleagues at The Forum Corporation, advise companies on customers and employees. They believe that the way to create brand loyalty and good customer experiences is to properly develop employees and to treat them well. "Creating a powerful customer experience requires the full and continual commitment of the people responsible for making it happen. People make the difference. If you concentrate on creating a great environment for your employees, they will focus on creating a great experience for your customers,"[5] the pair wrote in their aptly titled essay, "People First."

SET GOOD EXAMPLES

Senior management, of course, must set the example and reward employees for what they do right. You can't just reprimand workers for their mistakes. "The way they treat employees is reflective of how employees will treat customers," according to Smith and Wheeler. "Organizations that treat employees the way they treat customers understand what the customer experience and 'people power' are all about. Leaders must communicate a sense of purpose and constantly reinforce the values of the organization."[6]

At Krispy Kreme, no one does that quite like James Brumsey.

Brumsey is a longtime manager of the Krispy Kreme store on Virginia Beach Boulevard in Virginia Beach, Virginia. His store is one of the most successful in the chain, and his average employee tenure is 20 years.[7]

At six feet five inches tall, with a short, military-style haircut and a drill instructor's voice, Brumsey is no warm-and-fuzzy boss. He is by all descriptions, including his own, a disciplinarian who manages with a firm yet guiding hand. Still, Brumsey is among the best at training people to understand what Krispy Kreme is all about. He knows how to treat and develop employees to get the best possible work and customer service from them. He wants them to succeed and helps them move up the company ladder. And he gets what Krispy Kreme chief executive officer Scott Livengood calls "synergistic results."

Brumsey's employees are treated well; they understand what is expected of them from their boss; they work hard; they make a good product; and they treat customers well. They deliver on the Krispy Kreme promise. "Every person who comes into our store has a magic moment," Brumsey boasts.[8]

In fact, Brumsey is so good at getting stellar performance from workers that many management trainees and corporate employees work in Brumsey's store to learn the ropes of the company.[9] "The reason I have them go there is number one, they get to meet James and have him as a resource, and they also get great training in the fundamentals of business," Livengood says.[10]

Brumsey, who is in his mid-sixties and has worked for Krispy Kreme since 1966, leads his doughnut kingdom from a gray upholstered chair that sits just outside his office. Brumsey can watch everything from this chair—the kitchen, the front counter, the stockroom. Employees know the chair is off limits to anyone but their boss, just as they know what he expects from them every day.[11]

Brumsey is as precise—and predictable—as a time clock. He arrives at his store every day around six o'clock in the morning and stays until at least six o'clock at night. Each morning, Brumsey briefs employees on the "plan for the day" and then helps them with their work through the morning rush. He interacts with the customers daily, offering employees a good example of what is expected of them as Krispy Kreme employees. "Everyone here knows what to do," he says. "There's no lingering, no wondering. They've got the plan."[12]

"They know where James stands on issues," Livengood adds, explaining Brumsey's relationship with his employees. "They know what to do to elicit his praise. He's very consistent about priorities and responsibilities. They know if they deviate from what they're supposed to be doing, they're going to get a reaction."[13]

Though he's tough and strict, Brumsey isn't a bully. That's evidenced by his store's sales and the long tenure of his employees. Employees wouldn't stay if he were not a good and fair boss to work for, and that in turn would likely hurt store sales. It's also clear in both how he treats employees and how they feel about him in return. "He's mean as the devil," confesses Eva Phelps, a 31-year Krispy Kreme employee who is now a supervisor, with a twinkle in her eye. "But we love him. He's a good boss. I guess everybody in here, he's gotten them out of a bind."[14] The gruff, all-business Brumsey has helped employees pay overdue bills and fix broken-down cars, and he has often loaned or just plain given away money from his own pocket. His kindness shows in other, smaller ways, too, especially in his habit of pairing praise with instruction.

"First, I'm going to tell you good morning," Brumsey said early one day, as he spotted a new employee coming into Krispy Kreme through the wrong door. "Then I'm going to ask you a question: Did you come through that back door?"[15]

Yes, the employee nods, bracing for a reprimand. "That's a no-no," Brumsey instructs, gesturing to another entrance. "Always come through that [other] door. I haven't told you that before," the manager says, acknowledging his own oversight in training this new worker.[16]

"I heard compliments about you last night," Brumsey says in a booming voice as the employee walks away. "Keep it up."[17]

GOOD TRAINING IS ESSENTIAL

James Brumsey in Virginia Beach proves that managers are a very important ingredient to the success of each Krispy Kreme store.

Krispy Kreme requires each of its managers to complete an intensive Management 101 training course to make sure they're prepared for the responsibility of running a store. The class, taken by many new franchisees and corporate staff as well, begins with six weeks of on-the-job training at a certified training store, such as the one Brumsey runs. There, aspiring managers learn just what it takes to run a doughnut shop from the perspectives of both production workers and the retail specialists who serve customers.

During this initial period, managers must also complete online training courses and pass tests that were developed by the company and its consultant Handshaw & Associates in Charlotte, North Carolina.

Krispy Kreme hired Handshaw in September 1999, about seven months before its initial public offering, to revamp training procedures for managers. Before Handshaw was hired, new managers went through 12 weeks of on-the-job training and four weeks of classroom instruction at the company's Winston-Salem headquarters. But Krispy Kreme, with its rapid expansion plans, needed a quicker and better way to train its new employees.

Handshaw created an interactive online training course that Krispy Kreme managers could complete during their first six weeks of on-the-job instruction. The computer component prepares trainees for their next phase of schooling—a week of lectures from corporate employees and hands-on production and equipment training.

"At some point, somebody's got to put that doughnut in the hot oil. That's the stuff that's got to stay in the classes," says Dick Handshaw, president and managing partner for the consulting firm. But the computer system is great for teaching managers about other skills, like financial management, staffing, customer service, corporate culture, and sanitation.

By the time Handshaw's company was hired, Krispy Kreme had identified that it was not only in the doughnut business, but also in the customer experience business. Its new employee training had to support that and reflect the company's ideals of superior customer service.

"They wanted to make sure they carried the culture through," notes Handshaw, whose company worked to make the online course a primer on both practical skills and the more esoteric qualities valued by Krispy Kreme.

Handshaw's employees inserted videos from store openings and testimonials from Krispy Kreme customers into the online training program. "We really wanted to model that for the trainees and really put that picture in people's minds [of what creates] those magic moments."

Handshaw has received plenty of confirmation that the training program his company developed is working. The training numbers themselves are impressive. During the first year, Krispy Kreme trained 149 new managers using the online course, compared to 60 new managers the previous year. Executives have also praised the training system. Krispy Kreme hired Handshaw's company to create a similar interactive training course for hourly workers. Other companies have purchased the software training package Handshaw & Associates developed based on its experience with Krispy Kreme. But Handshaw himself became a true believer about the efficacy of the training programs while watching the news one night at home.

The manager of a new doughnut store was being interviewed. He told the reporter that Krispy Kreme was focused on creating "magic moments" for its customers. That was a key concept that the training courses aimed to teach, Handshaw notes, and here was a new manager talking about it on television.

Once managers have completed their initial on-the-job training—the online course and the first week of doughnut school at Krispy Kreme headquarters—they are sent back to a training store for another six weeks of in-the-trenches preparation. Then it's back to Winston-Salem for the final week of corporate classroom learning.

Once managers graduate from the formal training, they're given even more help from the company.

When developers open their first store in a region, Krispy Kreme sends out a seven-member traveling team to train new employees and help them during the initial doughnut-buying rush. These trainers instruct employees on how to make and serve doughnuts. They also emphasize the soft skills that Krispy Kreme values—friendliness, kindness, internal culture, and attentiveness to customers.

THINK ABOUT WHAT'S BEST FOR EMPLOYEES

At Krispy Kreme, the example of how to treat employees and customers comes from the top. Chairman and CEO Livengood, who joined the company's personnel department in 1977, studied industrial relations and psychology at the University of North Carolina at Chapel Hill. "Even then, the company had 1,800 employees and was a great place to work where you could see the impact of your contribution," Livengood notes.

As Krispy Kreme's top officer, Livengood is focused on making the company a good place to work. He emphasizes teamwork and takes into account how employees will be affected when making big corporate decisions. For example, he lingered over the decision of where to build Krispy Kreme's new corporate headquarters in Winston-Salem, North Carolina. Initially, Livengood wanted a suburban location that would accommodate his rapidly growing staff while also providing them easy access to restaurants and other community amenities. But when several suburban sites he had selected weren't available, Livengood and other corporate executives instead decided that Krispy Kreme should anchor a unique retail, business, and residential complex in downtown Winston-Salem. In addition to the 100,000-square-foot corporate headquarters, the development will house a performing arts center, a movie theater, townhomes, office space, and retail stores. "What we really wanted to do was to create an internal and external environment . . . that would be something that would be interesting and exciting for our employees to be a part of, something beyond the four walls of our office," Livengood asserts. "We wanted to accomplish it in such a way that it could be very special for the entire community and accomplish it in a way that would be symbolic of the city's commitment to progress. We wanted something that would demonstrate that Winston-Salem is a great place to locate a business and to communicate with equal strength that a business should never have to leave Winston-Salem to achieve its potential.

"We're proud of our heritage, and we're proud that we're from Winston-Salem, and there will be elements of the building that will reflect that, including a small museum," he says. Employees and visitors to the new headquarters, which is set to open in early 2005, "will clearly know that it's about Krispy Kreme."[18]

The example set by Livengood trickles down to his franchisees. That's no surprise, because these partners are chosen both for their business experience and because their values match those of the company.

Metz & Associates, which is building Krispy Kreme stores throughout the Pittsburgh, Pennsylvania, area, says its mission, in addition to offering good restaurant service for customers, is to provide its 2,000 employees with opportunities to excel through training and promotion. The company also rewards workers for good performance and works hard to retain them through a variety of pay and benefit programs. "Our employees are our greatest asset, and we strive to make them happy," the company asserts on the careers section of its web site.

At Rigel Corporation, the Krispy Kreme area developer for markets in Arizona and New Mexico, employees have long been treated as teammates who make valuable contributions. "The people that are working within Rigel are making the company successful," claims Darren Taylor, who was a regional manager for the company when it franchised Godfather's Pizza and Breugger's Bagel restaurants. Rigel has since sold its other restaurants to focus on the Krispy Kreme franchises. "[They] are great people to work for, and they send out the message to their people that they want everyone to be successful. In turn, people work a little harder because of it."[19]

Frank Musco, a regional manager for one of Rigel's other restaurant chains, says his bosses always gave him the authority and the latitude to run his territory. They never micromanaged. For example, Rigel principal Jim Morrissey wanted to close one of Musco's restaurants because it wasn't performing as well as his bosses would have liked. But he listened when Musco argued against the move. The restaurant's lease was about to expire, so it would have been easy to shut it down. Musco, arguing a strong case that he and his employees could improve the restaurant, convinced Morrissey to keep the location open for one more lease cycle.

In turn, Musco turned the restaurant around, as promised. "Now month after month, it is making good bottom-line money," Musco told a reporter at the time. "At any other company an owner wouldn't give a manager the autonomy to do something like that. It makes me feel like I am not just an employee. I am a real part of the company. And that is how I treat my people. I share [profit and loss statements] with our managers. I tell them to run their restaurants like they own them."[20]

BE VERY SELECTIVE ABOUT YOUR PEOPLE

The magic that Krispy Kreme creates with its employees isn't just the result of how well the company treats those workers. Krispy Kreme is also quite selective when drafting people for its own corporate team, and it trains them well. "We're in the people business," a recruiter told potential workers at an employment drive in California, explaining that every worker is expected to be an ambassador for the Krispy Kreme experience. "If you're not a people person, go get a job in a bank."[21]

Krispy Kreme's reputation is so tied up in the promise to provide fun, satisfying, and memorable experiences to its customers that the company hires only people who understand that promise and can deliver it. Barbara Thornton, the company's former director of human resources, explains, "What drives our work and the target that we're working on is the ultimate goal of being sure that we are creating magic moments for our customers. To do that, you have to find the right people, and they have to have the right fit, which means that the culture piece becomes very important."[22]

Alice Elliot, the New York–based headhunter, learned how important culture is to Krispy Kreme through the biggest assignment her search firm has handled for the company: convincing John Tate to leave retailer Williams-Sonoma to become Krispy Kreme's chief financial officer.

"Not every company is as fanatically focused on the quality of those they choose to work with," says Elliot. She herself had to survive a polite, but drilling and thought-provoking, interview with Krispy Kreme CEO Scott Livengood before winning the recruitment contract.

Livengood, who began his career at Krispy Kreme as a personnel trainee, quickly rose in the ranks. He was promoted to vice president of human resources in just three years. Livengood held that vice president's position for almost eight years, until August 1989, when he was tapped to lead corporate development. Elliot, who describes Livengood as a quiet, deep, and thoughtful man, said it was immediately clear to her that the CEO carried what he learned in the human resources department to Krispy Kreme's executive suite. "He has an understanding of the importance of teamwork," she observes.

"[You have to] realize you can't do it all yourself," Livengood advises. "Surround yourself with capable people and create an environment where everyone feels free to voice opinions different from yours. I encourage people to exercise initiative and take chances. They may fail, but failure is one step closer to success."[23]

Livengood hired Elliot to find a chief financial officer before the company's April 2000 initial public stock offering, when Krispy Kreme was little more than a regional brand with what it hoped was big potential. Livengood set his sights higher than most executives in his position would have, aiming to cherry-pick talent from the nation's best and most successful companies. Livengood "had an unswerving desire to build something great," Elliot says.

"Scott was not willing to compromise, particularly for that position," she remembers. "Scott said, 'What are some of the best brands in America? What are some of the best-run companies?' Scott was the one to mention companies like Williams-Sonoma, where John Tate came from, because they were best-of-class for the work they did."

Tate, who had also worked for Dole Foods, was chief financial officer at Williams-Sonoma, the San Francisco company that also includes Pottery Barn, when Krispy Kreme came calling. Elliot pitched the job to Tate, who was "very gracious in his amazement." That is, he was not interested in leaving a top executive position at a nationally known retailer like Williams-Sonoma to come to North Carolina to work for what was then a small doughnut company.

But Elliot couldn't let go of Tate. He certainly had the skills that Krispy Kreme was looking for in a chief financial officer. After all, you don't become the top money guy at Williams-Sonoma without that kind of talent. But Elliot also saw a bit of the Krispy Kreme spirit and friendliness in him, evidenced in the thoughtful attention he always paid to her assistant. Every time Tate called Elliot's office, he would talk to and listen to the assistant before asking for her boss.

"I just knew that John was a class guy," says Elliot, who finally cajoled a traveling Tate to meet her for lunch during a flight layover at the Newark, New Jersey, airport. "The minute I met John Tate was the minute I knew that Scott had to meet him."

That meeting eventually took place, and it was quickly followed by a job offer. Though Williams-Sonoma tried to convince him to stay, Tate chose to leave his high-level job there to join Livengood's team at Krispy Kreme. "Williams-Sonoma was one of the greatest brands out there," Elliot says, but that company had already achieved a fair amount of success by the time Tate joined it in July 1999. Krispy Kreme, by contrast, was just entering its growth period when Tate was hired in October 2000. This was Tate's opportunity to put his signature on something, she says, and to grow professionally with a fast-growing company.

It clearly was a smart move for Tate. He was quickly promoted to chief operating officer at Krispy Kreme, a position that gives him even more control of the company's growth and direction.

John Tate's success story happened in the corporate offices of Krispy Kreme. But employees at every level of the company have the chance to climb through the ranks. The company rewards good performance with decent pay, excellent benefits, promotions, praise, and genuine thanks. It recently launched a nine-month leadership development program for employees with senior management potential. Such benefits and good treatment help Krispy Kreme employees stay positive and happy. On average, they remain with the company much longer than their counterparts at other quick-service food chains.

As a result, Krispy Kreme has succeeded where other restaurants have failed. The company has created a high-morale atmosphere for its employees and a pleasant environment for customers at all of its stores around the world.

CHAPTER 11

Build on
Your Success

Vernon Carver Rudolph is a difficult man to characterize. His behavior and demeanor were so enigmatic and contradictory. In many pictures that Krispy Kreme displays of its founder, Rudolph wears the same expression—eyes bright and confident, staring straight ahead, lips drawn together in a straight, serious line. He is almost always wearing a dark suit and tie, and he rarely shows emotion. There is no upturn of a smile in his lips, no twinkle of amusement in his eyes. These pictures coincide with descriptions of Rudolph as a stern and serious man, short on demonstrable humor but long on ideals. It's not a stretch to imagine that this dour-faced man was a perfectionist, with a military-like intolerance for anything out of order.

Rudolph had a near photographic memory and a fine, almost controlling, attention to details. He worked out solutions to problems by drumming his pencil on the desk. Employees knew not to bother the boss when this nervous music was heard coming from his office. Rudolph couldn't pass by a crooked picture without straightening it, even just a fraction of an inch. Once, when a tractor-trailer driver who had been awake nearly 24 hours driving for Krispy Kreme reported to work wearing the previous night's beard stubble, Rudolph laid a dime on his desk. What was it for? "To buy a razor blade,"[1] Rudolph told the driver with a sly smile.

Yet, unlike so many bosses, Rudolph seemed to genuinely bond with his employees. He was clearly proud of the work they did for him, and he often credited Krispy Kreme's success and its future to their dedication and commitment to making a superior product. At a managers meeting shortly before his death in 1973, a member of the audience noticed Rudolph standing quietly by himself, sporting a satisfied look on his face. "Two cents for your thoughts," the man prodded Rudolph. "I am thinking of how proud I am of all these managers," Krispy Kreme's founder said, taking the two pennies he felt he had earned for giving his opinion. "Some of them are so young and are doing such a good job."[2]

Though Rudolph didn't like to take credit for such things, everyone around the office knew that he was generous with advice and could be relied on for other help in an emergency. Mattie DeBerry, who is now in her nineties, was the maid at Krispy Kreme's corporate headquarters for 30 years. Vernon Rudolph, she says, was one of the kindest men she ever met, always doing more for his employees than a boss is expected to do. Long before the federal government mandated that companies give employees family leave, Rudolph instituted his own policy to help employees deal with family or medical emergencies. When Rudolph found out that DeBerry's daughter was about to deliver her first child, he immediately called DeBerry away from her cleaning duties. Rudolph gave DeBerry a voucher for a plane ticket and cab fare and sent DeBerry to Brooklyn, New York, to be with her pregnant daughter for as long as she was needed there. That was just his way. Genuine kindness was as much a part of his personality as was seriousness and brusqueness.

Though Rudolph was full of contradictions, his business goals for Krispy Kreme were always crystal clear. Rudolph got into the doughnut business in the 1930s simply to make a living for himself. But as Krispy Kreme grew and as success rained on his little operation, Rudolph began thinking like a good businessman. He preached to employees about meeting change with change, about building Krispy Kreme into the biggest, best doughnut enterprise in the world. Rudolph was always conscious of moving Krispy Kreme forward. He was never content to settle for only the latest success, but instead was always looking ahead to the next one.

"We are in a growth industry. We have the best product line, the best technical, manufacturing, and marketing know-how. We expect to remain on top," Rudolph once said. "Only by full realization of our resources can we bring about results and achieve the goals we have been building toward these many years."[3]

NEVER BECOME COMPLACENT

From the moment he opened the first Krispy Kreme in 1937, Rudolph enjoyed a cascade of success. But Rudolph, who was raised in a family that valued hard work, was never complacent about that success. Every accomplishment was a nudge for the next one, and each was yet another stepping-stone to business preeminence. It was this ethic that turned Krispy Kreme from a small confectionary shop into the big business it is today.

Although Rudolph has been gone for more than three decades, his spirit and his work ethic still infuse the company. Krispy Kreme has unquestionably grown into an incredible company. Still, management constantly seeks ways to take the company one step further, just as Rudolph did. Whether it's expanding into additional countries or developing new product concepts, Krispy Kreme continually builds upon its own achievements and refuses to grow stale.

GROW FROM ADVERSITY

By the time Vernon Rudolph and his two friends arrived in Winston-Salem in the sultry summer of 1937, they were frustrated and nearly broke. The three men had left Nashville with $200 in cash, a gas stove, an iron kettle, a rolling pin, a galvanized washtub, doughnut cutters, and the Krispy Kreme recipe. They were full of dreams and wanted to strike out on their own. But the three cash-strapped men struggled to find a suitable location for their doughnut shop. In many cases, they were unable to pay the high rental rates that landlords demanded. By the time they arrived in Winston-Salem, the trio only had $25 between them to start their business and to pay for lodging, food, and other essentials. The $25 was soon gone, spent on the first month's rent for a 720-square-foot building on Winston-Salem's Main Street. With that payment, the business partners finally had their doughnut-making factory. But with no money left, they borrowed against tomorrow's success to buy ingredients for today, relying on credit and the goodwill of other local businesses to fund their fledgling enterprise. They convinced the landlady at a local boardinghouse to provide them with free food and lodging for a week. They promised to pay her at the end of the week with profits made from their first doughnut sales. Luckily, they were able to keep that promise and repay the debt. The business kept getting stronger each week, each month, each year.

At his first Krispy Kreme store, Rudolph built up such a strong, loyal customer base in Winston-Salem and in surrounding North Carolina towns that within a year the business had room to expand. In 1938, Rudolph's uncle opened a Krispy Kreme shop in Charlotte, North Carolina. That same year, the doughnut makers started cooking up fried apple, peach, and pineapple pies under the Old Timey Pie Company brand name.

Rudolph soon opened Krispy Kreme stores in the state capitals of Raleigh, North Carolina, and Charleston, West Virginia. Other entrepreneurs around the country were anxious to share in Krispy Kreme's success. In 1947, the company began its associates program, licensing franchisees to sell doughnuts under the Krispy Kreme trade name. These original franchisees needed between $3,200 and $3,500 to get started in the doughnut business.[4] By the end of 1948, in its eleventh year of business, Krispy Kreme had grown to include stores in 10 states, and annual sales topped $1 million.[5] By 1962, Rudolph told a newspaper reporter in Winston-Salem that Krispy Kreme was posting that much in sales every month.[6]

The intervening years have brought challenges for Krispy Kreme, the most significant in the 1970s after Vernon Rudolph died and his family sold Krispy Kreme to the conglomerate Beatrice Foods. That merger lasted only a few years, until 1982, when associate franchisees bought back the company. But the experience, which nearly ruined Krispy Kreme, stalled its growth. Executives had to pay off millions in debt and then had to remake their company into something special once again. Only in the past few years has Krispy Kreme been making the kind of headway and attempting the type of bold business leaps that Vernon Rudolph undertook in the company's first few decades.

HAVE A BIG VISION

The company has built upon the success of Vernon Rudolph and subsequent corporate leaders in many ways over the years. From that one store in Winston-Salem, it now has about 300 stores around the world. From the single original glazed doughnut, the company has created close to 30 different varieties. When coffee became a big seller in stores, it expanded by purchasing its own coffee business.

In late 1999, Krispy Kreme management decided it was finally time to take one of the biggest and boldest steps in its history. The company, which for so long had reveled in its small, private status, set in motion the process for going public.

Krispy Kreme's plan was to sell 3 million shares of its stock in order to spread ownership of the company beyond its base of 114 private shareholders. The public offering would also fortify Krispy Kreme financially, giving it millions of dollars that were needed to expand nationwide and to fully implement its new strategy as a specialty retailer bent on entertaining customers as well as feeding them.

The move was no surprise to friends and coworkers of CEO Scott Livengood. The quiet executive, who keeps a journal and even enjoys writing his own speeches, is a visionary, like his predecessor at Krispy Kreme. Those who know him say Livengood is a rare intellectual talent—a Renaissance man who has been clearing a path to success his entire life.[7]

"Somebody in Winston-Salem once told me he thought Scott Livengood was the smartest person he had ever met," reveals friend Ralph Simpson, whose public relations firm handles Krispy Kreme's hometown publicity. "I thought it was a pretty big statement at the time, but now I understand. Scott is first and foremost a thinker. He has an incredibly strategic mind. And he does all of this very quietly."[8]

As is customary before an initial public stock offering, Krispy Kreme managers hit the road to visit all the big investment houses and to meet with bankers and analysts. This time, executives and their IPO advisers were selling more than doughnuts; they were selling a company. Their job was to convince investors to gamble on Krispy Kreme's future profits and growth by taking an early ownership stake in the company. Executives showed off Krispy Kreme's strong and proven business model while touting its well-known consumer brand and its history as a steady moneymaker. In pitches to potential investors, they promoted their company as something special, a business with a following and huge potential, much like Starbucks, the coffee chain that had similarly built a wholesale distribution network to supplement its retail sales.

"It was really a brand with many channels of distribution, and we got investors to associate it with a special class of companies,"[9] says Mark

Goodman, managing director and head of the consumer banking group at Deutsche Bank Alex.Brown. His company was an underwriter for the stock offering. "That helped fuel the excitement of the IPO." Brokers and executives also wooed investors with Krispy Kreme–style southern charm and hospitality, giving away boxes of glazed doughnuts during each meeting and presentation. "We felt you couldn't understand the investment without sampling the product,"[10] Goodman says.

Still, it seemed that Krispy Kreme couldn't have chosen a worse time to go public. It scheduled its Nasdaq stock exchange debut in early April 2000, a time when most investors were still enamored of technology companies and not very interested in any old-economy businesses that offered a commodity consumers could actually put their hands around. Though Krispy Kreme's plans to become a public company were well publicized, few analysts and IPO experts pitched Krispy Kreme as a must-buy stock. They were still busy hyping high-technology businesses. Krispy Kreme, they said, just didn't have the growth potential of tech companies.

By the time Krispy Kreme staged its IPO, shares of all kinds of stocks were trading all over the place, as up and down as the weight on a yo-yo dieter's scale. Then, on the eve of Krispy Kreme's IPO, the markets tanked. The Dow Jones Industrial Average dropped 500 points, and the Nasdaq slid a whopping 60 points. It was such a bad day that one financial journalist opined, "The day Krispy Kreme Doughnuts went public may well be remembered as the end of the Internet bull market."[11] Many companies that were planning IPOs postponed them, withdrawing into private hibernation until the markets improved.

"When it came to pricing that night, conventional wisdom probably would have been to put the pricing off," says Deutsche Bank's Goodman, revealing the thought and debate that occurred just before the offering. Nevertheless, "We felt the facts and circumstances warranted pushing ahead and that the deal would be successful."[12] It turned out to be the right decision.

Investors grabbed for Krispy Kreme shares as if they were fighting over a plateful of hot doughnuts. Chief executive officer Scott Livengood rang the Nasdaq's opening bell. The stock quickly shot up from its $21 offering price, performing as few analysts expected it to. On the day of the IPO, Livengood, it seemed, was on as many television channels as the president of the United States is when delivering the State of the Union address. Livengood carried the Krispy Kreme message—and of course, free doughnuts—to the major news networks and to financial shows across the cable dial. By the end of the day, Krispy Kreme had given away thousands of doughnuts, and its shares had nearly doubled. Livengood had granted at least 25 interviews that day,[13] and though he's normally very restrained about showing his emotions, on that day the Krispy Kreme chief couldn't keep the smile off his face. The company raised $65.7 million through its initial public offering.

That was the first of many successes Krispy Kreme would achieve through its initial public offering. Publicity from the IPO fueled double-digit increases in sales and earnings during Krispy Kreme's first quarter as a public company.

The money Krispy Kreme raised through its IPO has enabled the company to partner with well-known, experienced, and heavily financed franchisees to build more than 100 stores in three years. Though the United States market is far from mature or saturated with Krispy Kreme stores, the chain already has big plans to spread internationally, to such places as Canada, the United Kingdom, Mexico, Australia, New Zealand, and Asia. "We decided to target those countries based on the popularity of American products in those markets, as well as the ease of doing business,"[14] explains CEO Livengood.

The fervor over Krispy Kreme, which began with its initial public offering, continues. People still line up in the dark and all kinds of weather for Krispy Kreme doughnuts, and its stock, now traded on the New York Stock Exchange, continues to do well.

Like other public companies, Krispy Kreme has experienced some peaks and dips in its stock value during the past three years, as investors responded to war, economic recession, terrorism, high unemployment rates, and other market triggers. Still, Krispy Kreme overall has remained a steady performer, rewarding its shareholders with the same consistency they would expect from its glazed doughnuts.

In late 2002, Krispy Kreme's stock was worth about 600 times its split-adjusted April 2000 offering price, which translated into huge riches for early investors and company executives. Such results, however, mean that the company's stock is trading at many times its potential future earnings. Because of the popularity of its stock, Krispy Kreme has a price-earnings ratio that is much higher than those of other companies within its industry, and that has some people worried.

"I don't address it," Livengood answers when asked the stock valuation question. "But I will say that we've been at this for a while, and I would hope that we've earned some credibility in the investment community. We've been very consistent each year in delivering more than what we've said we would accomplish."[15]

Many analysts have long been predicting that Krispy Kreme will surely stop rising and that its shares will fall like a spoiled soufflé to a level more in line with its growth potential. The bottom line among these analysts: Krispy Kreme's stock is valued too high and is primed for a downward correction in price.

Even so, opinions about Krispy Kreme's stock valuation vary as much as its doughnut flavors. Others contend that Krispy Kreme is a special and unique brand that deserves the premium valuation and can sustain it for as long as the company keeps its core promises to customers and continues to build on its success. "We knew our stock and our company would have to build up credibility with analysts as we told our story, then let our success rate speak for itself," Livengood has said. "The more people who have taken the time to investigate and research Krispy Kreme, the more they recognize the validity of our strategy and the vision we have for the company."[16]

"The stock has had such a great run, such a great performance," admits analyst David Geraty with RBC Capital Markets in Minneapolis, Minnesota. "It is one of the most premium priced stocks in the country. Investors are worried about earnings slowing down. They're worried about sales slowing down. They're worried about comp-store sales. Investors get paid to worry."

But in Geraty's mind, there's little reason to worry about Krispy Kreme, because the company's stock price is not built on a rocky foundation of promises and dreams of future sales and profits, like the razzle-dazzle Internet businesses that imploded few years ago, costing investors fortunes. Instead, Krispy Kreme, he insists, is a special company, much like two other restaurant chains that have basked in similar investor enthusiasm.

"Let's look at the two clearest examples of something really special and unique—Starbucks and The Cheesecake Factory. What's the value of those two companies?" Geraty asks. "You go back and do your homework. You'll see that investors also paid a very high premium—and still do—for both those companies. [In its first years as a public company, Starbucks stock traded for 50 to 100 times earnings.] So here's what I would say to people about Krispy Kreme: Generally investors have given it a valuation similar to other special, unique brands. As long as Krispy Kreme maintains those special characteristics—special growth, special brand characteristics—it will continue to be given that valuation. Even McDonald's used to have that high premium valuation at one time. The best companies have the highest valuation. I don't know how to get around that."

That's because the best companies continually build on their success.

There's no telling where Krispy Kreme's stock price will be when you read this book. It could be higher or lower, depending on the market's mood at the moment. But it's important to remember that a company's stock price is only one indication of how well it is doing. At the moment, all of Krispy Kreme's numbers—from earnings growth to stock price—seem to keep going up.

ALWAYS LOOK AHEAD

Though its doughnut empire is still growing, Krispy Kreme has already begun laying the foundation for its future by mortaring together the building blocks of its next potential big success.

On January 24, 2003, Krispy Kreme announced its intention to buy Montana Mills Bread Company, a small chain of bakeries based in Rochester, New York. "They do some things that are so reminiscent of Krispy Kreme," says John Tate, who is Krispy Kreme's chief operating officer and who served on Montana Mills board of directors for 14 months before the acquisition. "There were these amazing cultural similarities about how you think about your customer that resonated for all of us here."

At the time of the purchase, Montana Mills had about 30 stores, primarily in the Northeast. The stores have a relatively low average annual sales volume of $400,000 each. In fact, that's a much smaller average unit sales volume than Krispy Kreme had when it went public. Back then, Krispy Kreme stores were bringing in an average of $2.8 million a year, or $54,000 a week. Tate, a proponent of the partnership of the two companies, admitted that Montana Mills might have made some missteps during its early growth path. The company, in need of money, went public in the summer of 2002, selling its shares on the American Stock Exchange. Montana Mills probably staged its initial public offering sooner than it should have, Tate concedes. But executives from both companies believe the deal is a good one that will eventually help to bolster Krispy Kreme's financial situation and turn Montana Mills into a well-known brand.

"I think our goal, our hope, is really to leverage Krispy Kreme's unique capabilities," says Gene O'Donovan, Montana Mills cofounder and president. "They have done an outstanding job in the area of branding their business, of building up an incredible franchise network and just an overall world-class organization. Our goal is just to proliferate our brand and our business. We're looking forward to working with them to build the Montana Mills brand."

Investors weren't so convinced that Krispy Kreme made a good decision by buying the New York bread business. The company's shares dropped almost 9 percent on the day the sale was announced. Montana Mills stock also fell by 9 percent. But to be fair, on that day the markets in general performed poorly, and the price of an acquiring company's stock often falls on the day of such an announcement because of the impact a move like this has on short-term earnings.

Upon getting news of the sale, Andrew Wolf, an analyst with BB&T Capital Markets in Richmond, Virginia, cut his investment rating on Krispy Kreme from "strong buy" to "buy."

"It's unexpected," analyst Wolf said of the purchase. "While Montana Mills is a great potential concept, the problem is that it's potential, not yet profitable."[17]

Straying from its primary business of making and selling premium-quality doughnuts could hurt Krispy Kreme. It has certainly happened before to other food retailers that have ventured outside their area of expertise, observes marketing expert Craig Conroy. Wendy's purchase of Krispy Kreme rival Tim Hortons, a doughnut and coffee chain with units mostly in Canada, never achieved the potential both companies had anticipated. Many also viewed the purchase of Boston Market by McDonald's as an ill-advised move. "As a group, so many times when people in the food industry get away from their core business, they don't do well," observes Conroy, who is a regular business commentator on Fox television. "It seems at times when people leave their core business, they don't do as well because they maybe divide their attention."

But Krispy Kreme, Conroy says, just may be the company to buck the odds, with its overarching commitment to quality, its marketing and branding prowess, and its smart corporate stewardship. "I would believe they have the values to pull off something in a different, related industry," he said. "If they instill that with this acquisition, I can't see where they'd fail. Of course, it will be interesting to see down the road . . . how many Montana Mills stores there are and how the acceptance level is from the public."

Montana Mills is a "new twist on an old idea," says Gene O'Donovan, who founded the company in the mid-1990s with his wife, Suzy. Imagine a neighborhood bakery, warm and familiar and steeped in the perfume of homemade bread and sweets just pulled from the oven, and you have a basic idea of what each Montana Mills store is like. The restaurants each bake from a recipe book of about 100 hearty breads, including standards such as white, wheat, and rye, as well as such specialty loaves as pecan pie bread, cinnamon swirl, blueberry cobbler, peaches-and-cream, chocolate cherry, and cheese Danish. Montana Mills customers know which breads are being made fresh each day because the bakeries publish a daily baking schedule, which is available in stores and on the Montana Mills web site. The company's baking schedule beckons bread zealots in the same way that the Krispy Kreme hot light beckons doughnut lovers. The restaurants even take "bread reservations," so loyal customers are assured of getting a loaf of their favorite bread on the day it is baked.

Inside, Montana Mills stores are tiny, just like many old-fashioned bakeshops. The bakers begin their work early each day, arriving at around two o'clock in the morning to grind wheat into flour that will be used for that day's recipes. They stand in front of a bank of industrial ovens, mixing and kneading the bread dough on huge flour-dusted wooden tables in the center of the stores. Montana Mills has turned the preparation of its products into a performance it calls a "bread-baking theater," similar to Krispy Kreme's own "doughnut-making theater." Customers can peek into the wheat milling area, and they're also allowed to watch what goes on inside the kitchen at Montana Mills.

There are other similarities between Montana Mills and its new parent company, Krispy Kreme. O'Donovan and his wife, Suzy, are both certified public accountants by profession, but like Vernon Rudolph they dreamed of getting something else out of life. They started Montana Mills in a most modest way, crafting the first recipes in their kitchen at home. Suzy, who remains the company's principal baker, still begins most new bread recipes there. "Most of our products start out in our own kitchen at our house," Gene says. "Then we move them into our test kitchen and into our stores."

To introduce customers to its unique breads, Montana Mills gives away hefty samples, "slices the size of Montana," as they often say. Like Krispy Kreme, the company has learned that the more bread it gives away, the more it sells. Biting into a slice is something of an ethereal experience, insists founder Gene O'Donovan, because the bread is so fresh and tasty. "While it is bread, it's bread that's a little different," he maintains. "Our breads are so different and so unique that they stand alone."

"Have you ever tasted a hot Krispy Kreme?" asks Krispy Kreme's John Tate. "That's the feeling you get when you have a piece of Montana Mills bread. We have become convinced that they sell what must be the best breads in the world."

In Montana Mills, Krispy Kreme says it has found a good concept that can grow and become better with its guidance. Krispy Kreme knows how to build a strong brand, nurture it, and proliferate it, as evidenced by its own success. The company's management team believes it can replicate this same winning formula with other retail food concepts, beginning with Montana Mills.

"This acquisition is a natural outgrowth of the development of Krispy Kreme over the past five years," Krispy Kreme CEO Scott Livengood said, explaining his motivations for the $40.4 million acquisition that was expected to push Krispy Kreme's earnings down by about three cents in the first year.

"We view Krispy Kreme Doughnuts, first and foremost, as a set of unique capabilities," Livengood said. "The opportunity to create a wholesome, fresh-baked bakery and café concept the 'Krispy Kreme way' is obviously unique to [us]. I have long considered how to capitalize on this opportunity. In Montana Mills, we found the perfect foundation for this new concept—passionate bread bakers who have created a fiercely loyal customer following around a wide variety of fresh-baked goods, bread-baking theater, and sampling of large slices of bread. This is a great platform on which to build."

LOOK AT THE BIG PICTURE

For quite a while, Krispy Kreme's management team, led by Livengood, has been revising its ideas about what Krispy Kreme represents, explains chief operating officer Tate. The company is about more than great doughnuts and a network of clean, cozy, well-designed stores with a huge consumer following. "Scott has been thinking for a while about how to think more broadly about Krispy Kreme," Tate reveals. "We're not just the Krispy Kreme brand, but a set of great capabilities that could benefit other great brands." Among Krispy Kreme's key skills and strengths: unmatched marketing savvy; a strong network of experienced, rich franchisees; brand-building expertise; and a nationwide distribution network for its products. "Those are all key organizational competencies that sort of begged to be used to serve other brands," Tate insists. "They have that same ability to create another great concept. And bakeries seem to make the best sense."

Krispy Kreme's vision for Montana Mills will materialize after careful market review, testing, and planning. And it will be executed slowly and deliberately, just as Krispy Kreme's own growth plan was. Krispy Kreme will spend at least two years creating a menu and blueprint for the new Montana Mills stores, which will serve sandwiches, soups, salads, and specialty coffees. The bakery cafés are likely to compete with other fast-casual restaurants like Panera and Atlanta Bread Company. "I would say today it's like the neighborhood bakery," Tate notes. "Tomorrow, it's like a place in town where you go to get the freshest bread and the best-tasting sandwiches and the best coffee in town."

Once the concept is refined and the recipes formulated, Krispy Kreme will offer its area developers the chance to buy and build Montana Mills franchises across the United States and, eventually, internationally. Krispy Kreme also plans to introduce Montana Mills to its wholesale customers, moving the bread into supermarkets, convenience stores, and other off-premises marketplaces that sell its doughnuts. What the company won't do, though, is mix its two concepts. Krispy Kreme doughnuts won't be made or sold at Montana Mills cafés, and Montana Mills breads and treats won't be made or sold at Krispy Kreme shops.

The Montana Mills chain, because it will serve lunch and dinner, could eventually outnumber Krispy Kreme in terms of store locations. But the thrust of its growth is still five to six years away, at which time Krispy Kreme will be well into its own international expansion. "As we have indicated regarding our international expansion, we will always try to prepare for any type of expansion well before we need the growth," Livengood said. "We want the time to do it right. For this concept, I think that time is now."

TAKE NOTHING FOR GRANTED

As Krispy Kreme rounds out its sixth decade, the company is well positioned to build on its past successes. Its management team is moving carefully, yet thinking creatively, about how to leverage Krispy Kreme's powerful brand and its corporate skills in the future.

The core business of making and selling doughnuts to retail and wholesale customers still has plenty of room to grow in the United

States. The international market for Krispy Kreme stores is virtually untapped, with only a few stores now open in a handful of select foreign markets. The world literally awaits this specialty-retail-restaurant concept.

Yet, like their corporate predecessors, Krispy Kreme executives aren't taking any of this success for granted. Good publicity and a strong stock price are great for the ego—and sometimes for the company coffers as well—but they offer no promise of continued good fortune. That can be achieved only through planning, vision, and risk. Krispy Kreme's current management team has exhibited those attributes with the IPO, the national and international expansion plan, and, most recently, with the acquisition of Montana Mills Bread Company.

No one will ever know for sure, but the actions and plans of Livengood and his cohorts in Krispy Kreme's executive suite might just be bold enough to nudge a smile from founder Vernon Rudolph's pursed lips. They are, after all, meeting change with change and working hard to ensure that Krispy Kreme survives and thrives for generations to come.

CHAPTER 12

Keep Them Coming Back

Stewart Deck got hooked on Krispy Kreme doughnuts at an early age.

Deck grew up in Charlottesville, Virginia, in the 1970s. Back then, Charlottesville didn't have a Krispy Kreme store, so the hot original glazed doughnuts were a unique treat for Deck. And boy how he craved them! Unfortunately, it was a desire he could indulge only twice a year, during visits to his grandparents' home in Atlanta, Georgia.

Every summer, and again at Christmas, Deck's parents loaded their four children and the cat into the family station wagon for the 11-hour drive to Atlanta. "We would stop maybe once or twice along the way," remembers Deck, who is now 41. Sometimes, the station wagon would pull up to a High's Ice Cream shop that had a huge ice cream cone on its roof. Other times, the family stopped at Krispy Kreme and bought hot doughnuts to eat on the way. "This was in the early 1970s, when Krispy Kreme was a murmur, just known among people in the South," says Deck, who still connects Krispy Kreme with that warm, child-hood, sweet, cozy-car feeling. "Eating warm, sugary, sweet confections in a car traveling to see your grandparents is a really good childhood memory," he adds.

Today, Deck is a Krispy Kreme devotee of the highest order. He rarely eats any other kind of doughnut. In his mind, no other sweet quite compares to a Krispy Kreme. He even holds the title "Doughnut Editor" at a witty web site that is devoted to snack foods.

"I think that it's more than just eating a doughnut," waxes Deck, who weighs just 155 pounds despite his devotion to Krispy Kreme. "The whole experience of seeing them made, of standing out in the parking lot, or waiting in the car for the hot light to come on is so fun."

Though he was raised in the South—the land of Krispy Kreme—Deck's career as a magazine journalist eventually took him away from his doughnut heaven. He moved north to New England, a region that didn't get its first Krispy Kreme shop until late 2002. For years, Deck regrettably could find no quick fix for his Krispy Kreme cravings. He was an addict unfulfilled.

Thankfully, Deck's writing job required a lot of travel to the South and to other places within Krispy Kreme's growing territory. Once, he even negotiated a visit to Krispy Kreme's headquarters in Winston-Salem, North Carolina, for an interview with Frank Hood, the company's chief information officer. "We cut through the kitchen. On the counter were dozens and dozens of doughnuts sort of spread around," Deck remembers. "I almost couldn't wait to get out of there to tell people what it was like."

From then on, with every new out-of-town assignment, finding the nearest Krispy Kreme became nearly as important as booking a hotel room and setting up interviews with sources. "One of the first things I would do was look up in the phone book to see if there were any Krispy Kremes where I was going," he admits. "If I was going to cover a convention in Las Vegas, I would be quite pleased because I could find Krispy Kremes there."

Deck, who now lives in Arlington, Massachusetts, wouldn't return home from these towns without Krispy Kreme edible souvenirs for his friends and family. "Because we haven't had them in the region, I know a number of people who, when they travel, bring Krispy Kremes back with them. When you could have two carry-on bags on the airplane, I'd arrange my baggage so that one had two or three boxes of doughnuts in it."

Before long, Deck passed his love for and loyalty to Krispy Kreme doughnuts down to his oldest son, five-year-old Jacob. By the time he was three, Jacob had seen so many green-and-white boxes come into the house after his father's business trips that he thought Krispy Kremes were the only doughnuts in the world. The little boy didn't visit his first Krispy Kreme store until he was four, while vacationing at his grandparents' home in Charlottesville, Virginia. That experience was a sweet rite of passage, come full circle from father to son. "We got up early in the morning, and Jacob and I went to Krispy Kreme," Deck says. "He loved it. He has talked about it ever since then."

Like father, like son. The Decks are devoted and loyal Krispy Kreme customers for life.

CULTIVATE LOYALTY

A doughnut doesn't last long, especially if it's hot, fresh, and good. A single fluffy glazed confection can melt away in your mouth within seconds. A box of one dozen might disappear in mere minutes when placed before a few hungry people. Sometimes, customer loyalty can be just as fleeting, especially for companies that don't really listen to consumers, or those businesses that fail to use what they learn from customers to improve performance and cultivate repeat business.

In every industry, whether it's automobile manufacturing or the dessert business, companies hang their success on returning customers. In other words, they must convince people to keep buying their products or services again and again. Cultivating customer loyalty is a challenge, no matter what the industry. But Krispy Kreme has mastered this difficult and delicate task.

American consumers, in particular, have so many choices. Need a new car? There's BMW, Kia, Toyota, Nissan, Pontiac, Chevrolet, Ford, Honda, Acura, Mitsubishi, Mercedes, Volkswagen, and many more to choose from. Want something sweet to eat? Take your choice: You can get a huge chocolate chip cookie from Mrs. Fields, a grande latte from Starbucks, a hot glazed doughnut from Krispy Kreme, a tall slice of caramel cheesecake from The Cheesecake Factory, a bowl of homemade ice cream from Cold Stone Creamery, a pecan roll from Panera, a crunchy Butterfinger candy bar from 7-Eleven, or a slice of pumpkin pie from Marie Callender's.

With all those options and so many competitors chasing every precious spending dollar, consumers wield enormous power. There's a competitor for nearly every good and service, meaning consumers aren't bound by necessity to any one particular company. Therefore, they can pick and choose which companies to do business with based on such factors as price, quality, and service.

LISTEN TO YOUR CUSTOMERS

Despite all the available options, some companies have customers who keep returning again and again. These people are true brand loyalists who dismiss the competition, even if it is more convenient. How do some companies—Krispy Kreme among them—inspire such loyalty while also creating situations that are good for the bottom line?

Pete Blackshaw thinks he knows the answer. The best companies in every industry listen to their customers. And they respond to them, too.

Blackshaw, who graduated from Harvard Business School in 1995, is an experienced marketer. He worked for consumer products giant Procter & Gamble for four years, during which time he managed the Bounty paper towel brand. He also launched the company's interactive marketing department. He left Procter & Gamble in 1999 to start an online company.

A business school class called Service Management planted the seeds for Blackshaw's entrepreneurial venture. "Much of the premise of the course really was about the relationship between customer satisfaction and corporate profitability," he shares. For one class assignment, students were instructed to write two letters to two different companies. One had to be about a positive service experience, the other about a negative service experience. What emerged from the letters was striking: The most successful companies received the positive letters, while the negative letters were addressed to companies that were struggling. "Consumer feedback is the ultimate distant, early warning system for determining how companies are doing," Blackshaw maintains.

Blackshaw merged what he learned in the business school class with his Procter & Gamble marketing experiences to create Planet Feedback. The web site allows consumers to voice their compliments, complaints, questions, and suggestions about companies. It also provides valuable customer-service ratings and insight into the companies themselves for advertising agencies, corporate executives, competitors, and others who are interested in understanding customer behavior. "In the last three years, we have collected over 800,000 letters and another couple hundred thousand follow-up comments," Blackshaw says. "This has given us a really unique view into the world of customer service."

Planet Feedback has discovered that consumer experiences and comments can be harbingers of a company's impending success or failure. For example, McDonald's, WorldCom, and Kmart all received a slew of negative customer comments at Planet Feedback before making news about store closings, an accounting scandal, and a bankruptcy filing. "We're not suggesting that you can draw a line from angry consumers to accounting scandals" or other corporate failures, Blackshaw insists. But negative consumer feedback can point to "a deeper kind of corporate dysfunctionality."

Perhaps more important, Blackshaw and his colleagues at Planet Feedback have learned that companies that listen to customers have the best chance for success. This listening entails not only responding to questions and complaints, but also tapping into what consumers value in terms of service, products, and quality. Successful companies must deliver those prized attributes with consistency. "Players like Krispy Kreme or Nordstrom that pay attention to this will be disproportionately rewarded," Blackshaw maintains. "I call it 'service Darwinism.' "

It truly is survival of the fittest in the business world, and Krispy Kreme is a perfect example of this. The company receives about 5,000 e-mail messages a week from its customers,[1] some with photographs attached. It speaks to the company's folksy sensibilities that photographs, sent in by happy customers, of kids with chocolate-smeared faces and adults wearing paper Krispy Kreme hats are scattered throughout the corporate offices. But what really matters is that Krispy Kreme pays attention to these letters and to customer suggestions. In fact, the company actively solicits feedback in myriad ways. It uses mystery shoppers, conventional focus groups, and in-depth customer surveys to find out what consumers like and don't like about Krispy Kreme doughnuts, stores, and employees. Krispy Kreme also wants to hear about its customers' experiences and memories. At store openings and other big events, the company often has its own camera crews film customers as they eat doughnuts and share their best Krispy Kreme stories. The company then plays these videotaped testimonials during its annual shareholders' meetings, investor conferences, and presentations to financial analysts and the media.

It's obvious that Krispy Kreme values its customers' opinions, says Ellen Moore, a brand loyalty expert from Baltimore, Maryland. The company tells customers, "You're part of the Krispy Kreme family." And Moore notes that Krispy Kreme backs up this statement with actions, treating its customers with a familial respect and care. "You can't just put a label on it," she says of the family-like promise. "All of these things have to come from a genuine point within the company."

By listening to its customers, Krispy Kreme has been able to shape its brand and its stores. Consumers can be credited for the creation of the standard Krispy Kreme hot light that gleams whenever doughnuts are freshly made, as well as the doughnut-making theater that is central to every store. As previously mentioned, doughnut enthusiasts were always asking when they could get hot pastries. In response, Krispy Kreme adopted a twice-a-day cooking schedule at most stores and decided to flip on the neon light to alert customers. As they were transforming Krispy Kreme into a retail business, company executives also latched onto using customers' recollections about early visits to company stores. Because so many people talked about watching the doughnuts being made through a plate-glass window in the front of the store, Krispy Kreme management designed its new retail stores around the kitchen. Now patrons can witness every step in the creation of a Krispy Kreme doughnut. Executives also sought customer feedback on the redesigned store prototype, and they considered these comments before building the actual facilities.

Krispy Kreme has listened to its customers in other ways, too. Though the commentary was sometimes harsh, Krispy Kreme heeded what people said about its coffee. Frankly, a lot of people hated it. Zagat's, the famed New York restaurant guide, once called Krispy Kreme the best place in the world to get a doughnut, but advised diners to go elsewhere for a cup of coffee. Krispy Kreme responded by buying a small roasting company and brewing up three signature coffee blends to serve in its restaurants. Of course, there are now people who say they preferred the old java. But the response to Krispy Kreme's new coffee has been largely positive.

Krispy Kreme's attention to its customers has yielded strong results for the company. Of thousands of businesses across many industries, Krispy Kreme consistently ranks among the top 10 for customer satisfaction on Planet Feedback. Other companies in the top tier are Chick-fil-A, General Mills, Mars, the Kellogg Company, Nabisco, Gerber Products Company, Campbell's Soup, Tracfone Wireless, and Nestlé USA.

About 79 percent of letters posted by Planet Feedback users about fast-food and carryout restaurants are negative. Krispy Kreme letter writers, by comparison, register complaints only 49 percent of the time. Close to one-third of letter writers praise Krispy Kreme for its good doughnuts, quality service, consistency, and friendly and helpful employees. And happy customers keep coming back.

Keith Evans is one person who wrote in to Planet Feedback to compliment Krispy Kreme. Evans, a 25-year-old emergency 911 dispatcher, first learned about Krispy Kreme from his father, who suggested the company might be a good investment. "My dad mentioned he thought Krispy Kreme made a real good product in a market that really has only one other major competitor," recalls Evans, who lives in Stroudsburg, Pennsylvania. "With that in mind, I asked around. I was shocked that although I had not heard of these guys, everyone else knew about them and had good things to say."

In late 2002, Evans had a chance to taste his first Krispy Kreme in Clarks Summit, Pennsylvania. He and his brother-in-law were in Pittsburgh, Pennsylvania, taking a government civil service exam for jobs with the state police. After finishing the test, they rewarded themselves by stopping at the closest Krispy Kreme. Both were impressed.

"I was pleased enough to write a letter to Planet Feedback. What does that tell you?" quips Evans who exhorted the chain to build a store closer to his home.

"I had my first taste of a Krispy Kreme Doughnut and my first thought was, 'Now that's what a doughnut should taste like!' " he wrote. "I was extremely pleased with the quality of the food there and I can say with some certainty I will never go back to those other places again."

Though there is no Krispy Kreme in his town, Evans continues to occasionally buy the doughnuts from his local grocery store. "They make good doughnuts, no question. That's why I buy their product. I do prefer them over other places. Their food is better," he says. "I rarely went to Dunkin' Donuts or any other place before. I tried them a few times, but everything just tasted like mass-produced cardboard. As long as Krispy Kreme makes good food, I'll buy it. As long as Krispy Kreme stays responsive to its customers, namely Keith Evans, I'll be satisfied."

Evans is no expert in customer behavior, but he has hit upon a key component of brand loyalty. Keep Keith Evans—or any other patron—satisfied, and you'll keep a customer, most likely for life, unless you do something to spoil the relationship. Consumers have certain expectations for the companies they patronize. If a company makes promises about its products or services, consumers expect those promises to be kept.

KNOW WHAT'S EXPECTED OF YOU

From Krispy Kreme, customers have come to expect a delicious dough-nut—unmatched in taste—served by a friendly person in a pleasant atmosphere that harkens to a simpler time. The company clearly recognizes this. The word *promise* pervades its corporate materials, from the annual report to the web site to its packaging. Its doughnut boxes all carry the following message to customers: "Krispy Kreme Doughnuts has been making taste treats of the highest quality since 1937. Our promise is that we'll continue to make the best-tasting, highest-quality products because that's what you expect and deserve, and that's what we expect of ourselves." The box also invites customers to send their comments to Krispy Kreme by letter, e-mail, or telephone. "We'll respond," the company promises.

"Customers have an expectation, and they want to have that expectation delivered upon," says Ellen Moore, an advertising executive specializing in customer loyalty. "Trust is always the building block of brand loyalty."

Born in Birmingham, Alabama, and raised in Charlotte, North Carolina, Moore feels the tug of loyalty to Krispy Kreme.

She lives just around the corner from a Dunkin' Donuts shop in Baltimore. The nearest Krispy Kreme is a 15-minute drive out of the way. It's definitely not convenient, especially in a busy city like Baltimore, where traffic can be horrendous, stretching a 15-mile trip into an hour-long ordeal.

But when Moore craves doughnuts, she drives to Krispy Kreme. She doesn't even think about swinging by Dunkin' Donuts instead. In her mind, the cake-style doughnuts served by Dunkin' Donuts are simply not a suitable option.

"I will make the effort to go" to Krispy Kreme, says Moore, who can tie key memories from her past to the company. "That's loyalty when you become part of [a consumer's] life and they're going to choose you over a more convenient option whenever they can. That's the devout loyalty that you're looking for."

What else does Krispy Kreme do to secure such devotion from people like Ellen Moore, Keith Evans, and Stewart Deck?

Companies that enjoy strong repeat business all share at least one common attribute: a good, strong product. "You first have to start with a good product and then you have to build all these other things around it," explains Moore, who is the customer experience optimizer for Carton Donofrio Partners in Baltimore. "Do you have a good product that's worth being loyal to? In the case of Krispy Kreme, one of the reasons that people are so loyal to them is that they start with a fantastic product."

But a good product alone won't bring in business. A company and its brand must be properly managed and well tended, as Krispy Kreme is.

What makes Krispy Kreme successful and exemplary in other aspects of its business also contributes to the strong customer loyalty the company enjoys. For example, Krispy Kreme's monistic concentration on doughnuts and coffee allows the company to deliver the kind of consistent taste experience its customers demand. It can keep its promise. The company hasn't muddled its focus by attempting to sell anything else, at least not since the stormy Beatrice Foods years. Accordingly, customers know just what they'll get when they step inside a Krispy Kreme shop. "Companies need to stay focused on what they're best at. And boy howdy, Krispy Kreme has done that," says Moore, peppering her speech with southern colloquialisms. "What they're so good at is recognizing that every little thing they do contributes to their customers' experience of who they are." Interestingly, Stan Parker, Krispy Kremes' senior vice president of marketing, nearly mimics Moore's words when describing his company's primary branding strategy. "We look at every touch point with consumers as an opportunity to brand,"[2] Parker explains.

MAKE AN EMOTIONAL CONNECTION

Krispy Kreme's branding and marketing strategy indeed helps to explain why the company earns so much repeat business. Thanks to careful brand positioning and the company's deep community involvement, many customers feel an emotional connection to Krispy Kreme. In the same way Stewart Deck remembers his fun family car trips as a boy whenever he eats a Krispy Kreme doughnut, many customers link personal experiences and memories to the company. The desire to relive those pleasant times and to support a company that underwrites good causes draws people back to Krispy Kreme. "That's what makes people loyal, those memories," claims Moore, before invoking yet another example from her personal life.

Recently, the advertising executive was invited to an after-hours birthday party for a coworker. Hoping to be clever and unique, Moore decided to give her friend fresh doughnuts as a gift. Of course, only Krispy Kreme doughnuts would do. "I had to go out of my way to get those doughnuts," she recalls.

The extra effort was worth the response. Moore walked in, her arms loaded with as many dozen doughnuts as she could carry, only to have several other party guests rush up to her.

"Krispy Kremes! I love them!" her friends raved.

"Oh my gosh! I haven't had these since I was a kid," more than one person proclaimed.

Their reactions provided Moore with clear evidence that people feel an emotional connection with Krispy Kreme. The doughnuts are a special treat, and they invoke equally special memories—all of which translates into strong brand loyalty for the company.

"I would not have had that kind of reaction with another brand of doughnuts," Moore believes. "There's this wonderful warm feeling. It's emotional. It's deep down in you. The food itself is comforting and the brand is comforting."

Good companies also capitalize on immediacy, Moore says, and they give consumers a reason to buy their product right now. Few things can compare to the Krispy Kreme hot light, in terms of creating that gotta-have-it-now feeling. "The brand carries a great deal of loyalty," explains

Harry Heyligers, a Krispy Kreme store manager in California. "The one thing that makes us different than most other doughnut places is that we serve our glazed [doughnuts] hot. And I think that's where 90 percent of our loyalty comes from, just that it's a hot doughnut."[3]

Additionally, Moore says, Krispy Kreme's habit of selling its doughnuts through supermarkets, coffee shops, and other stores helps keep its customers satisfied and coming back for more servings. Grocery shoppers, for instance, are reminded of Krispy Kreme and have yet another chance to indulge in these famous treats at the store. "It sort of says, 'Even if you don't live near an actual company doughnut shop, we're going to get them to you fresh within 24 hours,'" Moore maintains.

The care that Krispy Kreme takes in selecting its employees is yet another factor that lures customers back. Krispy Kreme stores are generally happy places, filled with polite people willing to serve with a smile. "The staff at Krispy Kreme seems to be more consistently positive" than their counterparts at other food service establishments, Moore observes. "I can tell you that the experience the customers have with the employees is extremely important to whether they'll be back or not."

FACE UP TO CHALLENGES

The open kitchens that are central to all Krispy Kreme stores also help build the trust necessary for brand loyalty. "The doughnut-making theater, to me, is a metaphor for them being open," Moore says. By letting customers peek into its kitchens, Krispy Kreme proclaims, "We have nothing to hide." And that's vitally important, especially now that highly publicized corporate accounting scandals have shaken many people's trust in American businesses. "In today's business climate, everybody is questioning everything," Moore says.

One crisis won't necessarily cost a company customers. But how the business responds could. Think back to the 1980s, when cyanide-laced Tylenol pills killed several people. Manufacturer Johnson & Johnson was put to the ultimate test and passed with flying colors.

In the fall of 1982, seven people from the Chicago area died after taking Tylenol capsules that had been laced with cyanide. Investigators determined that the pill bottles had been purchased from various stores over a period of time. The perpetrator, who has never been found, emptied the capsules, refilled them with cynanide, and returned the bottles to the shelves of five stores.[4]

Johnson & Johnson responded by immediately pulling the pain medication out of stores. Company executives also talked openly about the crisis and owned up to their own culpability in the malicious tampering act. The company warned Americans not to consume any Tylenol-brand products and recalled about 31 million bottles of pain reliever, worth more than $100 million. For any consumer who asked, Johnson & Johnson replaced capsules with more tamper-resistant caplets and sent customers coupons for future purchases. Soon the company was making pills in triple-sealed, tamper-resistant packages, and the frightened public once again began buying Tylenol products because they trusted that the medicine was safe. Johnson & Johnson lost customers immediately after the poisonings, but within a few months, the company had regained its 35 percent market share.[5] "Because they handled it so quickly and so effectively, they actually probably built brand loyalty," Moore says.

Krispy Kreme reacted with similar speed and openness when addressing a potential scandal of its own. In late 2002, investors began questioning a synthetic lease the company used to finance the construction of a new doughnut mix manufacturing plant in Effingham, Illinois. The deal was perfectly legal. However, because of the way in which the project was financed, debt for the lease didn't show up on the company's balance sheet, according to chief governance officer Randy Casstevens. Still, the transaction raised questions and sparked concerns among investors already scarred by accounting malfeasance from the likes of Enron and WorldCom.

"We were somewhat shocked [by the negative reaction] because it is a common transaction," Casstevens told a class of accounting students at Wake Forest University in Winston-Salem, North Carolina. "The buzzwords [the media] were using were, 'accounting problems at Krispy Kreme.' Essentially, the stock was in freefall."

Within days of making headlines with its synthetic lease, Krispy Kreme responded by working out a more traditional bank financing deal to pay for the plant. "I think we try to put ourselves in the place of the investor out there who is going to buy 100 shares of Krispy Kreme stock or who invests in the stock market through their 401(k) at work," Casstevens says. "And a $35 million plant with no debt on your balance sheet, an average investor doesn't understand that."

In explaining the company's decision to change its financing for the plant, chief executive officer Scott Livengood said, "In the current economic climate, investors understandably are paying closer attention to the financial strength of their companies. There is no reason for us to do anything that could be misinterpreted, regardless of how legal and acceptable it may be." By being so up front about the confusing synthetic lease and acting quickly to change it, Krispy Kreme impressed its customers and investors while stoking their loyalty to the product, Moore surmises.

DO WHAT IT TAKES

It's clear that Krispy Kreme CEO Scott Livengood and his employees understand that it takes more than just a good product to lure people away from all of the other sweet temptations available to them. The company is constantly—and narrowly—focused on making the Krispy Kreme experience within its stores fun, consistent, comfortable, and, of course, tasty.

This approach wins Krispy Kreme new customers like Keri Maijala every day. Because she lives in California, Maijala hasn't been a Krispy Kreme customer for very long. But she has quickly become as much of a zealot as Stewart Deck.

Maijala nicknamed her first trip to Krispy Kreme "The Quest" because she had been yearning to taste the doughnuts for years.

A few years ago, she was visiting friends near Los Angeles. When they passed by a new Krispy Kreme store, Maijala could barely control her excitement. She just wanted to jerk the steering wheel toward the glowing Krispy Kreme sign. Maijala nagged and cajoled her friends until she convinced them to stop for the doughnuts she'd heard so many people rave about.

"It was really funny because I had been dying to try Krispy Kreme," she says. "It was kind of a myth. I heard people talking about it. Krispy Kreme, the company, is really good about creating a buzz. Everybody knows when one is coming and everyone is dying for the day when it opens."

The Krispy Kreme store Maijala visited in Van Nuys was so new and so popular that police officers were still lined up along Van Nuys Boulevard and in the parking lot directing traffic when her group arrived. The friends pulled their compact car into the drive-through lane, and Maijala documented the entire experience, snapping photographs with her new digital camera. With her first bite, Maijala knew that she'd be a Krispy Kreme customer for life.

"They're sweet on the outside, light and fluffy on the inside. If you get them right out of the fryer, they're just heaven. They are just little bits of sweetened frosted heaven," she raves. "The fact that they're not easily accessible makes them all the more alluring."

Maijala, who is a project manager for a multimedia company, lives in Corona, California, about 10 miles from the closest Krispy Kreme. Conscious about her health and her eating habits, Maijala tries to be sensible about her intake of the high-calorie Krispy Kreme doughnuts, although she constantly struggles with the temptation to visit the store more often. "I'm a Krispy Kreme snob. The ones that are in the grocery stores don't count. I won't buy out of the store," she confides.

But the hot doughnuts are another story—calorie counting be damned. "As long as that hot light's on . . . I'm bound to stop," she says. "I have to have them off the conveyor."

So, it seems, do millions of other satisfied Krispy Kreme customers who keep coming back for more from this popular company day after day, week after week, and year after year.

Milestones in
Krispy Kreme History

JULY 30, 1915: Founder Vernon Rudolph is born near Haitz in Marshall County, Kentucky, to Rethie Nimmo Rudolph and Plumie Harrison Rudolph.

1933: Ishmael Armstrong buys the Krispy Kreme name, secret recipe, and a doughnut shop from French chef Joe LeBeau of New Orleans, Louisiana. He later hires his 18-year-old nephew, Vernon Rudolph, to sell doughnuts door-to-door.

1935: Ishmael Armstrong sells his doughnut business to Plumie Rudolph, Vernon's father. Plumie and his sons, Vernon and Lewis, run doughnut shops in Nashville, Tennessee; Charleston, West Virginia; and Atlanta, Georgia.

SUMMER 1937: Vernon Rudolph, an idealistic 21-year-old hoping to make a career for himself, sets off from Nashville, Tennessee, with his good friend and a route salesman. The three idealistic young men are intent on starting their own doughnut business. They have $200 in savings, a few pieces of doughnut-making equipment, a green 1936 Pontiac, and the Krispy Kreme secret formula. The friends soon arrive in Winston-Salem, North Carolina, and use their last $25 to rent a small storefront on Main Street.

JULY 13, 1937: Vernon Rudolph, using ingredients he borrowed from a local grocer, cooks his first batch of Krispy Kreme doughnuts at the small production facility on Winston-Salem's Main Street. The locals are hooked, and retail and wholesale orders for doughnuts pour in. The handmade doughnuts retail for 5 cents each, or 25 cents a dozen. Wholesale customers get them for 20 cents a dozen.

DECEMBER 1, 1938: A local bank cashier praises Vernon Rudolph's promptness in repaying the loan. The banker's letter provides proof of how quickly Rudolph has transformed his dream into a successful business. The note begins, "Your check for $700.00 received for your note due this bank as of December 1," and goes on to say, "I am indeed proud that you are doing as well as you are, and trust that you will continue to do so. It gives me great pleasure to be of assistance to young men who are industrious and capable as I feel that you are, and watch them forge ahead and do things. We wish you the best of success in the time to come and shall be disappointed in you if you do not continue to make good."[1]

1938: Vernon Rudolph and an uncle pair up to open a second Krispy Kreme Doughnut Shop at 503 West Trade Street in Charlotte, North Carolina. Soon thereafter, they buy a fried pie recipe and start making apple, peach, and pineapple desserts under the Old Timey Pie Company brand name. The name is later changed to Krispy Kreme Pies. Through several commissaries in the South, Krispy Kreme continues to make fried fruit pies, honeybuns, and other pastries. These goods are packaged for wholesale distribution in the company's heritage markets only.

1939: Krispy Kreme's founder marries Ruth Ayers, a young woman he met in Atlanta, Georgia.

1941: Vernon Rudolph buys a doughnut shop in Charleston, West Virginia, that had been operated by others in his family. With this purchase, Rudolph owns three Krispy Kreme restaurants outright— one each in Winston-Salem, North Carolina; Raleigh, North Carolina; and Charleston, West Virginia. He also shares ownership of a fourth Krispy Kreme shop in Charlotte, North Carolina, with an uncle.

1944: Ruth Ayers Rudolph, Vernon's wife of five years, is killed in an automobile accident near her hometown of Orangeburg, South Carolina. Vernon Rudolph, who served an 18-month tour as a second lieutenant in the Army Air Corps, returns from World War II service. Out of grief for the loss of his wife and dedication to his business, he devotes all his energy to Krispy Kreme.

1946: Vernon Rudolph remarries. His new wife is Lorraine Flynt, a young woman from Winston-Salem.

1946: At considerable cost, Krispy Kreme is registered as a trademark with the U.S. Patent Office. "Don't look at the cost, look at the end result," Vernon Rudolph says at the time.[2]

OCTOBER 1, 1946: Krispy Kreme Doughnut Company is incorporated in North Carolina. Four days later, the new corporation acquires the assets of various doughnut shops throughout the country. This gives the new corporation control of seven Krispy Kreme stores in North Carolina, South Carolina, Tennessee, and West Virginia.

JUNE 3, 1947: Krispy Kreme Corporation is incorporated in North Carolina. The new corporation will manufacture the dry mix used to create Krispy Kreme doughnuts. It is also responsible for buying, selling, and manufacturing doughnut-making equipment and bakery supplies.

1947: Vernon Rudolph licenses the Krispy Kreme name to a number of associates who open their own doughnut shops. These first franchisees agree to buy mix from Krispy Kreme and to make and sell doughnuts under the parent company's strict standards. It takes about $3,500 to start one of the first Krispy Kreme franchises. This money purchases production equipment, 10 bags of doughnut mix, a Chevrolet panel truck, initial packaging supplies, and the installation and purchase of Krispy Kreme–approved sinks and water heaters. (By comparison, the average start-up cost for a new Krispy Kreme today is $350,000 to $500,000 for equipment alone.)

1948: Krispy Kreme establishes its mix department in a brick building on Ivy Avenue in Winston-Salem. Today, the company still uses this space to manufacture some of its doughnut mix and to roast its own brand of coffee.

1949: The Ivy Avenue plant is expanded so Krispy Kreme can make its own equipment. In the first year, the company manufactures fryer screens and doughnut racks. A year later, production capabilities have increased to the point that Krispy Kreme is making glazing machines, doughnut turners, cutting tables, and proof boxes that allow uncooked dough to rest and rise.

1949: Krispy Kreme opens a laboratory in which chemists test all ingredients that will be used in its doughnut mix. This gives the company control over quality and helps guarantee the consistency of doughnuts made at its operations throughout the South.

1951: Joseph McAleer spots a classified advertisement promising "excellent opportunities in the doughnut business"[3] and joins Krispy Kreme, working as an apprentice under Rudolph for $1 an hour.

JULY 5, 1951: The local newspaper, the *Winston-Salem Journal and Sentinel,* profiles Vernon Rudolph and Krispy Kreme in glowing terms. "Already a tobacco and textile center of considerable standing, Winston-Salem is making a strong bid for the title of 'World Doughnut Capital,' " the newspaper reports. "The company's chief concern is the doughnut itself—especially the yeast-raised variety, in the production of which it already leads the world."[4]

1951: Vernon Rudolph builds a brand-new model Krispy Kreme shop in downtown Greensboro, North Carolina. Previously when he planned to open a new location, Rudolph would buy an existing building and renovate it. This new Krispy Kreme, unlike other stores, has off-street parking, a loading dock, tiled floors throughout, and an office for the manager. Close to 25,000 people tour this new Krispy Kreme during a four-day grand-opening celebration.

1952: A Krispy Kreme franchisee—or *associate,* as they were called in those days—opens a doughnut shop with a coffee bar in Tampa, Florida.

1954: The corporate office copies the Florida associate's idea and builds a store with a coffee bar in Charlotte, North Carolina. The coffee bar becomes a gathering spot and draws customers into the store. It soon becomes a standard feature at all Krispy Kreme shops.

1955: Krispy Kreme hires a commercial artist to revamp its logo, which was likely designed by Plumie Rudolph, father of the founder. The artist adds a few flourishes to the original logo, but keeps it mostly intact. This design sets red and green as the company's official colors.

1955: The first orders come in from churches, clubs, and schools that want to sell doughnuts through the Krispy Kreme fund-raising program.

NOVEMBER 1957: The first issue of *Krispy Kreme News,* an employee newsletter, is published. For many years, it is written and edited by Louise Skillman Joyner, at that time the company's unofficial historian.

1958: Automatic doughnut-cutting tables, designed by Krispy Kreme engineers, are installed in 29 shops in 12 states. Each can cut 500 doughnuts an hour. Until this point, each Krispy Kreme doughnut was cut by hand, which limited the number of doughnuts that could be produced in an hour.

1959: With his company now in six states, Vernon Rudolph undertakes to standardize the appearance of Krispy Kreme stores. The company adopts a uniform look for its stores, and the first three standardized Krispy Kremes open. Each store has a green-tiled roof topped with a cupola. Large plate-glass windows allow customers to peek inside at the coffee bar and salesroom. All also use the same outdoor signs and green-and-white color scheme.

1962: The automatic doughnut cutter is replaced by another innovation—an air pressure extruder that forms perfect rings of dough. This device is similar to what is used in Krispy Kreme shops today.

1967: To further improve consistency, Krispy Kreme redesigns its mix production plant. The entire system is now automated, reducing the chance of human error and ensuring that every batch of doughnut mix is made in exactly the same way.

1970s: The signature Krispy Kreme "hot light" is born. During the 1970s, a franchisee in Chattanooga, Tennessee, buys a window shade and has the message "Hot Doughnuts Now" printed on it. When the doughnuts are freshly fried, he pulls down the shade. The corporate office learns of the innovation and its popularity with customers. The company has neon signs made for all its stores.[5]

AUGUST 16, 1973: Founder Vernon Rudolph dies in Winston-Salem at the age of 58. He is survived by his second wife, Lorraine Flynt Rudolph, two daughters, and three sons. After its founder's death, Krispy Kreme is held in trust by a bank for nearly three years.

MAY 28, 1976: Food conglomerate Beatrice Foods of Chicago, Illinois, purchases Krispy Kreme Doughnuts. This proves to be an ill-fated merger. Beatrice adds sandwiches, soups, and biscuits to Krispy Kreme's menu and changes the signature doughnut recipe.

1977: The company publishes *Krispy Kreme: A Man and an Enterprise,* a history of the corporation and a tribute to its late founder. It is written by company newsletter editor Louise Skillman Joyner.

1977: Scott Livengood, a native of Salisbury, North Carolina, and at the time a recent graduate of the University of North Carolina at Chapel Hill, joins Krispy Kreme's human resources department as a personnel traineee. He will later lead the company.

1981: Beatrice Foods puts Krispy Kreme up for sale.

FEBRUARY 28, 1982: Joseph A. McAleer, a longtime Krispy Kreme franchisee from Alabama, leads a leveraged buyout of the company, joining with other store owners. They pay close to $22 million for Krispy Kreme. The company returns to its original doughnut recipe.

MAY 1988: Joseph McAleer retires from day-to-day duties at Krispy

Kreme. J. A. "Mac" McAleer is selected to succeed his father as president and chief operating officer of the company.

1989: Under the leadership of president Mac McAleer and senior vice president Scott Livengood, Krispy Kreme changes its business model. The company, until then primarily a wholesaler, begins its transformation to becoming a much bigger doughnut retailer. McAleer begins answering queries from people interested in franchising Krispy Kreme restaurants.

MAY 9, 1995: Krispy Kreme opens its first store outside the Southeast, in Indianapolis, Indiana. Only 2 percent of the local population is familiar with the company, but the store thrives once residents taste the doughnuts.

JUNE 26, 1996: Krispy Kreme opens its first New York store on West Twenty-third Street. New Yorkers go crazy for the southern-made doughnuts, and Krispy Kreme's popularity soars, earning it status as a cult brand.

1997: Scott Livengood succeeds Mac McAleer as chief executive officer of Krispy Kreme.

JUNE 1997: Frank Hood, a native of Bessemer City, North Carolina, is hired as Krispy Kreme's first chief technology officer. He is charged with preparing the company for the change to the year 2000. He is also tasked with improving Krispy Kreme's technological capabilities in advance of its initial public stock offering.

JULY 17, 1997: In celebration of its sixtieth year in business, Krispy Kreme is inducted into the Smithsonian Institution's National Museum of American History. The company donates the Ring King Jr., its first automatic doughnut maker, and other artifacts to the museum.

1998: Stan Parker, Krispy Kreme's senior vice president of marketing, joins the company after 10 years with Winston-Salem-based Sara Lee Corporation, marketer of a broad range of consumer products.

1998: Krispy Kreme gets the Hollywood treatment in the Universal Pictures release *Primary Colors.* A Bill Clinton–like presidential candidate, played by John Travolta, pigs out on Krispy Kreme doughnuts in the film.

DECEMBER 6, 1998: Joseph A. "Mac" McAleer dies of lung cancer at the age of 74. He is eulogized as the "doughnut king" and is remembered as the man who helped turn Krispy Kreme around after the Beatrice Foods takeover.

1999: Popular singer Jimmy Buffett praises Krispy Kreme doughnuts in his song, "I Will Play for Gumbo." He later opens a Krispy Kreme franchise in southern Florida and becomes partners with one of the company's area developers.

JANUARY 26, 1999: Krispy Kreme opens its first California store in the Los Angeles suburb of La Habra. People line up for a taste of the hot glazed doughnuts.

SEPTEMBER 1999: *Advertising Age* magazine names Krispy Kreme one of the "21 Brands to Watch in the 21st Century." Others on the list are Wal-Mart, Amazon.com, Microsoft, and ESPN.

SEPTEMBER 1999: Krispy Kreme hires Handshaw & Associates, a consulting company in Charlotte, North Carolina, to develop an online training system for its managers. The software is completed and debuts on the same day Krispy Kreme's stock goes public the following year.

DECEMBER 16, 1999: Krispy Kreme files notice with the U.S. Securities and Exchange Commission that it plans to convert from a private firm to a company with publicly traded stock.

MARCH 2000: Kevin Boylan and Bruce Newberg, two men who had been negotiating with Krispy Kreme to build doughnut stores in northern California, file suit, accusing the company of breach of contract, intentional interference with contract and business relations, and other claims. The suit is filed after Krispy Kreme grants development rights for northern California to Brad and Maria Bruckman of Golden Gate Doughnuts.

APRIL 5, 2000: Krispy Kreme raises $65.7 million, after expenses, through its initial public stock offering. Shares begin trading on the Nasdaq under the ticker symbol KREM. It has the second-best performance of all new stock issues in 2000.

2001: Krispy Kreme engineers begin testing of a new hot doughnut machine that will allow the company to serve its just-cooked desserts hot whenever customers demand them. The company opens three stores, the first on November 13, 2001, to test the technology, saying it has discovered a way to "extend the hot doughnut experience to more people." This discovery will also help the company expand to smaller markets, well beyond the 750 stores projected at one time.

FEBRUARY 21, 2001: Krispy Kreme buys Digital Java, a small coffee roasting company in Chicago. Digital Java's founder, D. J. McKie, becomes vice president of Krispy Kreme's coffee and beverage division. He leads the development of three new blends of coffee for the company.

MAY 17, 2001: Krispy Kreme jumps to the New York Stock Exchange. Its ticker symbol changes to KKD. To celebrate the event, the company sets up a doughnut fryer on the street in front of the Exchange and serves 40,000 doughnuts and 70,000 cups of coffee to traders and passersby. NYSE chairman Dick Grasso and civil rights leader Jesse Jackson join in the festivities.

SEPTEMBER 11, 2001: A Krispy Kreme store in the World Trade Center in New York is destroyed when two planes crash into the Center's Twin Towers. The store's customers and employees escape unharmed. A damaged Krispy Kreme Doughnuts sign is later retrieved and returned to the company. Krispy Kreme plans to display the sign in a prominent spot at its corporate headquarters.

OCTOBER 30, 2001: A Krispy Kreme store opens in Issaquah, Washington. This store is special for two reasons: It sets an opening-week record, selling $454,125 worth of doughnuts, and the location is the first of a new store prototype, years in the making, that updates Krispy Kreme's look while keeping elements of its heritage.

DECEMBER 11, 2001: Krispy Kreme's first international store opens in the Toronto suburb of Mississauga, Ontario. Canadians line up under the hot light on opening day, proving that Krispy Kreme is a viable international export.

MARCH 2002: The company announces it will build a second mix manufacturing plant in Effingham, Illinois. The plant will provide doughnut mix and other supplies for Krispy Kreme stores in the midwestern United States.

APRIL 23, 2002: Krispy Kreme opens a store in Maple Grove, Minnesota. The area newspaper, the Minneapolis *Star Tribune,* assigns four reporters to cover the event. The store sells $480,693 worth of doughnuts and coffee in its first week—a new opening sales record.

MAY 2002: Krispy Kreme announces that it is starting a charitable foundation. The foundation, which could eventually have $10 to $20 million in assets, will likely fund family causes.[6] Paul Breitbach, a retired Krispy Kreme executive, will run the foundation.

JUNE 5, 2002: At its third annual meeting as a public company, Krispy Kreme reveals plans to expand into Australia and New Zealand. Area developers John McGuigan and Lawrence Maltz plan to open a total of 30 stores in both countries by 2008. At the same time, baseball great Hank Aaron announces that he will become Krispy Kreme's second celebrity franchisee.

JUNE 25, 2002: Sports legend Hank Aaron, who holds Major League Baseball's career home-run record, opens his Krispy Kreme shop in the impoverished, mainly minority, West End neighborhood of Atlanta, Georgia.

JULY 13, 2002: Krispy Kreme sets a Guinness world record by building the world's largest doughnut cake to celebrate its sixty-fifth anniversary. The 2,413-pound cake contains 14,832 Krispy Kreme doughnuts, 1,000 pounds of cake icing, and 330 pounds of candy decorations. It is unveiled in the historic village of Old Salem, North Carolina, near the site of the original Krispy Kreme doughnut factory.

SEPTEMBER 2002: Singer Ashanti poses with a box of assorted Krispy Kreme doughnuts in a *Jane* magazine advertisement for Candie's shoes.

SEPTEMBER 10, 2002: Krispy Kreme and Project Homestead in Greensboro, North Carolina, join forces to open the company's first doughnut shop partially owned by a nonprofit group. The store is part of an economic development project in east Greensboro, a once-thriving downtown business district.

NOVEMBER 2002: Krispy Kreme's CEO Scott Livengood files to sell $15 million worth of company stock.

NOVEMBER 14, 2002: Former *American Bandstand* host Dick Clark and several partners become Krispy Kreme's newest area developers. They will build stores throughout the United Kingdom.

JANUARY 2003: CEO Scott Livengood and his wife, Michelle, a former vice president at Krispy Kreme, donate $500,000 to Forsyth Country Day School in Lewisville, North Carolina, where two of their children are students. The money will help build an activity center and gymnasium for students at the private elementary school. The building will be named the Scott and Michelle Livengood Center.

JANUARY 23, 2003: Krispy Kreme announces it will become the anchor tenant in an $87 million mixed-use development in downtown Winston-Salem. After searching for nearly two years, the company has settled on a site for its new headquarters, set to open in 2005, which will include a visitors' museum honoring Krispy Kreme's heritage.

JANUARY 24, 2003: Krispy Kreme announces plans to acquire Montana Mills Bread Company, a Rochester, New York–based bakery concept. The doughnut maker pays $40 million for the bread business.

FEBRUARY 10, 2003: An arbitration panel awards $7.9 million to businessmen Kevin Boylan and Bruce Newberg. Two years earlier, the pair had filed a breach-of-contract lawsuit against Krispy Kreme and Golden Gate Doughnuts over franchising rights in northern California. Krispy Kreme said it had discussions with the men about becoming franchisees, but the company claimed it had never reached an agreement with them. Krispy Kreme takes a one-time, after-tax charge of 8 cents a share as a result of the arbitration judgment.

MAY 12, 2003: Krispy Kreme selects Grupo AXO to open 20 stores over the next 6 years in Mexico. Krispy Kreme Doughnuts retains a 30 percent equity interest in the joint venture.

JUNE 19, 2003: The first Australian Krispy Kreme store opens near Sydney.

Acknowledgments

Only two names appear on the cover of this book, but plenty of other people deserve credit for the completion of this manuscript.

The first thanks, of course, must go to Krispy Kreme for making such delicious doughnuts and having such a great business model. The company was a joy to write about, and its people—specifically Stan Parker, Jay Jung, Brooke Smith, Frank Hood, D. J. McKie, Fred Mitchell, Gerard Centioli, John Tate, and John Underwood—provided crucial information and insights into the company. They were friendly, to boot.

Additional thanks from Kirk Kazanjian: The process of writing a book requires the help and talents of a wide array of people. At the top of my list, I must thank Amy Joyner for being such a great coauthor. Her impeccable research skills and excellent writing are the reason this book exists. I look forward to working with her again in the future.

What's more, I want to acknowledge Tom Perricone, who accompanied me on doughnut taste-testing missions at Krispy Kremes around the country, along with the entire team at Literary Productions. I also want to thank our editor Debra Englander, plus Joan O'Neil, Peter Knapp, Elke Villa, and everyone at John Wiley & Sons for believing in this project and supporting our efforts to bring Krispy Kreme's unique story to life.

Finally, I'm grateful to Dick Clark for writing the book's foreword. Dick's not only a great entertainer, he's also a very successful businessman and nice guy to boot. His Krispy Kreme recollections are a terrific addition, and it was a pleasure working with him on this project.

Additional thanks from Amy Joyner: My biggest appreciation goes to my family and friends who supported me through this project. Though I doubted my abilities and myself many times, my parents Betsy and Bob, and brothers, Ryan and Patrick, offered me unwavering support and encouragement. Bruce Buchanan deserves thanks as well, for helping me through the rough spots, celebrating my writing successes, and for just simply being there. My grandparents were also supportive cheerleaders.

Friends Kerry Hall and Allison Foreman were great first editors on early chapters, as was Bruce. *News & Record* researchers David Bulgin, Marcus Green, and Diane Lamb helped me suss out sources and photographs, and they gave me direction when I hit reporting walls.

I'm grateful for the tips that coworkers and friends Dan Nonte, Dick Barron, Meredith Barkley, Liam Sullivan, Scott Andron, Tom Taylor, Jim Buice, Elma Sabo, Emily Sollie, Maria Johnson, Stephen Carlson, Margaret Bell, Val Nieman, and others passed on about doughnuts, reporting, Krispy Kreme events, book writing, and publicity. Special thanks to August Leger Meyland for taking my author photograph and understanding that it had to be perfect.

The public libraries in Greensboro and Winston-Salem, North Carolina, provided valuable source material. The staffs at both places were very helpful and patient. The Smithsonian Institution in Washington also housed a wealth of information about Krispy Kreme history and heritage.

I am, of course, thankful, grateful, and indebted to every person who agreed to be interviewed for this book. Several offered more help than I ever expected, and they deserve special acknowledgment. Great thanks to marketing expert Craig Conroy, who scouted out Krispy Kreme and Montana Mills locations for me, and even sent pictures and a loaf of Montana Mills bread; to Eric Whittington, who arranged interviews with numerous professors at Wake Forest University; to analysts Kathleen Heaney and David Geraty, who offered their comments and research; to advertising executive Ellen Moore, who provided great insight into customer loyalty; to Pete Blackshaw and Sue MacDonald at Planet Feedback, who shared their knowledge and data with me; to Alice Elliot and Dick Handshaw, who talked in detail about their partnerships with Krispy Kreme; to Phil Averitt, Lydian Bernhardt, and their children, Peyton and Caroline, who shared their family time with a writer; and to Stewart Deck, the Krispy Kreme fan extraordinaire, who offered unique insights as doughnut lover and a journalist.

Kirk Kazanjian, as well, deserves recognition for coming up with a wonderful concept and outline for this book, for being a great coauthor and editor, and for giving a newspaper reporter a shot at becoming an author.

And, finally, thanks to all you readers who made writing this book worthwhile. I hope you enjoyed reading it as much as I enjoyed writing it.

$\mathcal{N}otes$

INTRODUCTION

[1] Tara Weingarten, "A Tasty Stock Offering: Bill Clinton Loves Them, but Will Wall Street?" *Newsweek,* September 27, 1999, p. 45.

[2] Juliette Arai, Krispy Kreme Doughnut Corporation Records, ca. 1937–1997, Smithsonian Institution American History Archives.

[3] David A. Taylor, "Ring King," *Smithsonian Magazine,* March 1998.

[4] Byron McCauley, "Doughnut Man Ready to Lead Company Back to the Future," *News & Record,* July 31, 1989.

[5] Scott McCormack, "Sweet Success: The Hottest Indulgence Since Martinis and Cigars Is the Lowly Doughnut—Brought to You by Krispy Kreme," *Forbes,* September 7, 1998, pp. 90–91.

[6] "Back to Basics," *News & Record,* January 6, 1983.

[7] Dan Malovany, "Kreme de la Kreme," *Snack Food & Wholesale Bakery,* February 2002, p. 19.

[8] John Tate, Speech at CIBC World Markets Second Annual Consumer Growth Conference, July 9–10, 2002.

[9] Scott Livengood, speech at Krispy Kreme 65th Birthday Celebration, July 13, 2002.

CHAPTER 1

[1] Valerie Bauerlein, "Joseph McAleer Is Remembered for Role in Shaping Krispy Kreme," *Winston-Salem Journal,* December 9, 1998, p. B1.

[2] Byron McCauley, "Doughnut Man Ready to Lead Company Back to the Future," *News & Record,* July 31, 1989.

[3] Byron McCauley, "Krispy Kreme Will Test New Look in Greensboro," *News & Record,* July 11, 1989.

[4] Dan Malovany, "Kreme de la Kreme," *Snack Food & Wholesale Bakery,* February 2002, p. 19.

[5] Scott Hume, "Model Behavior: Krispy Kreme's Scott Livengood Enjoys Dozens of Hot Opportunities," *Restaurants and Institutions,* July 2001, pp. 28–38.

[6] Hume.

[7] Malovany.

[8] Malovany.

[9] Hume.

[10] Hume.

CHAPTER 2

[1] Bob Krummert, "Out of Its Shell: ICON Opens the Doors at Joe's Seafood, Prime Steak & Stone Crab in Chicago," *Restaurant Hospitality,* November 2000, p. 54.

[2] Krummert.

[3] Carli Cutchin, "Better than Sex?" *Reno News and Review,* December 13, 2001.

[4] Martha Sherill, "The Doughnut That Saved Las Vegas," *Esquire,* September 1998.

[5] Sherill.

[6] Sherill.

[7] Sherill.

[8] Gilbert Chan, "Sacramento, Calif.-Based Doughnut King Wins Again," *Sacramento Bee,* May 29, 2001.

[9] Chan.

[10] Chan.

[11] Chan.

[12] "Canadian Donut War: Krispy Kreme vs. Tim Hortons," *NACS Online,* July 13, 2002.

[13] Krispy Kreme, *2002 Annual Report,* Winston-Salem, NC, Krispy Kreme Doughnut Corporation, 2002.

[14] "Canadian Donut War: Krispy Kreme vs. Tim Hortons," *NACS Online,* July 13, 2002.

[15] Dan Malovany, "Kreme de la Kreme," *Snack Food & Wholesale Bakery,* February 2002, p. 19.

[16] Scott Hume, "Model Behavior," *Restaurants and Institutions,* July 1, 2001, p. 28.

[17] Ben Van Houten, "Glazed Days: Donut Chain's Growth Hinges on Full-Service Franchisees," *Restaurant Business,* June 1, 2000, p. 14.

[18] Van Houten.

[19] Carlye Adler, "Would You Pay $2 Million for This Franchise?" *Fortune Small Business,* May 1, 2002, p. 36.

[20] Adler.

[21] Adler.

[22] Adler.

CHAPTER 3

[1] Scott Hume, "Model Behavior," *Restaurants & Institutions,* July 2001, p. 28–38.

[2] Richard Reinis, "Krispy Kreme Doughnuts, LA Style," *Franchising World,* November–December 2001, p. 18–20.

[3] Reinis.

[4] Sheridan Hill, "The Dough Boys," *Business North Carolina,* August 1994, p. 50.

[5] *Krispy Kreme: A Man and an Enterprise,* Krispy Kreme, 1977, p. 9.

[6] Dan Malovany, "Kreme de la Kreme," *Snack Food & Wholesale Bakery,* February 2002, p. 19.

[7] Krispy Kreme, *2002 Annual Report,* Winston-Salem, NC, Krispy Kreme Doughnut Corporation, 2002.

[8] Malovany.

[9] Carlye Adler, "Would You Pay $2 Million for This Franchise?" *Fortune Small Business,* May 1, 2002, p. 36.

[10] Brean Murray Research Company Report: Krispy Kreme Doughnuts, Inc., New York, NY, Brean Murray Research, 2002.

CHAPTER 4

[1] Scott Hume, "Model Behavior," *Restaurants & Institutions,* July 1, 2001, pp. 28–38.

[2] "Does Krispy Kreme Bring Joy to Your Heart?" *Display & Design Ideas,* May 2001, p. 102.

[3] Dan Malovany, "Kreme de la Kreme," *Snack Food & Wholesale Bakery,* February 2002, p. 19.

[4] Hume.

[5] Malovany.

CHAPTER 5

[1] Scott McCormack, "Sweet Success: The Hottest Indulgence Since Martinis and Cigars Is the Lowly Doughnut, Brought to You by Krispy Kreme," *Forbes,* September 7, 1998, p. 90.

[2] *Krispy Kreme: A Man and an Enterprise,* Krispy Kreme Doughnut Corporation, 1977.

[3] *Krispy Kreme: A Man and an Enterprise.*

[4] Byron McCauley, "Doughnut Man Ready to Lead Company Back to the Future," *News & Record,* July 31, 1989.

[5] Sheridan Hill, "The Dough Boys," *Business North Carolina,* August 1994, p. 50.

[6] McCauley.

[7] "Back to Basics," *News & Record,* January 6, 1983.

[8] Valerie Bauerlein, "Joseph McAleer Is Remembered for Role in Shaping Krispy Kreme," *Winston-Salem Journal,* December 9, 1998, p. B1.

[9] Bauerlein.

[10] Hill.

[11] McCauley.

[12] Brian O'Keefe, "Kreme of the Crop: While Tech Stocks Are Soaking in the Deep-Fat Fryer, Krispy Kreme Keeps on Rising," *Fortune,* July 23, 2001, p. 247.

[13] Ann Stone, "Holey Rollers: Doughnuts Are Glazing New Trails, Appealing to Consumer Taste for Sweet Nostalgia," *Restaurants and Institutions,* October 1, 1997, p. 40.

[14] Stone.

[15] Margaret Littman, "Cultivating the Krispy Kreme Cachet," *Bakery Production and Marketing,* October 15, 1997, p. 35.

[16] Littman.

CHAPTER 6

[1] Kathy Mulady, "Countdown Begins for Krispy Kreme's Arrival," *Seattle Post-Intelligencer,* August 1, 2001.

[2] Tricia Duryee, "Long Lines, Happy Patrons Greet Opening of Issaquah Krispy Kreme," *Seattle Times,* October 30, 2001.

[3] Duryee.

[4] "Don Stahurski: Colorado's Krispy Kreme Man," *Colorado Biz,* March 2001, p. 93.

[5] Emily Fromm, "From Soup to Doughnuts, This Marketer Gives a Small-Town Franchise Big-City Appeal," *Brandweek,* March 26, 2001, p. 21.

[6] Nora Ephron, "Sugar Babies," *New Yorker,* February, 1997.

[7] Roy Blount Jr., "Southern Comfort," *New York Times Magazine,* September 8, 1996, p. 67.

[8] Krispy Kreme, *2002 Annual Report,* Winston-Salem, NC, Krispy Kreme Doughnut Corporation, 2002.

[9] "Word of Mouth Tastes Pretty Sweet to Krispy Kreme," *PR Week,* October 20, 2001, p. 14.

[10] Lisa Lockwood, "Krispy Kreme's Hole in One," *WWD,* June 13, 2001, p. 24.

[11] Scott Woolley, "Primary Calories," *Forbes,* April 20, 1998, p. 39.

[12] Tim Schooley, "The Doughnut Connection," *Pittsburgh Business Times,* July 27, 2001, p. 11.

[13] Krispy Kreme, 2002.

[14] Buck & Pulleyn, "Introducing Krispy Kreme to Rochester," www.pulleyn.com, 2001.

[15] Sid Smith, "Selling of a Doughnut: Krispy Kreme Crafts a Mythology Around Its 210-Calorie Pastry," *Chicago Tribune,* May 6, 2002.

[16] Smith.

[17] Richard Reinis, "Krispy Kreme Doughnuts, LA Style," *Franchising World,* November–December 2001, p. 18.

[18] Reinis.

CHAPTER 7

[1] Juliette Aria, Krispy Kreme Doughnut Corporation Records, ca. 1937–1997, Smithsonian Institution American History Archives.

[2] Charles Fishman, "The King of Kreme," *Fast Company,* October 1999, p. 262.

[3] Krispy Kreme, *2002 Annual Report,* Winston-Salem, NC, Krispy Kreme Doughnut Corporation, 2002.

[4] Krispy Kreme.

[5] Krispy Kreme.

[6] Krispy Kreme.

CHAPTER 8

[1] Lorraine Fry, "The Top 25 IPOs of 2000," *Red Herring,* May 31, 2001.

[2] Edward Cone, "Krispy Kreme's Essential Ingredient," *Baseline,* November 1, 2002.

[3] Cone.

[4] Melissa Solomon, "Energizing the Troops," *Computerworld,* March 12, 2001.

[5] Stewart Deck, "Big Brands, Small I.T.," *CIO,* November 15, 2000, p. 238.

[6] Deck.

[7] Corechange, "Case Study: Krispy Kreme."

[8] "Return on Investment," *CIO,* August 15, 2002.

[9] Cone.

[10] "Return."

[11] Kim Kiser, "On the Rise," *Online Learning,* April 2002, p. 12.

[12] Kiser.

[13] Kiser.

CHAPTER 9

[1] Todd Cohen, "Charity Hot at Krispy Kreme," *Philanthropy Journal,* May 14, 2002.

[2] Cohen, "Charity."

[3] Laura Williams-Tracy, "Giving and Getting," *North Carolina Magazine,* January 2, 2003.

[4] Cohen, "Charity."

[5] Todd Cohen, "Krispy Kreme Promotes Films by N.C. Students in L.A., N.Y.," *Philanthropy Journal,* June 27, 2001.

[6] Todd Cohen, "Krispy."

[7] Carey Hamilton and Brian Louis. "Unity Place Details Revealed: Community Leaders Hail Project as Major Step for Downtown," *Winston-Salem Journal,* January 24, 2003, p. A1.

[8] American Tribute Foundation.

[9] "Krispy Kreme Doughnut Corporation Helps Georgia Flood Victims," *PR Newswire,* July 19, 1994.

[10] Susan Selasky, "Check It Out," *Detroit Free Press,* December 3, 2002.

[11] Krispy Kreme, *Krispy Kreme Enewsletter,* January 2003.

[12] "Krispy Kreme Donates Portion of Sales to Sacramento Children's Home," *PR Newswire,* October 6, 2000.

[13] "Krispy Kreme Donates."

[14] Cohen, "Charity."

[15] Cohen, "Charity."

[16] Mark Binker, "Eateries Could Lift E. Market," *News & Record,* May 19, 2002, p. B1.

[17] Stephen Martin, "Store to Sweeten East-Side Renewal," *News & Record,* May 23, 2002, p. B9.

[18] Krispy Kreme press release, "Krispy Kreme Awards Franchise to Greensboro, NC Community Development Corporation," May 22, 2002.

[19] Krispy Kreme, "Krispy Kreme Awards."

CHAPTER 10

[1] Deborah Crowe, "Krispy Kreme Recruiters Seeking Personable People for Oxnard, Calif., Store," Knight-Ridder/Tribune Business News, September 5, 2001.

[2] Leigh Harrington, "Krispy Kreme Workers Show Sweet Side by Volunteering," *Voice-Tribune,* July 18, 2001.

[3] "No Holes in Doughnut Success Story," University of California at Irvine Graduate School of Management.

[4] Melissa Solomon, "Energizing the Troops," *Computerworld,* March 12, 2001, p. 50.

[5] Shaun Smith and Joe Wheeler, "People First," Customer Focus Consulting web site.

[6] Smith and Wheeler.

[7] Kris Stefansky, "Virginia Krispy Kreme Manager Praised for Firm Hand and Role as a Mentor," *Knight-Ridder/Tribune Business News*, February 18, 2002.

[8] Stefansky.

[9] Stefansky.

[10] Stefansky.

[11] Stefansky.

[12] Stefansky.

[13] Stefansky.

[14] Stefansky.

[15] Stefansky.

[16] Stefansky.

[17] Stefansky.

[18] Brian Louis, "Krispy Kreme Scours Winston-Salem, N.C., for Place to Build New Headquarters," *Knight-Ridder/Tribune Business News*, October 6, 2002.

[19] "Rigel Corp.: Driven by Unique Management Style and an Ability to Adapt," *Nation's Restaurant News,* January 1998, p. 150.

[20] *Nation's Restaurant News.*

[21] Crowe.

[22] Smith and Wheeler.

[23] "Retail Entrepreneurs of the Year," *Chain Store Age Executive* with *Shopping Center Age,* December 2000, p. 59.

CHAPTER 11

[1] Krispy Kreme, *Krispy Kreme: A Man and an Enterprise,* 1977, p. 26.

[2] *Krispy Kreme: A Man and an Enterprise,* p. 26.

[3] *Krispy Kreme: A Man and an Enterprise,* p. i.

[4] *Krispy Kreme: A Man and an Enterprise,* p. 20.

[5] Harold Ellison, "Rudolph Began Doughnut Business in Salem, but Not Before 1830, *Winston-Salem Journal,* March 3, 1963.

[6] Ellison.

[7] Doug Campbell, "America's Doughnut Kings," *Denver Business Journal,* August 25, 2000, p. 29A.

[8] Campbell.

[9] Avital Louria Hahn, "Krispy Kreme Hits IPO Jackpot: While NASDAQ Crumbles, Doughnuts Rise," *Investment Dealers' Digest,* January 2, 2001.

[10] Hahn.

[11] Hahn.

[12] Hahn.

[13] Campbell.

[14] "Krispy Kreme's Hole Earth Strategy: The Doughnut Maker Says It Can Refute Street Skeptics by Sustaining Growth and Conquering the World. Meanwhile, Fancy a Tasty Dot-Com?" *Business Week Online,* December 9, 2002.

[15] Beth Belton, "His Doughnut Stores Are His 'Children': That's How Krispy Kreme CEO Scott Livengood Thinks about His Expanding Outfit and the Sweet Spot It Has Carved for Itself," *Business Week Online,* December 9, 2002.

[16] Richard Craver, "Krispy Kreme's Market Value Keeps Growing," Knight-Ridder/Tribune Business News, May 27, 2002.

[17] Shad Elam, "Krispy Kreme to Buy Montana Mills for about $40.4 Million," *Bloomberg Business News,* January 24, 2003.

CHAPTER 12

[1] Chris Penttila, "Brand Awareness," *Entrepreneur,* September 2001, p. 49.

[2] Penttila.

[3] Lee Zion, "D'oh! Doughnuts Have 'Em Standing in Line," *San Diego Business Journal,* December 18, 2000, p. 1.

[4] Sally Roberts, "Tragedy Spurred Innovation; Looking Back at Lessons Learned in the Tylenol Poisonings," *Business Insurance,* October 21, 2002, p. 1.

[5] Roberts.

MILESTONES IN KRISPY KREME HISTORY

[1] *Krispy Kreme: A Man and an Enterprise,* Krispy Kreme, 1977, p. 8.

[2] *Krispy Kreme: A Man and an Enterprise,* p. 13.

[3] Valerie Bauerlein, "Joseph McAleer Is Remembered for Role in Shaping Krispy Kreme," *Winston-Salem Journal,* December 9, 1998, p. B1.

[4] *Krispy Kreme: A Man and an Enterprise,* p. 14.

[5] Scott Hume, "Model Behavior: Krispy Kreme's Scott Livengood Enjoys Dozens of Hot Opportunities," *Restaurants and Institutions,* July 2001, p. 28–38.

[6] Todd Cohen, "Charity Hot at Krispy Kreme," *Philanthropy Journal,* May 14, 2002.

Index